Gender Justice

GENDER JUSTICE

Edited by
Subhash Chandra Singh

SERIALS PUBLICATIONS
NEW DELHI (INDIA)

First Published - 2009

ISBN: 978-81-8387-284-3

Published by

SERIALS PUBLICATIONS
4830/24, Prahlad Street, Ansari Road
Darya Ganj, New Delhi-110002 (India)
Phone : 23245225 Fax : 91-11-23272135
E-mail: serials@satyam.net.in

CONTENTS

PREFACE

Gender justice is fundamental to fostering gender equality and gender mainstreaming. Gender equality is not one issue but denotes many facets. It is a complex concept shaped by different layers of injustice and oppression. Gender justice incorporates gender equitable promotion and protection of civil, political, economic and social rights. It also includes protection from gender-based violence and discrimination. This necessitates gender awareness and gender analysis of women's rights as well as the obstacles to the enjoyment of these rights.

In India, as throughout the world, gender inequality continue to undermine democracy and human rights, impede development and compromise people's lives in dramatic ways. The high level of gender discrimination and gender violence are threat to our democracy and human rights, which ultimately undermine women's ability to enjoy their constitutional rights.

The papers in this volume show that policies promoting sex equality seek fundamental social change. The contributors challenge historical patterns of state-society interaction concerning the organization of the societal structure, economy, and the respective rules of the state, religion, and cultural groups. The role of civil society, mass media and the authorities of the state involved in the protection and promotion of women's rights are also discussed thoroughly by contributors.

Empowerment of women has many facets. Empowerment is a socio-economic and political concept that goes beyond formal political participation and conscious raising schemes. **D. Lenin & Kirubakaran Samuel** conducted their study on "Attainment of Women's Rights through Empowerment". This study brings out that empowerment cannot be achieved through the handling of just money since the credit by itself does not bond women together enough to unleash a process of empowerment. Other social and development concerns are required to cement groups so that they can metamorphose into vehicles of empowerment. There is a need to reduce the structural constrains to make women free to exercise their constitutional and legal rights.

Gender justice and empowerment of women denote a process of acquiring knowledge and awareness of one's legal rights. Some women's and other progressive groups working with law have suggested that law can be an important catalyst that can mobilize women into action. Lack of awareness about law is seen as a major factor in the gap between the formal rights of women and the continuing social and economic inequality of women. Again, **D. Lenin & Kirubakaran Samuel**, in another study on "Women's Knowledge and Awareness on Legal Rights" focuses that knowledge of law and awareness about their rights under the law are essential for real empowerment. Those who possess legal knowledge are less likely to be victimized. The researchers have presented occupation-wise legal awareness data and showed that government women employees have greater awareness about their constitutional and legal rights than other groups of women. The study shows that legal literacy programme is essential at the gross root level if we intend to bring a *de facto* equality in the society.

Anupam Ahluwalia's paper is on "Custom, Law and Violence against Women in India". This study brings out that the laws in isolation cannot do the miracles. There is need of social awakening and change in the attitude of the masses, so that respect and equal status can be given to women. This awakening can be brought about by education campaign among youth making them aware of existing social evils and the means to eradicate them.

Devinder Singh & Dinesh Kumar in their paper on "Role of Judiciary in Promotion and Protection of Rights of Women under the Constitution of India" discusses the role of higher courts in the promotion of women's rights in India. The struggle of women's rights in India can be characterized is a fight for human rights—a fight against poverty, ignorance and inequality and all other factors which negate the forces of progress. So, all efforts need to be made to fight with these constrains. In the past few decades the Indian constitutional courts have played pro-active role in the promotion and protection of human rights of women.

Domestic violence against women appeared to be a serious threat to the lives of Indian women. **Pushpa Sinha's** contribution is on "Domestic Violence against Women and Girls and Human Rights". The author argues that domestic violence is a health, legal, economic, educational and developmental and above all, a human rights issue. By defining various key concepts, the author shows, how women and girls face discrimination and gender-based violence throughout their life cycle. Through her study she suggests that women need to be empowered through education, employment opportunities, and legal literacy and inheritance rights. Human rights education and information should be provided to them so that they can take a self decision in all matters relating to their well-being.

There can be little doubt that the status of women has been a cause of concern in every society, whether developing or developed. Like other societies, Nigerian society has also appeared to be a gender discriminatory. Women in Nigeria face discrimination almost in all walks of life, including politics. **Hakeem Ijaiya's** paper on "Feminist Jurisprudence: The Role of Women in Politics in Nigeria" addresses the problem of gender inequality in politics in Nigeria. To address the problem of gender inequality in Nigerian politics, the author suggests three things, viz. liberating women, centering women, and empowering women. To liberate and empower women mean to participate women in politics.

K. B. Rangappa, S. Suchitra & N. Geetha's contribution is on "Gender Inequality in Education and Economic Development: An Empirical Analysis of District Level Data in Karnataka". The authors see the impact of gender inequality in education on socio-economic indicators like fertility, child mortality, maternal mortality rates, HIV/AIDS infections, and women's participation rates in labour force. Finally, the authors concluded that the education in general and women's education in particular plays a vital role in the emancipation and development of women.

Himani Vaid & Ajay Kumar's contribution is on "Empowerment of Women through Rights, Ideas and Initiatives". The areas of discussion in this paper are the initiatives taken by the government through their policies, plans and different programmes for the empowerment of women in the society. The study supports the idea that multidimensional approach needs to be adopted to improve the status of women. The government policies, plan of action and programmes should be designed in such a way that both men and women play an active role in the development of nation.

The paper, "Plural Legalities, Human Rights and Gender Justice in India: Issues and Prospects", by **Yogetha Kunver & Nanjunda D C**, focuses on constitutional provisions and plurality of laws which have been adopted by the government for the welfare of women. The authors are of the view that using law and the legal system can only be one of the many remedies to be used to change the unequal status of women. To bring a complete change, our social structure has to be changed and attitudes of people in society have to be altered before equality can become real for women.

Contributions from disciplines with environmental and ecological orientation would be particularly valuable to understand women's problems. Ecology and environment play an important role in shaping the culture of a particular society. In Indian philosophy and culture, both men and women are seen as indispensable part of nature. The role of women in maintaining ecological balance has been the subject of discussion today. **Bindu Ramachandran's** paper on "Gender and Bio-diversity Management in a Food-gathering Society of Kerala" correlates gender with ecological issues. The study is an attempt to explain the role of gender in the management of bio-diversity, in Kattunaicken society, one of the food gathering societies of Kerala.

Through another contribution titled "Human Rights: Gender Discrimination against Female Children in Nigeria", **Hakeem Ijaiya,** discusses that female children in Nigeria are subjected to all forms of gender discrimination such as early marriages, female genital mutilation, etc. The traditional practices such as female genital mutilation have negative impact on the reproductive and health rights of the female children in Nigeria, as observed by the author.

R. R. Prasad, in his paper titled "Economic Efficiency versus Equity in Gender and Development Approach" has examined how liberal thoughts give priority to economic efficiency over equality, resulting inequality in economic institutions. The author advocates that efficiency approach reflects distributional issues with serious implications for gender equality. In author's view gender and development approach challenges distortions caused by efficiency approach in various areas impinging on gender relations.

Social and economic development of any nation depends very much on the development and growth of education. Education plays an important role in the development of women. It is one of the tools through which we can examine gender justice index of any country. In his paper titled "Gender Gap in Education: A Case Study in Karnataka", **M.H. Hullur** critically examines the gender gap in literacy scenario in the State of Karnataka. In his study, the author found gender gap in the growth and development of education in Karnataka. Disparities are being found both in primary and higher education.

The traditional social structure, cultural norms and value system continues to place women in the situation of disadvantage in terms of role, relationship and decision-making. Their inferior status is shrouded by a variety of institutional complexes. Despite having equal status in early Vedic period there was degeneration in their status in the later period. In his paper, "Bottle Necks to Gender Justice: A Study with Special Reference to India", **R. N. Sharma** discusses the various factors which are responsible for this degeneration. The author gives a detailed account of women's subordination in the Indian society, beginning from the pre-Vedic period to modern era.

Changes in the global political economy since 1980s have had a dramatic effect on the lives of women who have become increasingly integrated as players in the world's production and consumption processes. Women have been affected by globalization in the most diverse aspects of their lives. The effects have been multiple and contradictory, inclusionary and exclusionary. The relationship between globalization and gender is thoroughly studied by **P. Srinivas Subbarao** in his paper titled "Globalization and its Impact on Indian Working Women". The study shows that the process of globalization has opened new avenues and better opportunities of jobs for women. This, in turn, can promote equality between the sexes, something that Indian woman have been struggling for a long time.

It is said that Indian economy is predominantly an agricultural in nature. Indian agriculture is a symbiosis of crops and animal production. The dairy sector today provides productive employment as family labour. In India, women accounted for 93 per cent of the total employment into dairy sector. Despite their productive role, women play fewer roles in decision-making. It is always male who participates in the activity where cash economy is involved. The paper titled "Gender Inequality in Dairy Sector in Agra District of Uttar Pradesh", contributed by **Jyoti Gogia**, shows how women in dairy sector are lacking control of both management and economic returns with the use of modern techniques and commercialization of this sector. According to author, training of women in animal husbandry is found to be totally neglected. The level of improved household technology, too, is very unsatisfactory, more especially in backword regions, where the majority of women are still working with age-old tools. Finally, the author suggested some measures through which we can improve the condition of women in dairy sector.

The paper, "Growing Intersectoral Imbalances and Gender Inequalities in Wages and Incomes in India", by **Geetanjali Sharma,** focuses on multidimensional context of gender inequalities as prevalent in Indian labour markets, stemming from the socially derived structures, division of labour, sex segregation and labour market segmentation that provide the basis for propagation and perpetuation of wage and income inequalities. Wages and incomes in India have been rising over time; however the gender inequalities have not been bridged. Changes in women's workforce participation have influenced the remuneration and returns due to them; however the wage imbalances across men and women remain.

The widespread entry of women into the paid labour force represents one of the major social changes of the last quarter of the twentieth century. Industrial revolution led large number of women to work outside the home to augment their family income. In male dominated organizational set up women face work-related sexual abuse and harassment. The paper, "Sexual Harassment of Working Women: A Critical Analysis", by **Gurpreet Pannu,** takes a critical look at the gravity of the problem with possible solutions. The study has tried to explain sexual harassment from many different but interrelated perspectives. A sequential discussion of the problem from different dimensions may illuminate pathways and stimulate research activity in this area.

The paper, "Sarva Shiksha Abhiyan and Gender Equality in Education: Reaching the Unreached", by **M. Sugirtha & K. Madeswaran,** deserves a special merit in the context of the role of elementary education in the development of children. The study captures the picture of girls and women's education in India, especially in the state of Tamil Nadu. The paper discusses the challenge of ongoing and proposed policies and programmes of central and state governments, highlighting the problems and prospects of universalizing elementary education. The main focus has been placed on the educational needs of the girls, SCs, STs, and other children in difficult circumstances.

Neaz Ahmed's contribution on the "Legal Procedures of Marriage and Divorce among the Muslims between Bangladesh and India: A Comparative Analysis", deals with procedural aspects of marriage and divorce laws, as applicable to Muslims in Bangladesh and India. As observed by the author, in the matters of marriage and divorce among Muslims in Bangladesh and India, same laws are not followed although both the countries possess mostly *sunni* faith. Regarding changes in the Muslim personal law of marriage and divorce in Bangladesh and India, the author argues that there is a need to make law considering the need of the changing society. In author's view, the divorce should be granted on certain grounds, not without any reason at the will of one, without the intervention of court.

D. Pulla Rao's paper on "Violence against Women with Special Reference to Sexual Harassment at the Workplace in India", discusses that unequal power relations have led to discrimination and violence against women both within and outside family circle. One of the most serious impediments to women's development is the phenomenon of continuing and increasing violence against them within the family and at the workplace. The author suggests that multidimensional intervention programmes both at individual and organizational level needs to be emphasized to protect women in general and working class in particular.

The paper titled "Violence against Women", by **P. Sundara Pandian & R. Shobanadevi**, discusses that despite their significant contribution in the national freedom struggles, Indian women have been deprived of their due share in various areas of activities and have been subjected to inhuman and humiliating wrongs from birth to death for no sin. The authors emphasize the need to review the balance of power between women and men at all levels of society. Combating violence against women requires challenging the way that gender roles and power relations are articulated in society. Further, they emphasized that breaking the cycle of violence and abuse require concentrated collaboration and action between government and non-governmental actors, including educators, healthcare authorities, legislators, the judiciary and the mass media.

Undoubtedly the position of women during the Vedic period was glorious on account of freedom and equality. During this period women participated in every walk of life. Women started to bear hardship in post-Vedic period, but their status became highly deteriorated in medieval period. Through their contribution, "Women and Law", **Himani & Rajneesh**, thoroughly reviewed the position of Indian women, right from the Vedic period to modern era. The authors suggest that bringing about more and more legislations to ensure better opportunities to grant more rights and concessions, is of no benefit unless there is a basic change in the people's attitude towards women and women's role in society.

Gender justice and women's empowerment in India still has a long way to go, as the World Economic Forum report has put the country among the bottom ten, when it comes to their participation in economic agenda. In India religion is seen as a major agent in the oppression of women as well as the source of inequality. Decision-making has traditionally been regarded as a male domain in most religions. Often using customs and traditions as a tool, women have been sidelined from most decision-making process. Many social evils such as the devadasi system of temple prostitution, child marriage, sati (widow immolation), and lack of inheritance still persist in the face of legislation. Rape, sexual molestation, bride-burning, and unrelenting physical and psychological abuse within and outside the family have become a part of women's life in India. Insecurity within and outside the household is today the greatest obstacle in the path of women's progress. Women all over the world face worse than men. No society can claim to be a gender-just society unless physical integrity of women is guaranteed and fully secured by the state.

At a broader level, this volume attempts to mitigate the negativity, which has come to be associated with gender inequality. This is reflected through the choice of papers and the inclusion of ethnographic and inter-sectional studies. Taking it further, is the use of data to show the ground reality. This volume is a conscious attempt directed at simply viewing reality for the sake of reality, and bringing out gender issues on forefront.

Varanasi **Subhash Chandra Singh**

2008

ATTAINMENT OF WOMEN'S RIGHTS THROUGH EMPOWERMENT

D. LENIN* & KIRUBAKARAN SAMUEL**

INTRODUCTION

Empowerment is the most frequently used term in development dialogue today. It is also the most nebulous and widely interpreted concept. Advocates of micro finance claim the very process of forming self-help groups is empowering and a critical mass is formed which can be harnessed to pull households out of poverty traps. The corresponding side of the debate around this issue, is that, the same critical mass can usurped by larger political and economic interests to promote their own mandates, by which women become instruments and are further disempowered. Further, empowerment cannot be achieved through the handling of just money since credit by itself does not bond women together enough to unleash a process of empowerment. Other social and development concerns are required to cement groups so that they can metamorphose into vehicles of empowerment.

In the context of development, empowerment cannot be given to anyone, nor is it a goal that can be reached by an organisation or state. It is a process that takes place wherein an inequality moves towards becoming equality. The inequality that has to alter into equality is the inequality in participation in the various processes of development. These can range from education, health services, housing, livelihoods, employment, remuneration; etc. Empowerment is a process whereby constraints that impede equal participation are reduced so that the inequality starts moving towards becoming equality. The next question that comes to mind is, 'what are these constraints which impede equal participation in development processes?' These constraints are most often structural and connected to both the larger environment that the woman finds herself in. Since it is connected to structural constraints, empowerment and the conditions that have to be generated for it are contextual and specific to the location and situation, in all its dimensions-geographical, socio-cultural, and political. That is primarily the reason for the myriad understandings of the

---

* *Research Scholar, Department of Sociology, Annamalai University, Tamilnadu, India.*

** *Professor of Sociology, Directorate of Distance Education, Annamalai University, Tamilnadu, India.*

term and the fuzziness that affords activists the freedom to interpret and act according to the situation they face in their respective fields. Interventions such as those of micro finance self-help groups can play an important role in reducing structural constraints.

METHODS AND MATERIALS

This study is undertaken in 5 blocks in Cuddalore district, viz. Bhuvanagiri, Keerapalayam, Parangipettai, Cuddalore and Virudhachalam. From each block, 60 rural women are selected as sample. The relevant primary data are collected from the SHGs women respondents by employing a well-structured interview schedule. The collected data are classified and tabulated with the help of computer programming. The general data interpretation is done with the help of percentage and average analysis.

RESULTS AND DISCUSSION

A study of data in Table 1 indicates the occupation wise respondents' socio culture dimension of empowerment. It can be assessed with the help of 8 factors on a 5 point rating scale. These include freedom of movement, lack of discrimination against daughters, commitment to educate daughters, visibility in and access to social species, access to modern transportation, participation in extra familial groups and social network, shift in patriarchal norms such as son preference and symbolic representation of the female in myth and ritual.

It could be noted that out of the chosen 8 factors of socio cultural dimension of empowerment women respondents rate commitment to educate daughters as their first order empowerment. In this perception they secure mean score 4.16 on a 5 point rating scale. The second order form of socio culture empowerment is observed in terms of shift in shift in patriarchal norms such as son preference as per the respondents' secured mean score 3.88 on a 5 point rating scale. The women respondents rate third order of socio culture empowerment in terms of lack of discrimination against daughters as per the respondents' secured mean score 3.85. on a 5 point rating scale. The freedom of movement is rated at fourth order of socio culture empowerment as per the respondents' secured mean score 3.56 on a 5 point rating scale. The respondents have fifth order of socio culture empowerment towards participation in extra familial groups and social network as per the respondents' secured mean score 3.55 on a 5 point rating scale. The access to modem transportation is rated at sixth order of socio culture empowerment as per the respondents' secured mean score 3.14 on a 5 point rating scale. The visibility in and access to social activity takes the seventh order of socio culture empowerment as per the respondents' secured mean score 2.94 on a 5 point rating scale. The women respondents have last order form of socio culture empowerment in the form of symbolic representation in rituals and ceremonies.

It is interesting to note that among the chosen occupation groups, the respondents of Government employees group stand at the first position of socio

Table 1
Occupation Wise Respondents' Socio Cultural Dimension of Empowerment

Variables	*Government*	*Private*	*Business*	*Agriculture*	*labour*	*Total*
Visibility in and access to social activities	3.65	3.16	2.66	2.16	3.05	2.94
Symbolic representation of the female in rituals and ceremonies	3.24	3.42	1.96	1.88	2.42	2.58
Access to modern transportation	3.79	3.56	3.52	2.06	2.76	3.14
Shift in patriarchal norms such as son preference	4.52	4.61	4.44	2.96	2.89	3.88
Participation in extra familial groups and social network	4.45	3.96	2.89	3.89	2.55	3.55
Lack of discrimination against daughters	4.56	2.41	4.44	3.88	3.96	3.85
Freedom of movement	4.56	3.15	2.86	4.05	3.18	3.56
Commitment to educate daughters	3.32	3.79	4.42	4.72	4.56	4.16
Total	4.01	3.51	3.40	3.20	3.17	3.46

Source: computed

ANOVA

Source of Variation	*SS*	*df*	*MS*	*F*	*F crit*
Rows	9.940098	7	1.420014	2.915687	2.359258
Columns	3.686685	4	0.921671	1.89245	2.714074
Error	13.63671	28	0.487026		
Total	27.2635	39			

culture empowerment as per their secured mean score 4.01 on a 5 point rating scale. The private employee group women come to the second position with respect to their overall socio culture empowerment as per their secured mean score 3.51 on a 5 point rating scale. The women belonging to business group take the third position with respect to their overall socio culture empowerment as per their secured mean score 3.40 on a 5 point rating scale. The agriculture group respondents hold the fourth position of socio culture empowerment as per their secured mean score 3.20 on a 5 point rating scale. The labour respondents slip down to the last position of socio culture empowerment as per their secured mean score 3.17 on a 5 point rating scale.

The Anova two way model is applied for further discussion. At one point, the computed Anova value is 2.91 which is greater than its tabulated value at 5 per cent level of significance. Hence, there is significant variation among the chosen occupation groups with respect to respondents' socio culture dimension of empowerment. At another point, the computed Anova value is 1.89, which is lesser than its tabulated value at 5 per cent level of significance. Hence, variation among the components relating to socio culture empowerment is statistically identified as insignificant.

A study of data in Table 2 indicates the income wise respondents' socio cultural dimension of empowerment. It is interesting to note that among the chosen income groups, the respondents in the income group Rs. 20,000 and above stand at the first position of socio cultural empowerment as per their secured mean score 4.21 on a 5 point rating scale. The respondents in the income group Rs. 15,000 -20,000 come to the second position with respect to their overall socio cultural empowerment as per their secured mean score 3.49 on a 5 point rating scale. The respondents in the income group Rs. 10,000 -15,000 take the third position with respect to their overall socio cultural empowerment as per their secured mean score 3.47 on a 5 point rating scale. The respondents in the income group Rs. 5,000 -10,000 hold the fourth position of socio cultural empowerment as per their secured mean score 3.09 on a 5 point rating scale. The respondents in the income group up to Rs.5,000 fall in to the last position of socio cultural empowerment as per their secured mean score 3.04 on a 5 point rating scale.

The Anova two way model is applied for further discussion. At one point, the computed Anova value is 3.85 which is greater than its tabulated value at 5 per cent level of significance. Hence, there is significant variation among the chosen income groups with respect to respondents' socio cultural dimension of empowerment. At another point, the computed Anova value is 4.76, which is greater than its tabulated value at 5 per cent level of significance. Hence, variation among the components relating to socio cultural empowerment is statistically identified as significant.

A study of data in Table 3 indicates the education wise respondents' socio cultural dimension of empowerment. It is interesting to note that among

Table 2
Income Wise Respondents' Socio Cultural Dimension of Empowerment

Variables	*Up to Rs. 5,000*	*5000-10,000*	*10,000 15,000-*	*15,000-20,000*	*20,000 and above*	*Total*
Visibility in and access to social activities	2.65	2.16	3.05	3.16	3.66	2.94
Symbolic representation of the female in rituals and ceremonies	1.96	3.24	2.42	1.88	3.42	2.58
Access to modern transportation	2.76	3.52	3.56	2.06	3.79	3.14
Shift in patriarchal norms such as son preference	2.89	2.96	4.44	4.61	4.52	3.88
Participation in extra familial groups and social network	2.89	3.96	2.55	3.89	4.45	3.55
Lack of discrimination against daughters	3.88	2.41	3.96	4.44	4.56	3.85
Freedom of movement	2.86	3.15	3.18	4.05	4.56	3.56
Commitment to educate daughters	4.42	3.32	4.56	3.79	4.72	4.16
Total	3.04	3.09	3.47	3.49	4.21	3.46

Source: computed.

ANOVA

Source of Variation	*SS*	*df*	*MS*	*F*	*F crit*
Rows	9.940098	7	1.420014	3.851411	2.359258
Columns	7.01981	4	1.754953	4.759843	2.714074
Error	10.32359	28	0.3687		
Total	27.2835	39			

Table 3
Education Wise Respondents' Socio Cultural Dimension of Empowerment

Variables	*Primary*	*Secondary*	*Higher secondary*	*Under graduate*	*Post graduate*	*Total*
Visibility in and access to social activities	3.16	2.16	2.65	3.05	3.66	2.94
Symbolic representation of the female in rituals and ceremonies	2.42	3.42	1.96	1.88	3.24	2.58
Access to modern transportation	2.76	3.56	3.79	2.06	3.52	3.14
Shift in patriarchal norms such as son preference	2.89	2.96	4.44	4.61	4.52	3.88
Participation in extra familial groups and social network	2.55	3.96	2.89	3.89	4.45	3.55
Lack of discrimination against daughters	3.96	2.41	4.44	3.88	4.56	3.85
Freedom of movement	3.18	3.15	2.86	4.05	4.56	3.56
Commitment to educate daughters	4.56	4.72	4.42	3.79	3.32	4.16
Total	3.19	3.29	3.43	3.40	3.98	3.46

Source: computed.

ANOVA

Source of Variation	*SS*	*df*	*MS*	*F*	*F crit*
Rows	9.940098	7	1.420014	2.775185	2.359258
Columns	3.016285	4	0.754071	1.473709	2.714074
Error	14.32711	28	0.511683		
Total	27.2835	39			

the chosen education groups, the post graduate degree level respondents achieved the top position of socio cultural empowerment as per their secured mean score 3.98 on a 5 point rating scale. The respondents with higher secondary education come to the second position with respect to their overall socio cultural empowerment as per their secured mean score 3.43 on a 5 point rating scale. The respondents with under graduation take the third position with respect to their overall socio cultural empowerment as per their secured mean score 3.40 on a 5 point rating scale. The respondents with secondary level education hold the fourth position of socio cultural empowerment as per their secured mean score 3.29 on a 5 point rating scale. The respondents with primary level education slip down to the last position of socio cultural empowerment as per their secured mean score 3.19 on a 5 point rating scale.

The Anova two way model is applied for further discussion. At one point, the computed Anova value is 2.78 which is greater than its tabulated value at 5 per cent level of significance. Hence, there is significant variation among the chosen education groups with respect to respondents' socio cultural dimension of empowerment. At another point, the computed Anova value is 1.47, which is lesser than its tabulated value at 5 per cent level of significance. Hence, variation among the components relating to socio cultural empowerment is statistically identified as insignificant.

A study of data in Table 4 indicates the caste wise respondents' socio cultural dimension of empowerment. It is interesting to note that among the chosen caste groups, the forward caste respondents stand at the first position of socio cultural empowerment as per their secured mean score 4.10 on a 5 point rating scale. The backward caste respondents come to the second position with respect to their overall socio cultural empowerment as per their secured mean score 3.50 on a 5 point rating scale. The most backward caste respondents take the third position with respect to their overall socio cultural empowerment as per their secured mean score 3.35 on a 5 point rating scale. The scheduled caste respondents with secondary level caste went down to the last position of socio cultural empowerment as per their secured mean score 2.87 on a 5 point rating scale.

The Anova two way model is applied for further discussion. At one point, the computed Anova value is 6.78 which is greater than its tabulated value at 5 per cent level of significance. Hence, there is significant variation among the chosen caste groups with respect to respondents' socio cultural dimension of empowerment. At another point, the computed Anova value is 12.21, which is greater than its tabulated value at 5 per cent level of significance. Hence, variation among the components relating to socio cultural empowerment is statistically identified as significant.

A study of data in Table 5 indicates the occupation wise respondents' economic dimension of empowerment. It can be assessed with the help of 8 factors on a 5 point rating scale. These include control over income, relative contribution to family support, access to and control of family resources, access

Table 4
Caste Wise Socio Cultural Dimension

Variables	*Forward caste*	*Backward caste*	*Most backward caste*	*Scheduled caste*	*Total*
Visibility in and access to social activities	3.7	2.79	3.11	2.15	2.94
Symbolic representation of the female in rituals and ceremonies	3.2	3.01	2.14	1.96	2.58
Access to modern transportation	3.92	3.12	3.15	2.38	3.14
Shift in patriarchal norms such as son preference	4.25	4.12	3.74	3.39	3.88
Participation in extra familial groups and social network	4.76	3.75	3.62	2.05	3.55
Lack of discrimination against daughters	4.15	3.95	3.63	3.66	3.85
Freedom of movement	4.25	3.07	3.05	3.86	3.56
Commitment to educate daughters	4.55	4.21	4.34	3.54	4.16
Total	4.10	3.50	3.35	2.87	3.46

Source: computed

ANOVA

Source of Variation	*SS*	*df*	*MS*	*F*	*F crit*
Rows	7.926222	7	1.132317	6.781861	2.487582
Columns	6.115759	3	2.038586	12.20984	3.072472
Error	3.506216	21	0.166963		
Total	17.5482	31			

Table 5
Occupation Wise Respondents' Economic Dimension of Empowerment

Variables	*Government*	*private*	*Business*	*Agriculture*	*Labour*	*Total*
Control over income	4.11	3.96	3.65	3.52	3.24	3.70
Relative contribution to family support	4.22	3.98	3.77	3.77	3.17	3.78
Access to and control of family resources	3.96	3.55	2.86	2.96	2.46	3.16
Access to employment	3.52	4.07	2.52	2.77	2.45	3.07
Ownership of assets and land	4.22	4.07	3.77	2.52	3.65	3.65
Access to credit	4.33	4.22	3.99	3.87	3.81	4.04
Involvement and representation in local trade associations	4.02	3.96	4.05	3.79	3.97	3.96
Access to markets	3.98	3.48	4.05	4.21	3.77	3.90
Total	4.05	3.96	3.58	3.43	3.32	3.66

Source: computed

ANOVA

Source of Variation	*SS*	*df*	*MS*	*F*	*F crit*
Rows	4.56996	7	0.652851	4.935075	2.359258
Columns	3.127535	4	0.781884	5.910465	2.714074
Error	3.704065	28	0.132288		
Total	11.40156	39			

to employment, ownership of assets and land, access to credit, involvement and representation in local trade associations and access to markets.

It could be noted that out of the total 8 factors of economic empowerment, the respondents rate access to credit as first order economic empowerment. In this aspect, they secure mean score 4.04 on a 5 point rating scale. The involvement and representation in local activities takes the second order of economic empowerment as respondents secure mean score 3.96 on a 5 point rating scale. The access to market ranks third order of economic empowerment as it secure a mean score 3.90 on a 5 point rating scale. The economic empowerment in terms of relative contribution to family support takes the fourth order as women respondents secure mean score 3.78 on a 5 point rating scale. The control over household income occupies the fifth order of women empowerment as per respondents secured mean score 3.70 on a 5 point rating scale. The women respondents rate sixth order of economic empowerment with respect to ownership of assets and land as per their secured mean score is 3.65 on a 5 point rating scale. The economic empowerment in terms of access to control of family resources ranks seventh order as per the respondents' secured mean score 3.16 on a 5 point rating scale. The women respondents consider last order of economic empowerment in terms of access to employment as per the respondents' secured mean score 3.07 on a 5 point rating scale.

It is interesting to note that among the chosen occupation groups, the respondents of Government group stand at the first position of economic empowerment as per their secured mean score 4.05 on a 5 point rating scale. The private employee group women come to the second position with respect to their overall economic empowerment as per their secured mean score 3.96 on a 5 point rating scale. The women belonging to business group take the third position with respect to their overall economic empowerment as per their secured mean score 3.58 on a 5 point rating scale. The agriculture respondents hold the fourth position of economic empowerment as per their secured mean score 3.43 on a 5 point rating scale. The labour group respondents slip down to the last position of economic empowerment as per their secured mean score 3.32 on a 5 point rating scale.

The Anova two way model is applied for further discussion. At one point, the computed Anova value is 4.93 which is greater than its tabulated value at 5 per cent level of significance. Hence, there is significant variation among the chosen occupation groups with respect to respondents' economic dimension of empowerment. At another point, the computed Anova value is 5.91, which is greater than its tabulated value at 5 per cent level of significance. Hence, variation among the components relating to economic empowerment is statistically identified as significant.

A study of data in Table 6 indicates the income wise respondents' economic dimension of empowerment. It is interesting to note that among the chosen income groups, the respondents in the income group Rs. 20,000 and above

Table 6
Income Wise Respondents' Economic Dimension

Variables	*Up to Rs. 5,000*	*5000- 10,000*	*10,000- 15,000*	*15,000- 20,000*	*20,000 and above*	*Total*
Control over income	3.24	3.62	3.55	4.01	4.06	3.70
Relative contribution to family support	3.27	3.67	3.77	4.12	3.88	3.78
Access to and control of family resources	2.46	3.96	2.91	2.96	3.5	3.16
Access to employment	2.45	2.83	2.52	3.57	4.07	3.07
Ownership of assets and land	3.65	2.52	3.67	4.22	4.17	3.65
Access to credit	3.81	3.87	4	4.33	4.21	4.04
Involvement and representation in local trade associations	3.97	3.79	4.02	4.02	3.99	3.96
Access to markets	3.77	4.21	4.08	3.98	3.45	3.90
Total	3.33	3.56	3.57	3.90	3.92	3.66

Source: computed.

ANOVA

Source of Variation	*SS*	*df*	*MS*	*F*	*F crit*
Rows	4.399977	7	0.628568	3.80133	2.359258
Columns	2.028025	4	0.507006	3.066172	2.714074
Error	4.629935	28	0.165355		
Total	11.05794	39			

stand at the first position of economic empowerment as per their secured mean score 3.92 on a 5 point rating scale. The respondents in the income group Rs.15,000 -20,000 come to the second position with respect to their overall economic empowerment as per their secured mean score 3.90 on a 5 point rating scale. The respondents in the income group Rs. 10,000 -15,000 take the third position with respect to their overall economic empowerment as per their secured mean score 3.57 on a 5 point rating scale. The respondents in the income group Rs. 5,000 -10,000 hold the fourth position of economic empowerment as per their secured mean score 3.56 on a 5 point rating scale. The respondents in the income group up to Rs.5,000 slip down to the last position of economic empowerment as per their secured mean score 3.33 on a 5 point rating scale.

The Anova two way model is applied for further discussion. At one point, the computed Anova value is 3.80 which is greater than its tabulated value at 5 per cent level of significance. Hence, there is significant variation among the chosen income groups with respect to respondents' economic dimension of empowerment. At another point, the computed Anova value is 3.07, which is greater than its tabulated value at 5 per cent level of significance. Hence, variation among the components relating to economic empowerment is statistically identified as significant.

A study of data in Table 7 indicates the education wise respondents' economic dimension of empowerment. It is interesting to note that among the chosen education groups, the post graduate degree level respondents stand at the first position of economic empowerment as per their secured mean score 4.14 on a 5 point rating scale. The respondents with under graduation come to the second position with respect to their overall economic empowerment as per their secured mean score 3.75 on a 5 point rating scale. The respondents with higher secondary level education take the third position with respect to their overall economic empowerment as per their secured mean score 3.66 on a 5 point rating scale. The respondents with secondary level education hold the fourth position of economic empowerment as per their secured mean score 3.58 on a 5 point rating scale. The respondents with primary level education slip down to the last position of economic empowerment as per their secured mean score 3.15 on a 5 point rating scale.

The Anova two way model is applied for further discussion. At one point, the computed Anova value is 6.56 which is greater than its tabulated value at 5 per cent level of significance. Hence, there is significant variation among the chosen education groups with respect to respondents' economic dimension of empowerment. At another point, the computed Anova value is 10.15, which is greater than its tabulated value at 5 per cent level of significance. Hence, variation among the components relating to economic empowerment is statistically identified as significant.

A study of data in Table 8 indicates the caste wise respondents' economic dimension of empowerment. It is interesting to note that among the chosen

Table 7
Education Wise Respondents' Economic Dimension

Variables	*Primary*	*Secondary*	*Higher secondary*	*Under graduate*	*Post graduate*	*Total*
Control over income	3.24	3.65	3.52	3.96	4.11	3.70
Relative contribution to family support	3.17	3.77	3.77	3.98	4.22	3.78
Access to and control of family resources	2.46	2.86	2.96	3.55	3.96	3.16
Access to employment	2.45	2.52	3.52	2.77	4.07	3.07
Ownership of assets and land	2.52	3.77	3.65	4.07	4.22	3.65
Access to credit	3.81	3.99	3.87	4.22	4.33	4.04
Involvement and representation in local trade associations	3.79	4.05	3.97	3.96	4.02	3.96
Access to markets	3.77	4.05	3.98	3.48	4.21	3.90
Total	3.15	3.58	3.66	3.75	4.14	3.66

Source: Computed

ANOVA

Source of Variation	*SS*	*df*	*MS*	*F*	*F crit*
Rows	4.56996	7	0.652851	6.556814	2.359258
Columns	4.043685	4	1.010921	10.15303	2.714074
Error	2.787915	28	0.099568		
Total	11.40156	39			

Table 8
Caste wise Respondents' Economic Dimension of Empowerment

Variables	*Forward caste*	*Backward caste*	*Most backward caste*	*Scheduled caste*	*Total*
Control over income	4.1	3.9	3.61	3.29	3.70
Relative contribution to family support	4.21	4.01	3.71	3.17	3.78
Access to and control of family resources	3.9	3.44	2.85	2.46	3.16
Access to employment	3.62	3.9	2.53	2.25	3.07
Ownership of assets and land	4.23	3.99	3.77	2.61	3.65
Access to credit	4.33	4.07	3.99	3.81	4.04
Involvement and representation in local trade associations	4.41	3.96	4.05	3.97	3.95
Access to markets	4.35	3.98	3.95	3.77	3.90
Total	4.14	3.91	3.56	3.17	3.66

Source: computed.

ANOVA

Source of Variation	*SS*	*df*	*MS*	*F*	*F crit*
Rows	4.264397	7	0.6092	7.104504	2.487582
Columns	4.355809	3	1.451936	16.93253	3.072472
Error	1.800716	21	0.085748		
Total	10.42092	31			

caste groups, the forward caste respondents stand at the first position of economic empowerment as per their secured mean score 4.14 on a 5 point rating scale. The backward caste respondents come to the second position with respect to their overall economic empowerment as per their secured mean score 3.91 on a 5 point rating scale. The most backward caste respondents take the third position with respect to their overall economic empowerment as per their secured mean score 3.56 on a 5 point rating scale. The scheduled caste respondents with secondary level caste went down to the last position of economic empowerment as per their secured mean score 3.17 on a 5 point rating scale.

The Anova two way model is applied for further discussion. At one point, the computed Anova value is 7.1 which is greater than its tabulated value at 5 per cent level of significance. Hence, there is significant variation among the chosen caste groups with respect to respondents' economic dimension of empowerment. At another point, the computed Anova value is 16.93, which is greater than its tabulated value at 5 per cent level of significance. Hence, variation among the components relating to economic empowerment is statistically identified as significant.

CONCLUSION

Women respondents have high level of socio culture empowerment with respect to commitment to educate daughters, shift in patriarchal norms such as son preference and lack of discrimination against daughters. The respondents have moderate level of socio culture empowerment with respect to freedom of movement, participation of extra familial groups and social network and access to modern transportation. The respondents have low level of socio culture empowerment with respect to visibility in and access to social activities and symbolic representation in rituals and ceremonies.

Among the chosen occupation groups, the women belonging to government employee group rank the first position of socio culture empowerment, private employee group the second, business group the third, agriculture respondents group the fourth and labour group the last. There is a correspondence between income status of the respondents and their ratings on socio cultural dimension of women empowerment. It could be noted that higher the income status, higher the positive perception towards their ratings on socio cultural dimension of women empowerment. There is a correspondence between education status of the respondents and their ratings on socio cultural dimension of women empowerment. It could be noted that higher the education status, higher the positive perception towards their ratings on socio cultural dimension of women empowerment. There is a correspondence between caste status of the respondents and their ratings on socio cultural dimension of women empowerment. It could be noted that higher the caste status, higher the positive perception towards their ratings on socio cultural dimension of women empowerment.

Women respondents have high level of economic empowerment with respect to access to credit, involvement and representation in local trade associations and access to markets. The women respondents have moderate level of economic empowerment in terms of relative contribution to family support, control over income and ownership of assets and land. The women respondents have low level of economic empowerment in terms of access to and control of family resources and access to employment. Among the chosen occupation groups, the women belonging to government employee group rank the first position of economic empowerment, private employee group the second, business group the third, Agriculture group the fourth and labour group the last. There is a correspondence between income status of the respondents and their ratings on economic dimension of women empowerment. It could be noted that higher the income status, higher the positive perception towards their ratings on economic dimension of women empowerment. There is a correspondence between education status of the respondents and their ratings on economic dimension of women empowerment. It could be noted that higher the education status, higher the positive perception towards their ratings on economic dimension of women empowerment. There is a correspondence between caste status of the respondents and their ratings on economic dimension of women empowerment. It could be noted that higher the caste status, higher the positive perception towards their ratings on economic dimension of women empowerment and the vice versa.

SUGGESTIONS

1. There is a need to increase the confidence level among women, as their confidence level is a low though capacity building programme.
2. Efforts should be made to increase the regular participation of women in development programmes as their regular participation level is low.
3. There is a need to conduct awareness training programme for the benefit of rural women.
4. Efforts should be made to provide the benefits of right to information act among the rural women.
5. Efforts should be made to provide the benefits of rural employment guarantee act.
6. There is a need to conduct legal awareness training programme for the benefit of rural women.

REFERENCE

Dr. (Mrs) V. Mohini Giri (1999), *Kanya: Exploitation of Little Angels* by Gyan Publishing House, New Delhi.

Sreenath Lalitha (1996), Victimisation of Girl-child in the Home, *Journal of the Indian Law Institute*, Vol. 38, p. 101-107.

Bhadra Mita (1999), ***Girl Child in Indian Society,*** Rawat Publications.

Kishwar Madhu (1995), ***Where Daughters are Unwanted,*** Manushi, No. 86, Jan-Feb., p. 15-22.

Bhargavi V. Davar (Edited by) (2001), Mental Health from a Gender Perspective, New Delhi, Sage Publication, p. 427.

Kishwar, Madhu (1992), ***Sex Harassment and Slander as Weapons of Subjugation,*** Manushi, No. 62, Jan-Feb., p. 2-15.

B. Sivaramayya (Ed. by) (1983), Status of Women and Social Change, in *Journal of Indian Law Institute,* Vol. 25, p. 270.

Chowdhary Prem (1994), Widow Remarriage in Haryana, *Manushi,* No. 82, May-June, .p. 12-18

Dutt, Anuradha (1993), In the Name of the Mother, *Manushi,* No. 79, p. 23-26, Nov.-Dec.

Masoodi, Saqlain G. and Dhar Lalita (1998), Womens Rights in Christianity: Some Reflections on Divorce Laws , *Cochin University Law Review,* Vol. 22, p. 16-44.

Raju, K. N. M. and Bhat T. N. (1996-1997), Gender Issues in the Choice and Adoption of Family Planning Methods , *Indian Journal of Gender Studies,* Vol. 3-4, 57-70.

WOMEN'S KNOWLEDGE AND AWARENESS ON LEGAL RIGHTS

D. Lenin* & Kirubakaran Samuel**

INTRODUCTION

The Constitution of India guarantees equality of sexes and in fact grants special favours to women. These can be found in three articles of the Constitution. Article 14 says that the government shall not deny to any person equality before law or the equal protection of the laws. Article 15 declares that government shall not discriminate against any citizen on the ground of sex. Article 15 (3) makes a special provision enabling the State to make affirmative discriminations in favour of women. Moreover, the government can pass special laws in favour of women. Article 16 guarantees that no citizen shall be discriminated against in matters of public employment on the grounds of sex. Article 42 directs the State to make provision for ensuring just and humane conditions of work and maternity relief. Above all, the Constitution imposes a fundamental duty on every citizen through Articles 15 (A) (e) to renounce the practices derogatory to the dignity of women.

All these are fundamental rights. Therefore, a woman can go to the court if one is subjected to any discrimination. When we talk about constitutional rights of women in India, we mainly pertain to those areas where discrimination is done against women and special laws formulated to fight those bigotries. The most important issues stand as those pertaining to marriage, children, abortion, crimes against women, and inheritance.

Before modern Hindu laws were passed, child marriages were the norms, inter-caste marriages were banned, the girl became a part of the husband's family, and polygamy was common. In the 19th century, the British rulers passed several laws to protect customs and traditions while abolishing detestable practices like Sati. Some such revolutionary laws were Hindu Widows Remarriage Act 1865 and the Brahmo Samaj Marriage Act 1872, the forerunner of the present Special Marriage Act. In the beginning, the Act sets four essential conditions for a valid Hindu marriage. They are monogamy, sound mind, marriageable age and the parties should not be too closely related.

---

* *Research Scholar, Department of Sociology, Annamalai University, Tamilnadu, India.*

** *Professor of Sociology, Directorate of Distance Education, Annamalai University, Tamilnadu, India.*

Polygamy was permitted among Hindus before the Act was passed in 1955. However, after the act was passed, any man marrying again while his wife is living will be punished with fine and imprisonment up to seven years. Formerly, child marriages were common. The Child Marriage Act of 1929 was not very effective as such marriages were continued to be performed. Now, however, the bridegroom must be 21 years old and the bride 18 years. However, there is a separate Muslim Code of Conduct, which allows polygamy of up to four wives as per Islamic laws.

There are some grounds available to the wife only, both in Hindu and civil marriages. One such ground available exclusively to the wife is her husband's commission of rape, sodomy or bestiality. Under the Hindu Adoptions and Maintenance Act 1956, a Hindu wife is entitled to be maintained by her husband. Section 125 of the Criminal Procedure Code also deals with maintenance of wife and children. If there is a decree of maintenance against the husband and the couple have been living apart for over one year, it would be a ground for the wife to seek dissolution of marriage. Here again the Muslim Personal Law has a different set of conditions for the annulment of an Islamic marriage.

The Dowry Prohibition Act of 1961 says that any person who gives, takes, or abets the giving or taking of dowry shall be punished with imprisonment, which may extend to six months or with fine up to Rs. 5,000 or with both. Dowry that started off as a practice to give away presents to the departing daughter, usually some resources to begin her new married life, slowly assumed extraordinary proportions and turned into a social evil. Brides were expected to bring the "gifts" regardless of their personal willingness. The bride's family could no longer have an individual say; lists were prepared and sent to the girl's house before the final agreement between the two families. The condition being that the boy would marry the girl only if the demands were met. Such a custom is being practiced not only in India but also in other countries like Bangladesh and Nepal. The reason behind this custom is the poor economical condition of the people along with a lack of education; unawareness of legal rights among women and a general bias against the women.

Crimes like rape, kidnapping, eve teasing and indecent exposure can be grouped as crimes against women. Rape is the worst crime against women after murder and the maximum punishment under the Indian Penal Code (IPC) is life imprisonment. An abortion or miscarriage due to natural causes is not an offence. Therefore, the law does not deal with it. However, violent and forceful abortion is a crime. Sections 312 and 316 of the Indian Penal Code deal with abortion as crime. Section 313 deals with abortion without the consent of the woman. The punishment could even be life imprisonment. The Hindu Succession Act gives male and female heirs almost equal right to inheritance. Section 14 says that any property possessed by a female Hindu shall be held by her as full owner and not as a limited owner.

METHODS AND MATERIALS

This study is undertaken in 5 blocks in Cuddalore district, viz. Bhuvanagiri, Keerapalayam, Parangipettai, Cuddalore and Virudhachalam. From each block, 60 rural women are selected as sample. The relevant primary data are collected from the SHGs women respondents by employing a well-structured interview schedule. The collected data are classified and tabulated with the help of computer programming. The general data interpretation is done with the help of percentage and average analysis.

RESULTS AND DISCUSSION

Data presented in Table 1 indicate the occupation wise respondents' awareness on rights of women in Indian constitution. It could be noted that out of the total 300 respondents, 60.67 per cent of them are aware of right to equality in Indian constitution article 14 and 16 and the rest 39.33 per cent of them are ignorant of this fact. Majority of the labour group (66.67%) and agriculture group (58.33%) respondents are not aware of right to equality provision in Indian constitution. Out of the total 300 respondents, 56.33 per cent of them are aware of right to means of livelihood enshrined in article 39 (A) of the Indian constitution and the rest of them are not aware of the same. The labour group respondents (58.33%) and business group respondents (57.69%) have no awareness on right to means of livelihood enshrined in article 39 (A) of the Indian constitution. Out of the total 300 respondents, 53.33 per cent of them possess knowledge on right to life enshrined in article 21 of the Indian constitution and the rest 46.67 per cent of them do not possess such knowledge. The respondents of government employees (70.77%) occupy the first position with respect to knowledge on right to life enshrined in article 21 of the Indian constitution. Out of the total 300 respondents, 59 per cent of them possess knowledge on right to equal protection before the law as enshrined in article 15 of the Indian constitution and the rest 41 per cent of them have no such knowledge. The labour group (61.67%) and agriculture group (54.17%) respondents have no knowledge right to equal protection before the law as enshrined in article 15 of the Indian constitution.

In this study, 45.67 per cent of the respondents have knowledge of laws against discrimination of women enshrined in article 15(3) of the Indian constitution and the rest 54.33 per cent of them do not possess such knowledge. Majority of the Government employees (56.92%) and private employees have knowledge of laws against discrimination of women enshrined in article 15(3) of the Indian constitution. Out of the total 300 respondents, 48.67 per cent of them have knowledge of law and work and maternity relief enshrined in article 42 of the Indian constitution and the rest 51.33 per cent of them have no such knowledge. Majority of the labour group (65%), agriculture group (66.67%) and business group (57.69%) have no knowledge of law and work and maternity relief enshrined in article 42 of the Indian constitution. Moreover, 55.67 per

Table 1
Occupation wise Respondents' Knowledge on Rights of Women in Indian Constitution

	Knowledge of right to equality		*Knowledge of right to means of livelihood*		*Knowledge of right to life*		*Knowledge of right to equal protection before the law*	
Occupation	*Yes*	*No*	*Yes*	*No*	*Yes*	*No*	*Yes*	*No*
Labour	20	40	25	35	22	38	23	37
	(33.33)	(66.67)	(41.67)	(58.33)	(36.67)	(63.33)	(38.33)	(61.67)
Agriculture	20	28	25	23	20	28	22	26
	(41.67)	(58.33)	(52.08)	(47.92)	(41.67)	(58.33)	(45.83)	(54.17)
Business	30	22	22	30	27	25	26	26
	(57.69)	(42.31)	(42.31)	(57.69)	(51.92)	(48.08)	(50.00)	(50.00)
Private employees	57	18	52	23	45	30	58	17
	(76.00)	(24.00)	(69.33)	(30.67)	(60.00)	(40.00)	(77.33)	(22.67)
Government employees	55	10	45	20	46	19	48	17
	(84.62)	(15.38)	(69.23)	(30.77)	(70.77)	(29.23)	(73.85)	(26.15)
Total	182	118	169	131	160	140	177	123
	(60.67)	(39.33)	(56.33)	(43.67)	(53.33)	(46.67)	(59.00)	(41.00)

Contd...

	Knowledge of laws against discrimination of women		Knowledge of law on work and maternity relief		Knowledge of law renounce practices derogatory to the dignity of women		
Occupation	*Yes*	*No*	*Yes*	*No*	*Yes*	*No*	*Total*
Labour	19 (31.67)	41 (68.33)	21 (35.00)	39 (65.00)	24 (40.00)	36 (60.00)	60
Agriculture	15 (31.25)	33 (68.75)	16 (33.33)	32 (66.67)	21 (43.75)	27 (56.25)	48
Business	18 (34.62)	34 (65.38)	22 (42.31)	30 (57.69)	27 (51.92)	25 (48.08)	52
Private Employees	48 (64.00)	27 (36.00)	49 (65.33)	26 (34.67)	49 (65.33)	26 (34.67)	75
Government Employees	37 (56.92)	28 (43.08)	38 (58.46)	27 (41.54)	46 (70.77)	19 (29.23)	65
Total	137 (45.67)	163 (54.33)	146 (48.67)	154 (51.33)	167 (55.67)	133 (44.330	300

Source: Computed.
Figures in parenthesis denote percentages.

Contd...

Chi Square Summary Result

Occupation group	*Chi square calculated value*	*Degrees of freedom*	*Chi square tabulate value*
Knowledge of right to equality	49.25	4	9.43
Knowledge of right to means of livelihood	19.31	4	9.43
Knowledge of Right to life	18.64	4	9.43
Knowledge of right to equal protection before the law	32.12	4	9.43
Knowledge of laws against discrimination of women	24.8	4	9.43
Knowledge of law on work and maternity relief	20.68	4	9.43
Knowledge of law renounce practices derogatory to the dignity of women	17.87	4	9.43

cent of the respondents have knowledge of law renounce practices derogatory to the dignity of women enshrined in article 51(a)(e) of the Indian constitution and the rest 44.33 per cent of them have no such knowledge. Majority of the government employees (70.77%), private employees (65.66%) and businessmen (51.92%) possess knowledge of law renounce practices derogatory to the dignity of women enshrined in article 51(a)(e) of the Indian constitution.

The chi square test is applied for further discussion. The computed chi square value is 49.25 which is greater than its tabulated value at 5 per cent level of significance. Hence there is an association between occupation status and respondents' knowledge of right to equality. A similar result has been observed with respect to respondents' knowledge of right to means of livelihood, knowledge of right to life knowledge of right to equal protection before the law, knowledge of laws against discrimination of women, knowledge of law on work and maternity relief, and knowledge of law renounce practices derogatory to the dignity of women.

A study of data in Table 2 indicates the occupation wise respondents' knowledge on laws related to dowry, marriage and divorce. It could be noted that out of the total 300 respondents, 70.67 per cent of them aware of dowry prohibition act, 1961 and the rest 29.33 per cent of them are ignorant of this act. Majority of the labour group (58.33%) and agriculture group (58.33%) have no knowledge on dowry prohibition act, 1961. Out of the total 300 respondents, 44 per cent of them have knowledge on foreign marriage act and the rest 56 per cent of them have no such knowledge. Majority of the government employees (61.54%) and private employees (56%) possess knowledge on foreign marriage act. In this study, 42 per cent of the respondents are familiar with special marriage act, 1954 and the rest 58 per cent of them do not possess such knowledge. Most of the labour group (80%) and agriculture group (79.17%) have no knowledge on special marriage act, 1954. It could be observed that 62.33 per cent of the respondents have knowledge on Hindu Marriage Act, 1955 and the rest 37.67 per cent of them are ignorant of this act. Most of the government employees (81.54%) and private employees (84%) have knowledge on Hindu marriage act, 1955. Out of the total 300 respondents 59 per cent of them possess knowledge on Indian divorce act, 1869 and the rest 41 per cent of them have no such knowledge. Majority of the labour group (51.67%) and agriculture group (52.08%) have no knowledge on Indian divorce act, 1869. In this study, 37.33 per cent of the respondents are familiar with converts' marriage dissolution act, 1866 and the rest majority of them are ignorant of this act. A more than half of the government employees (61.545%) and private employees (52%) are familiar with converts' marriage dissolution act, 1866. Moreover, 59.33 per cent of the respondents are known to prohibition of child marriage act, 2006 and the rest 40.67 per cent of them do not have such knowledge. Majority of the labour group (60%) and agriculture group (56.25%) have no knowledge on prohibition of child marriage act, 2006.

Table 2
Occupation wise Respondents' Knowledge on Laws Related to Dowry, Marriage and Divorce

	Dowry Prohibition Act, 1961		*Foreign Marriage Act, 1969*		*Special Marriage Act, 1954*		*Hindu Marriage Act, 1955*	
Occupation	*Yes*	*No*	*Yes*	*No*	*Yes*	*No*	*Yes*	*No*
Labour	25	35	15	45	12	48	23	37
	41.67	58.33	25.00	75.00	20.00	80.00	38.33	61.67
Agriculture	20	28	13	35	10	38	22	26
	41.67	58.33	27.08	72.92	20.83	79.17	45.83	54.17
Business	40	12	22	30	27	25	26	26
	76.92	23.08	42.31	57.69	51.92	48.08	50.00	50.00
Private employees	67	8	42	33	40	35	63	12
	89.33	10.67	56.00	44.00	53.33	46.67	84.00	16.00
Government employees	60	5	40	25	37	28	53	12
	92.31	7.69	61.54	38.46	56.92	43.08	81.54	18.46
Total	212	88	132	168	126	174	187	113
	70.67	29.33	44.00	56.00	42.00	58.00	62.33	37.67

Contd...

Occupation	*Indian Divorce Act, 1869*		*Converts' Marriage Dissolution Act,1866*		*Prohibition of Child Marriage Act, 2006*		*Total*
	Yes	*No*	*Yes*	*No*	*Yes*	*No*	
Labour	29	31	11	49	24	36	60
	48.33	51.67	18.33	81.67	40.00	60.00	
Agriculture	23	25	10	38	21	27	48
	47.92	52.08	20.83	79.17	43.75	56.25	
Business	28	24	12	40	27	25	52
	53.85	46.15	23.08	76.92	51.92	48.08	
Private employees	48	27	39	36	55	20	75
	64.00	36.00	52.00	48.00	73.33	26.67	
Government employees	49	16	40	25	51	14	65
	75.38	24.62	61.54	38.46	78.46	21.54	
Total	177	123	112	188	178	122	300
	59.00	41.00	37.33	62.67	59.33	40.67	

Source: Computed
Figures in parenthesis denote percentages.

Contd...

Chi Square Summary Result

Occupation group	*Chi square calculated value*	*Degrees of freedom*	*Chi square tabulate value*
Dowry Prohibition Act, 1961	72.09	4	9.43
Foreign Marriage Act, 1969	26.92	4	9.43
Special Marriage Act, 1954	32.75	4	9.43
Hindu Marriage Act, 1955	48.86	4	9.43
Indian Divorce Act, 1869	13.82	4	9.43
Converts' Marriage Dissolution Act,1866	42.53	4	9.43
Prohibition of Child Marriage Act, 2006	31.26	4	9.43

A study of data in Table 3 indicates the occupation wise respondents' knowledge on laws related to crimes against women crimes identified under the Indian penal code. It could be noted that out of the total 300 respondents, 59 per cent of them aware of punishment for rape under 376 of the Indian penal code and the rest of them do not have such awareness. Majority of the labour group (68.33%) and agriculture group(60.42%) have no awareness on punishment for rape under 376 of the Indian penal code. In this study, 48 per cent of the respondents are familiar with punishment for kidnapping and abduction under section 363 and 373 of the Indian penal code and the rest of the respondents do not possess such awareness. Out of the total 300 respondents, 60.67 per cent of them have knowledge on punishment for homicide and dowry death under 302 and 304(b) of the Indian penal code and the rest of the respondents do not possess such knowledge. Most of the government employees (86.15%) and majority of the private employees (73.33%) and businessmen (51.92%) have awareness on punishment for homicide and dowry death under 302 and 304(b) of the Indian penal code.

It could be noted that 45.67 per cent of the respondents have known about punishment for torture both mental and physical under section 498(a) of the Indian penal code and the rest of the respondents do not possess such awareness. A more than two third of the labour group(78.33%) and agriculture group (75%) respondents are ignorant of punishment for torture both mental and physical under section 498(a) of the Indian penal code. Out of the total 300 respondents, 43.33 per cent of them are familiar with punishment for molestation under Sec 354 of the Indian penal code and the rest of the respondents do not possess such awareness. A more than half of the government employees (52.31%) and private employees (60%) respondents have awareness on punishment for molestation under Sec 354 of the Indian penal code. It is observed that 55 per cent of the respondents have knowledge on sexual harassment under section 509 of the Indian penal code and the rest of the respondents do not possess such knowledge. A more than half of the labour group (63.33%) and agriculture group (56.25%) respondents have awareness on punishment for sexual harassment under section 509 of the Indian penal code. Moreover, 37.33 per cent of the respondents possess knowledge on punishment for importation of girls under section 9 and 366(b) of the Indian penal code and the rest of the respondents do not possess such knowledge. A more than half of the government employees (52.31%) and private employees (60%) respondents have awareness on punishment for importation of girls under section 9 and 366(b) of the Indian penal code.

A study of data in Table 3 indicates the income wise respondents' knowledge on laws related to crimes against women crimes identified under the Indian penal code. It could be noted that highest income group respondents take the first position in their awareness on punishment for rape under section 376 of the Indian penal code(86.84%), punishment for torture both mental and

Table 3
Occupation wise Respondents' Knowledge on Laws Related to Crimes against Women Crimes Identified Under the Indian Penal Code

	Rape (Sec. 376 IPC)		*Kidnapping and Abduction for Different Purposes (Sec. 363-373 IPC)*		*Homicide for Dowry, Dowry Death or their Attempts (Sec.302/304-B of IPC)*		*Torture, both Mental and Physical (Sec. 498-A of IPC)*	
Occupation	*Yes*	*No*	*Yes*	*No*	*Yes*	*No*	*Yes*	*No*
Labour	19	41	20	40	24	36	13	47
	31.67	68.33	33.33	66.67	40.00	60.00	21.67	78.33
Agriculture	19	29	20	28	20	28	12	36
	39.58	60.42	41.67	58.33	41.67	58.33	25.00	75.00
Business	29	23	22	30	27	25	26	26
	55.77	44.23	42.31	57.69	51.92	48.08	50.00	50.00
Private employees	56	19	45	30	55	20	48	27
	74.67	25.33	60.00	40.00	73.33	26.67	64.00	36.00
Government employees	54	11	37	28	56	9	38	27
	83.08	16.92	56.92	43.08	86.15	13.85	58.46	41.54
Total	177	123	144	156	182	118	137	163
	59.00	41.00	48.00	52.00	60.67	39.33	45.67	54.33

Contd...

	Molestation (Sec. 354 of IPC)		*Sexual Harassment (Sec.509 of IPC)*		*Importation of Girls (up to 21 years of age) 9Sec. 366.B of IPC)*		
Occupation	*Yes*	*No*	*Yes*	*No*	*Yes*	*No*	*Total*
Labour	21	39	22	38	11	49	60
	35.00	65.00	36.67	63.33	18.33	81.67	
Agriculture	12	36	21	27	12	36	48
	25.00	75.00	43.75	56.25	25.00	75.00	
Business	18	34	27	25	10	42	52
	34.62	65.38	51.92	48.08	19.23	80.77	
Private employees	45	30	49	26	45	30	75
	60.00	40.00	65.33	34.67	60.00	40.00	
Government employees	34	31	46	19	34	31	65
	52.31	47.69	70.77	29.23	52.31	47.69	
Total	130	170	165	135	112	188	300
	43.33	56.67	55.00	45.00	37.33	62.67	

Source: Computed.
Figures in parenthesis denote percentages.

physical (65.38%), punishment for molestation under section 354 of Indian penal code (63.46%), punishment for sexual harassment under section 505 of Indian penal code, and punishment for importation of girls under section 9 and 366(b) of the Indian penal code. The respondents in the income group Rs. 15,000-20,000 stand at the first position in their knowledge on punishment for kidnapping and abduction under section 363 and 373 of the Indian penal code (72.86%) and punishment for homicide and dowry death under 302 and 304(b) of the Indian penal code (83.05%).

Table 4
Occupation wise Respondents' Views on Measures to Safeguard the Legal Rights of Women

Occupation	*Legal awareness programme*	*Review of laws and legislative measures*	*Under-taking investiga-tion*	*Preparing new laws*	*Law reform in marriage and main-tenance*	*Total*
Labour	10 (16.67)	11 (18.33)	8 (13.33)	23 (38.33)	8 (13.33)	60
Agriculture	12 (25.00)	9 (18.75)	10 (20.83)	7 (14.58)	10 (20.83)	48
Business	9 (17.31)	8 (15.38)	16 (30.77)	12 (23.08)	7 (13.46)	52
Private employees	16 (21.33)	11 (14.67)	26 (34.67)	10 (13.33)	12 (16.00)	75
Government employees	23 (35.38)	9 (13.85)	13 (20.00)	13 (20.00)	7 (10.77)	65
Total	70 (23.33)	48 (16.00)	73 (24.33)	65 (21.67)	44 (14.67)	300

Source: Computed
Figures in parenthesis denote percentages

A study of data in Table 4 indicates the occupation wise respondents' views on measures to safe guard the legal rights of women. It could be noted that out of the total 300 respondents, 23.33 per cent of them suggest that women's legal rights can be promoted through conducting legal awareness programme. This view draws major attention among the respondents of government employees (35.38%). In this study, 16 per cent of the respondents suggest that proper review of laws and legislative measures can protect the legal rights of women and 24 per cent of the respondents hold the view on undertaking investigation on status of women can protect the rights. A considerable number of private employees (34.67%) and business group respondents (30.27%) emphasize on need of investigation on legal status of women as measure to protect their rights. In this study, 21.67 per cent of the respondents state that there is a need to prepare new laws and the rest 14.67 per cent of them emphasize the need for law reform in marriage and maintenance.

CONCLUSION

The respondents possess first order knowledge of right to equality enshrined in 14 and 16 of the Indian constitution, knowledge of right to equal protection enshrined in 15 of the Indian constitution the second, knowledge of right to means of livelihood enshrined in article 39 (A) of the Indian constitution the third, knowledge of law and renounce practices derogatory to the status of women enshrined in 51(a) (e) of the Indian constitution the fourth. Knowledge of right to life enshrined in article 21 of the Indian constitution the fifth, knowledge of law on work and maternity relief enshrined in article 42 of the Indian constitution the sixth, and knowledge of laws against discrimination of women enshrined in article 15(3) of the Indian constitution the last.

The respondents possess first order form of knowledge on dowry prohibition act, 1961, knowledge of Hindu marriage act, 1955 the second, knowledge of prohibition of child marriage act, 2006 the third, knowledge of Indian divorce act, 1869 the fourth, knowledge of foreign marriage act, 1969 the fifth, knowledge of special marriage act, 1954 the sixth, and knowledge of converts' marriage dissolution act, 1866 the last. A more than half of the respondents have knowledge on punishment for rape under section 376 of the Indian penal code, punishment for sexual harassment under section 354 of the Indian penal co]de and punishment for homicide and dowry death under section 302 and 304(b) of Indian penal code. Majority of the respondents have no knowledge on punishment for kidnapping and abduction under section 363 and 373 of the Indian penal code, punishment for torture both mental and physical under section 498(a) of the Indian penal code, punishment for molestation under Sec 354 of the Indian penal code and punishment for importation of girls under section 9 and 366(b) of the Indian penal code. In general, government employees occupies the first position in their awareness on knowledge on Laws related to crimes against women Crimes identified under the Indian penal code, private employees the second, businessmen the third, agriculture group the fourth and labor group the last. The respondents make first order suggestion of undertaking investigation on legal status of women as measure to protect the rights, conducting legal awareness programme follows the next order suggestive measure, enacting new laws the third, review of laws and legislative measures the fourth and making law reforms in marriage and maintenance the last.

REFERENCES

Dr. (Mrs) V. Mohini Giri (Ed.) (1999), *Kanya: Exploitation of Little Angels*, Gyan Publishing House, New Delhi.

Sreenath Lalitha (1996), Victimisation of Girl-Child in the Home, *Journal of the Indian Law Institute*, Vol. 38, p. 101-107.

Bhadra Mita (1999), Girl Child in Indian Society, Rawat Publications.

Kishwar Madhu (1995), Where Daughters are Unwanted, Manushi, No. 86, Jan.-Feb., p. 15-22.

Bhargavi V. Davar (2001), *Mental Health from a Gender Perspective*, Edited by, New Delhi, Sage Publication, p. 427.

Kishwar, Madhu (1992), Sex Harassment and Slander as Weapons of Subjugation, *Manushi*, No. 62, Jan.-Feb., p. 2-15.

B. Sivaramayya (1983), Status of Women and Social Change, *Journal of Indian law Institute*, Vol. 25, pp. 270.

Chowdhary Prem (1994), Widow Remarriage in Haryana, *Manushi*, No. 82, May-June, p. 12-18.

Dutt, Anuradha (1993), In the Name of the Mother, *Manushi*, No. 79, p. 23-26, Nov.-Dec.

Masoodi Saqlain G. and Dhar Lalita (1998), Womens Rights in Christianity: Some Reflections on Divorce Laws, *Cochin University Law Review*, Vol. 22, p. 16-44.

Raju K. N. M. and Bhat T. N. (1996-97), Gender Issues in the Choice and Adoption of Family Planning Methods, *Indian Journal of Gender Studies*, Vol. 3-4, 57-70.

CUSTOM, LAW AND VIOLENCE AGAINST WOMEN IN INDIA

ANUPAM AHLUWALIA*

INTRODUCTION

Women have been an easy victim of violence. A peep into the history reveals the fact that since times immemorial she has been subjected to different kinds of violence. Crime against women is a universal phenomenon and the difference from a society to another society lies only in the frequency, quantum and nature of such violence. So long we trace the written records of the human civilization the fact is quite evident that Women have been victims of gender discrimination. There is no woman in this world who has not suffered any kind of violence at one time or the other in her life. It is a bitter truth that though all men are not molesters, batterers, assaulters, murderers but all women are prospective victims of the violence because of their belonging to weaker sex. From quite a few decades the need for giving her due to her was felt and women issues have gathered importance both at national and international fronts. Crime against woman has gathered the main platform in these concerns, the basic reason behind this issue attracting the attention of the masses and the people in power is that the frequency of such crimes has increased to a great extent and that fact has shocked the sensibility of mankind.

DEFINITION OF VIOLENCE AGAINST WOMEN

An attempt was made by the United Nations to define "Violence Against Women" in 1993 in Declaration On the Elimination Of Violence Against Women. It defines it as 'any act of gender-based violence that results in, or is likely to result in, physical, sexual or psychological harm or suffering to women, including threats of such acts, coercion or arbitrary deprivation of liberty, whether occurring in public or in private life[1]. Further it says, Violence against women shall be understood to encompass, but not be limited to, the following:

(a) Physical, sexual and psychological violence occurring in the family, including battering, sexual abuse of female children in the household, dowry-related violence, marital rape, female genital mutilation and

* *Lecturer Law, School of Legal Studies, Guru Nanak Dev University Regional Campus, Jalandhar, Punjab.*

other traditional practices harmful to women, non-spousal violence and violence related to exploitation;

(b) Physical, sexual and psychological violence occurring within the general community, including rape, sexual abuse, sexual harassment and intimidation at work, in educational institutions and elsewhere, trafficking in women and forced prostitution;

(c) Physical, sexual and psychological violence perpetrated or condoned by the State, wherever it occurs.'[2]

UNITED NATION'S CONCERN FOR THE SAFETY OF WOMEN AROUND THE GLOBE

The globe has unitedly come forward for giving her protection and respect. The United Nations from time to time has come up with different conferences and has made numerous conventions with an aim of giving special status and rights to the women folk of the world which would help them improving there fate in their world. On December 10, 1948 the General Assembly of the United Nations adapted and proclaimed the Universal Declaration of Human Rights which states that all human beings are born free and they have an equality in dignity and rights.[3] Unlike the French Declaration of the Rights of Man, 1789[4], The Universal Declaration of Human Rights grants the rights to all human beings i.e. men and women both irrespective of their sex. Further the UDHR under Art.2 declares that there shall be no distinction among humans on the grounds of race, colour, sex, language, religion, political or other opinion, national or social origin, property, birth or other status.[5] The Convention for the Elimination of All Forms of Discrimination against Women 1979 (CEDAW), prohibits any form of discrimination against women as an offence against humanity.[6] It defines what constitutes discrimination against women and sets up an agenda for national action to end such discrimination. By accepting the Convention, States commit themselves to undertake a series of measures to end discrimination against women in all forms.

Violence against women is a major hindrance in the enjoyment of human rights by the women through out the world. The same issue was talked upon in *Beijing Platform for Action* which stated that, 'Violence against women is an obstacle to the achievement of the objectives of equality, development and peace' Violence against women both violates and impairs or nullifies the enjoyment by women of their human rights and fundamental freedoms. The long-standing failure to protect and promote those rights and freedoms in the case of violence against women is a matter of concern to all States and should be addressed.[7] It also emphasized the importance of reliable statistical data[8] in understanding violence against women and recommended that work be done to promote research, collect data and compile statistics, especially concerning domestic violence relating to the prevalence of different forms of violence against women, and encourage research into the causes, nature, seriousness and consequences of violence against women and the effectiveness of measures implemented to prevent and redress violence against women.[9]

All these instruments aim at providing safe guard to women's human rights and have promised her an environment suitable for safety of her person, property and for the development of her personality. It is worth mentioning here that India along with majority of the countries of the world is signatory to these instruments and thus it is mandatory for the member countries to follow the provisions of the said conventions. More over India is a modern welfare state, and one of the most important essential of a modern state is to provide equality and freedom to its inhabitants and develop an environment in which its citizens can lead a progressive life.

NATIONAL CONCERN

The Preamble of the Constitution provides "the equality of Status and opportunity." The Indian Constitution has ensured equal status to all i.e. not only between men and men but also between men and women.[10] Article 14[11] provides for equality in general. Article 15[12] prohibits discrimination. Article 15 (3)[13] provides for special protective discrimination in favor of women and children. Art. 23 (1)[14]prohibits the traffic in human beings and all forms of bonded labour,[15] but authorises the State to impose compulsory service for 'public interest'.[16] Traffic in human beings obviously includes traffic in women and children[17] for immoral and other purposes, e.g. to make them Devdasis[18] In *Gaurav Jain v/s Union of India*[19] the Hon'ble SC observed that:

> "The fallen victims in the flesh trade are no less than a slave trade.
> The fallen/trapped victims of flesh trade are subjected to cruel,
> inhuman and degrading treatment which are obnoxious,
> abominable and an affront to article 5 of the said declaration
> (UDHR, 1948) and also Article 21 of Indian Constitution".

Article 46[20] directs the State to promote the educational and economic interests of the women and weaker sections of the people and that it shall protect them from social injustice and all forms of exploitation. Exploitation which means the utilization of person's for ones own ends, is opposed to the dignity of the individual to which the preamble of the Constitution refers. It is opposed to the Directive principles of the State Policy, which provide respectively that the State shall secure the health and strength of workers, men and women and the tender age of children are not abused, and that citizens are not forced by economic necessity to enter avocations unsuited to their age or strength; that childhood and youth are protected against exploitation and against moral and material abandonment.[21]

A part from granting many fundamental rights to its citizens equally Indian Constitution empowers the legislature to make special laws for the protection of women and granting them special privileged status so that they can be helped in progressing and improve their social and economic status.[22] Thus Indian legislature from time to time has come up with special laws like The Dowry Prohibition Act,1961 (28 of 1961) The Commission of Sati (Prevention) Act, 1987 (3 of 1988) The Immoral Traffic (Prevention) Act, 1956 ,The Indecent Representation of Women (Prohibition) Act, 1986 , The Child Marriage Restraint Act, 1929 ,The Medical Termination of Pregnancy Act, 1971 (34 of 1971), The Pre-Natal Diagnostic Techniques Act, The Prevention of Domestic Violence Against Women Act, 2005 etc, all these laws aim at providing protection and safety to the women of India. Apart from these the various provisions of the Indian Penal Code,1860, Code of Criminal Procedure, 1973 stand for safe guarding her from various types crimes committed against her.

Despite the fact that so many laws exist on the paper for the protection of the rights of women and her security of her person, the fact remains that due to the poor enforcement of these legal provisions we have not been able to achieve the object behind these legislations. What is more ironical is that irrespective of the various safeguards provided to them many times they are constant victims of harassment of the enforcement agencies when they approach them for the redressal of their complaints.

The fact is evident from the figures relating to crime against women collected by the National Crime Record Bureau. A total of 1,85,312 incidents of crime against women (both under IPC and SLL) were reported in the country during 2007 as compared to 1,64,765 during 2006 recording an increase of 12.5% during 2007. These crimes have continuously increased during 2003-2007 with 1,40,601 cases in 2003, 1,54,333 cases in 2004,1,55,553 in 2005, 1,64,765 cases in 2006 and 1,85,312 cases in 2007. The rate of crime has increased marginally from 14.7 during the year 2006 to 16.3 during 2007. The proportion of IPC crimes committed against women towards total IPC crimes has increased continually during last 5 years from 7.6% in 2003 to 8.8% during 2007. It is quite shameful for the nation that the capital of the country, New Delhi is the most unsafe city for the women. Delhi has reported the highest rate at 7.0 as compared to the National average of 1.8.[23] Though the figures show an alarming situation yet many of us rarely acknowledge that violence against women and girls, many of whom are brutalized from cradle to grave simply because of their gender, is the most pervasive human right violation in the world.

CLASSIFICATION OF CRIME AGAINST WOMEN

In common the crime against women constitutes several forms of atrocities against them. It is very difficult to give the term a precise definition since it is influenced by various socio-legal aspects. Generally speaking these are such acts of violence which are directed specifically against the person of women. These crimes can be classified on two basis:

On the Basis of Area of Commission of Crime

(i) Crimes committed against women in society, like physical hurt, sexual assault, rape, kidnapping , murder etc.

(ii) Sexual harassment in educational institutions, work place.

(iii) Crimes committed against women in the home like wife battering, physical abuse at the hands of her partner/relatives, dowry related harassment, dowry deaths, sexual crimes in form of rape, incest etc.

(iv) Crimes committed against women in the custody, like forcible surrender for sex, rape, physical assault etc.

On the Basis of Laws Governing the Various Crimes

(i) *Crimes identified under Indian Penal Code 1860:* Rape,[24] Kidnapping and Abduction for different purposes,[25] Culpable Homicide,[26] Murder,[27] Dowry Death,[28] Cruelty by Husband and his Relatives,[29] Molestation,[30] Sexual Harassment[31]referred in the past as Eve Teasing, Importation of girls (up to 21 years of age)[32].

(ii) Crimes identified under Special and Local laws.

REASONS FOR LOWER REPORTING OF CRIMES AGAINST WOMEN

The figures though give shocking picture about the rising crime rate but the fact remains that is it just the tip of the ice burg. The true picture is much more scaring as the number of incidents actually taking place is much higher that the ones reported. The reasons for lower reporting of these crimes are as under:

1. Cases of domestic violence specifically are less reported because of the social acceptability of violence and men's dominance coupled with privacy and sanctity of the family affairs and self sacrificing womanhood which stops a woman to report. National Crime Bureau in its report pointed out that it is estimated that closer to 5crore women face domestic violence in their homes however only 0.1% are courageous to report against them.[33]

   As age old saying explains the situation

   " Those within the four walls do not wish to speak about it and those outside do not want to listen about it."

2. Economic dependence of women on men forces them to tolerate such acts of violence since they don't have any other choice except of tolerating it.

3. In case of crimes committed out of home women generally do not report because of family prestige. No wonder we boast of living in the modern society but our hypocratic attitude is quite evident when we link the loss of virginity of the victim of a sexual crime with the loss of honour and respect of her family. The irony in such a case is though

she being a victim deserves all support, help, strength and sympathy from her family and society at large, but what she gets is hatred, disgrace, neglect and insult. Resultantly many women who fall a prey to the sexual crimes prefer to hide them and choose not to report.

4. Even the legal framework and the enforcement mechanism some where is responsible for low reporting. It is a nude truth that police in our country does not carry a clean picture. Many times the victims of these crimes are subjected to further harassment and humiliation by the police. Not only this there are a number of reported incidents speaking about the atrocities committed by the police on the women in their custody.

The result of such lesser or under reporting is two fold. One the true picture of the problem is not revealed, which one way or the other affects the policy making for the protection of the woman. Secondly when the violence is tolerated and goes unreported the perpetrator and the like minded persons gains more courage which results in the repetition of such acts against the same person or another.

PREVENTIVE MEASURES

Only legislation and law enforcement agencies cannot prevent the incident of crime against women. There is need of social awakening and change in the attitude of the masses, so that due respect and equal status is given to women. Its a time when the woman needs to be given her due. This awakening can be brought by education campaign among youth making them aware of existing social evils and the means to eradicate same. Mass media can play an active role here as in the present days it has reached every corner of the nation. Various N.G.O's can hold a responsible position here by assigning them with the task of highlighting socio-economic causes leading to such crimes and by disseminating information about their catastrophic effect on the womanhood and the society at large. It must not be forgotten that the most important role in granting the protection to the woman against such crime has to be done by law enforcement agencies. These agencies can take a deterrent step to curb these crimes since they have power and legal authority behind their actions. Bureau of Police Research and Development, Ministry of Home Affairs, Government of India in a study has stressed upon three measures to curb and check the crimes against women. Accordingly they lay three ways to check and control this menace. Firstly by reforms in law, secondly by issue of executive instructions and thirdly by strengthening woman police and setting up special cells in the States and U.T's to deal with the problem.

Laws in isolation cannot do miracles and this is but for sure. So what else needs to stand by the laws is social awakening. Of course this social awakening needs to be backed by strong and stringent laws and governmental instructions, sufficient financial assistance and infra structural framework, skilled and trained police personnel, establishment of fairly large number of special cells dealing with the crime against women, speedy disposal of these cases and above all a will in the womanhood of India that they will no longer tolerate such acts of violence.

NOTES

1. Article 1 Declaration on the Elimination of Violence against Women.
2. Article 2 Declaration on the Elimination of Violence Against Women.
3. Article 1. UDHR, All human beings are born free and equal in dignity and rights. They are endowed with reason and conscience and should act towards one another in a spirit of brotherhood.
4. Article 1. Men are born and remain free and equal in rights. The said declaration in its entire text fails to use the term women, considering them not worth giving any right.
5. Article 2. Everyone is entitled to all the rights and freedoms set forth in this Declaration, without distinction of any kind, such as race, colour, sex, language, religion, political or other opinion, national or social origin, property, birth or other status. Furthermore, no distinction shall be made on the basis of the political, jurisdictional or international status of the country or territory to which a person belongs, whether it be independent, trust, non-self-governing or under any other limitation of sovereignty
6. Art. 1 Discrimination against women, denying or limiting as it does their equality of rights with men, is fundamentally unjust and constitutes an offence against human dignity.
7. Beijing Platform for Action, paragraph 12.
8. In India the data is collected by National Crime Record Bearue. Until the year 1988 there was no separate record of the crime against women. It was for the first time in 1988 that NCRB started collecting the statistics separately on crime against women.
9. *Supra note* 8 paragraph 129a.
10. Art. 14-16 of the Constitution of India.
11. Art. 14. The State shall not deny to any person equality before law or equal protection of the laws within the territory of India.
12. Art. 15. The State shall not discriminate against any citizen on grounds only of religion, race, caste, sex, and place of birth or any of them.
13. Art. 15 (3). Nothing in this article shall prevent the State from making any special provisions for women and children.
14. Art. 23. Traffic in human being and begar and other similar forms of forced labour are prohibited and any contravention of this provision shall be an offence punishable in accordance with law.
15. Vide Bonded Labour System(Abolition) Act,1976 the word 'Bonded Labour' means any labour or service rendered under the bonded labour system.
16. Basu Durga Das, Shorter Constitution of India, 13th edn., Wadhwa and Company, Nagpur, 2002, p. 325.

17. Raj Bhadur v. Legal Remembrances of the Govt. of W.B. AIR 1953 Cal. 522 ; Nihal Singh v. Rambai, AIR. 1987 MP. 126 (para 12).
18. Vishaljeet v. Union of India, (1990) 3 SCC 318 (paras 3,7,18): AIR 1990 SC 1412.
19. AIR 1997 SC 3021.
20. Art. 46. The State shall promote with special care the educational and economic interests of the weaker sections of the people, and in particular, of the Scheduled Castes and the Scheduled Tribes, and shall protect them from social injustice and all forms of exploitation.
21. Seervai H.M, Constitutional Law of India, Vol. 2, Universal Book Traders, Delhi, 2002. p.1234.
22. Art. 15 (3) Constitution of India.
23. *http://ncrb.nic.in/cii2007/cii-2007/CHAP5*
24. Sec. 376 Indian Penal Code, 1860.
25. Sec. 363-373 Indian Penal Code,1860.
26. Sec. 299 Indian Penal Code, 1860.
27. Sec. 300 Indian Penal Code, 1860.
28. Sec. 304 B Indian Penal Code, 1860.
29. Sec. 498 A Indian Penal Code, 1860.
30. Sec. 354 Indian Penal Code,1860.
31. Sec. 509 Indian Penal Code, 1860.
32. Sec 366-B Indian Penal Code,1860.
33. *http://ncrb.nic.in*

ROLE OF JUDICIARY IN PROMOTION AND PROTECTION OF RIGHTS OF WOMEN UNDER THE CONSTITUTION OF INDIA

DEVINDER SINGH* & DINESH KUMAR**

"One could judge the degree of civilization of a country by the social and political position of its women".

Charles Fourrier (1772-1837)

INTRODUCTION

The Indian society lacks homogeneity, as there exist differences of religion, language, culture etc. There are sections of people who are comparatively weaker than others-economically, socially and culturally-and their lot can be ameliorated only when the state makes a special effort to that end. Mutual suspicion and distrust exists between various religious and linguistic groups in the society.[1]

In our country women are worshipped as goddess as mother and as 'creator'. It is presumed that the best creation belongs to women. Half of our population too is women. Women always been discriminated, suffered and are suffering in silence. Self-sacrifice and self denial are their nobility and fortitude and yet they have been subjected to all inequities, indignities and discrimination.[2]

The Indian Constitution is dominantly egalitarian and equalitarian. It is egalitarian because it believes in the equality of all men. In other words, it provides for an egalitarian socio-political system in which there will be no discrimination on grounds of race, religion, sex, caste or place of birth. It is equalitarian because its provisions can be used to maintain equality and to prevent discrimination and also to bring about equality where inequality or discrimination exists.[3] Certain sections of Indian society including the Indian women have been victim of social injustice since centuries. With a view to all aviating the lots of such socially handicapped sections of society, the framers of the constitution have laid down specific constitutional guarantees.[4]

* *Reader, Department of Laws, Panjab University, Chandigarh-160 014.*

** *Lecturer, Department of Laws, Panjab University, Chandigarh 160 014.*

The Constitution of India enjoins equality of sexes but unfortunately Indian society is still harsh to women in the same way as it was during the period of Manu. The Constitution sets up an effective institutional machinery to oversee that these safeguards are properly effectuated by the various governments in the country. However, even after 61 years of India's independence, the condition of women is still vulnerable.

The purpose of this article is to highlight the main provisions of the Indian Constitution regarding 'women' in brief and role-played by judiciary. In the end of it some suggestion shall be given to improve the condition of the women.

WOMEN AND THE LAW

The condition of woman in law, full of disabilities and disqualification the world over is described in vivid terms in legal history and also in encyclopedias. Under the old Christian law, she was not considered a 'person'. Thus, she had no rights to join a college (only a 'person' could do so). She could not be enrolled as a medical practitioner or a lawyer for the same reason. Until the twentieth century, she had no right to vote in Christian countries. In some Muslim countries, she still has no right to vote. In the ancient law of Christian countries, she labored under various disabilities. Their participation in the civic life, in the work force, in industries, in education and administration was minimal; and in Muslim countries insignificant.[5]

In ancient India alone throughout the ancient civilizations, they occupied the proud place of equal partners. There is a reference regarding more than twenty women rishis (religious leaders), who have composed the hymns of *Rigved*. In ancient Bharat, they were elected representatives and took part in debates and *shastrartha* (learned discourse). There is reference to their taking part in sports and training in martial arts. This appears to have been lost in the struggle of a thousand years or so against foreign invasions.[6]

The position of women in India has not been very sound in the preceding few hundred years. During British rule, certain attempts were made to improve the lot of women. For this purpose certain laws were enacted. These include the Hindu Widow's Remarriage Act, 1856 (repealed in 1983) the Child Marriage Restraint Act, 1929, and the Hindu Women's Right to Property Act, 1937 (repealed in 1956 and replaced by the Hindu Succession Act).[7]

Since Independence, All India Women's Conference became interested in constructive work and left its agitational attitude of pre-independence era. Its activities since Independence led to the various constitutional measures, different state's legislations, judicial decisions, the democratic policy, the awakening on the part of certain section of women, the influence of the feminist movements in the west, all these have helped to initiate the women's liberation in India. Some significant ones are: Act of Woman's Legal Rights, 1952; the Suppression of Immoral Traffic in Women and Children Act, 1954; the Special Marriage Act, 1954; the Hindu Marriage and Divorce Act, 1956; Intestate

Succession Act, 1956; the Orphanages and Widow Home Act [The Orphanages and other Charitable Homes (Supervision and Control) Act, 1960]; and the Dowry Prohibition Act, 1961, the domestic violence act, to cite a few.[8] But we have miles to go before we can claim that there is gender justice in India. Despite all these efforts to promote the welfare of women, one has to admit that even now women in India are not treated with dignity. They are neither allowed, nor encouraged to enjoy their basic rights, and they are not accepted by men as equal to them. The pitty is that women themselves have not realized that they are equal to men.

India is the largest functioning democracy in the world. It is axiomatic to say that the true spirit of democracy cannot be achieved unless there is equality between all sections of the people. Viewed from the perspective that women constitute over 49 per cent of the Indian population and 50 per cent of the world population, it becomes even more apparent that humanity cannot progress unless equal rights are not only conferred but implemented in a manner which makes the constitutional guarantee of equality before the law and equal protection of the laws a living reality.

The struggle of the Indian women can thus be characterized as a fight for humanism - it is a fight against poverty, ignorance, inequality and all other factors which negate the forces of progress and an assertion of all healthy and positive norms and attitudes which spell out advancement, equality, progress and freedom from any kind of social bondage.[9]

WOMEN AND THE INDIAN CONSTITUTION

The Constitution of India per se does not make specific provisions on women's rights. In fact the word 'women' has been scarcely used in the Constitution. The Preamble of the Constitution accepted sex-equality in principle. It guarantees to all citizens, irrespective of sex, "justice, social, economic and political; liberty of thought, expression, belief, faith and worship; equality of status and opportunity."[10]

However, equality before the law and equal protection of laws is guaranteed under Article 14. Non-discrimination on the ground of religion, race, caste, sex or place of birth is guaranteed under Article 15 (1). Although Article 15(1) enjoins non-discrimination on the ground of sex, Article 15(3) provides that this shall not prevent the State from making any special provision for women and children. So that, while their can be no discrimination against women on the basis of sex in view of Article 15(1), special legislation in favour of women is permissible. Article 15(3) has been so interpreted as permitting discrimination in favour of women but not against women. Every special law for women necessarily carries with it discrimination in favour of women or sex-based discrimination. This kind of discrimination alone is permissible - presumably as a means of strengthening the weak position of women in the social, legal and political spheres and to be looked at not as an exception to equality, but as a promoter of equality. In this sense Article 15(3) can be considered as a charter for affirmative action in favour of women.[11]

This perception is strengthened by the Directive Principles of State Policy. Article 39 enjoins the State to direct its policy towards securing that men and women equally have the right to an adequate means of livelihood, that there is equal pay for equal work for both men and women, and that health and strength of working men and women and the tender age of children are not abused and the citizens are not forced by economic necessities to enter on vocations unsuited to their age or strength. Article 42 directs the State to make provision for securing just and humane conditions of work and to provide for securing just and humane conditions of work and to provide for maternity relief. The Constitution also casts a duty upon the citizens of this country to denounce practices derogatory to the dignity of women (Article 51A (e)).

The Directive Principles as well as Article 15(3) have focused on the vulnerability of children and women in our society and have recognised that those who are in unequal socio-economic and political positions cannot be treated as equals. In this sense, even Article 15(3), though drafted as an exception, flows from Articles 14 and 15(1) because Article 14 which enjoins equality before the law and equal treatment under the laws can be applied fairly, only on the basis that the laws operates alike on persons who are similarly situated in the context of the law in question. All persons similarly circumstanced can be treated alike both regarding privileges conferred and liabilities imposed, but not those who are dissimilar in material respect in the context of the law. That is why the principle of classification has been read into Article 14.[12]

The Indian Constitution also contains some provisions for woman to effectively participate not only in rule making process but also to represent the women section in a more better manner, by making reservation of seats for her in local bodies. The Constitution (Seventy-third Amendment) Act, 1992 has been enacted to give constitutional status to the Panchayati Raj. It seeks to provide "democracy of grassroots" as it intends "to give power to the people." Under Article 243-D (3), out of total seats to be filled by direct election in every Panchayat, not less than one-third (including the seats reserved for SC's and ST's Women) seats shall be reserved for women. Such seats may be allotted by rotation to different constituencies in a Panchayat.[13]

Part IX-A has been added to the Constitution by the Constitution (Seventy-fourth Amendment) Act, 1992. It provides for the setting up of three types of Municipal Corporations. Of the total seats (including the seats reserved for Women belonging to SC's & ST's) to be filled by direct election in every Municipality, not less than one-third shall be reserved for women and such seats may be allotted by rotation to different constituencies in a Municipality.[14]

However, despite the above-mentioned constitutional provisions and other laws relating to women, the factual situation of women is not satisfactory. The sharp decline in juvenile sex ratio; continuing high maternal mortality rate and infant mortality rate; high gender gap in literacy at all levels; high rate of dropouts of girl students; and increasing incidence of crime against women raises many questions about the role of institutional machinery to implement the law. It is unfortunately true that a woman has, even in her own home given a rather subordinate role to play.

Consequently, the access of women particularly those belonging to weaker sections including SC/ST/OBC and minorities, majority of whom are in the rural areas and in the informal, unorganized sector-to education, health and productive resources, among others, is inadequate. Therefore, they remain largely marginalized, poor and socially excluded. The economic empowerment of women through poverty eradication, provision of micro-credit, strategies to save them from the negative impact of globalization etc. was stressed.[15]

ROLE OF THE JUDICIARY

Indian judiciary has applied the principle of social justice in some areas like dealing with *stridhan,* divorce, and proprietary rights for women and has also appreciated the protection discrimination in favour of women. Whenever necessary, the Supreme Court has not failed to warn the Union Government as well as State governments of their responsibility towards women's rights which must not be trampled upon. It is proved from number of judgement pronounced by Supreme Court which can be termed as stepping stones towards the promotions of women's rights in socio-economic and political environment. A few of them are worth-mentioning here.

In *Yusuf Abdul Aziz v. The State of Bombay,*[16] the validity of Section 497 of the Indian Penal Code was challenged. This Section makes an abettor of adultery punishable, but provides that, "in such case the wife shall not be punishable as an abettor". It was argued that clause (3) of Article 15 should be confined to provisions which are beneficial to women and could not be used to give them a licence to commit and abet crimes. The Court found neither such restriction under clause 15(3) nor a licence to commit offence of which punishment has been prohibited.

The provision under Order 5, Rule 15 of Civil Procedure Code, 1908 for making service for summons on any male member of the family, if the defendant could not be found was held not discriminatory of Article 15(3) which covers any provision either for betterment or for some other purpose specially made for women. It was held that there was no discrimination between a woman and man simply on the ground of his or her sex in receiving a notice on behalf of some other member of the family.[17]

In *Ranghubans Saudagor Singh v. State,*[18] an order of the Governor of Punjab rendered women ineligible to posts in men's jails other than those of clerks and matrons. The order was assailed as violative of Article 16(2). The Court turned down this plea and held what is forbidden under the Constitution is discrimination on the ground of sex alone, but when the peculiarities of sex added to a variety of other factors and consideration from a reasonable nexus with the object of classification then the Constitutional bar under Articles 15 and 16(2) cannot be attracted.

Article 14 of the Constitution recognizes 'women' as a class. The Court has declared that women as a class were different from men as a class; and for this the legislature had merely removed the disability attaching to women by passing the Hindu Succession Act, 1956.[19] Upholding sex as a sound basis for classification while making laws that favour women under Article 15(3), however, took a curious turn in the case of Air India International v. Nargesh Mirza.[20] Mr. Justice Fazal Ali observed that termination of services of an Air Hostess under such circumstances was not only a callous and cruel act but also an open insult to Indian Womanhood. No civilized Society could ever allow it because it was unfair to women.

The writ by Miss Muthamma, a senior member of Indian Foreign Service, speaks a story that makes one wonder whether Articles 14 and 16 belong to myth or reality. In this case, the Indian Foreign Service (Conduct and Discipline) Rules 1961 provided that the woman in service should seek permission before her marriage is solemnized; and further she may be required to resign if the Government is satisfied that her family and domestic commitment comes in the way of her duties. Justice Krishana Iyer while delivering the judgement has observed that "Discrimination against woman, in traumic transparency, is found in this rule..... In these days of nuclear families inter-continental marriages and unconventional behaviour one fails to understand the naked bias against the gender of species".[21] Similarly, preference in favour of women for certain posts in exclusive girls college was held to be not violative of Article 14 and 16.[22]

In Randhir Singh v. Union of India,[23] applying the principle of 'equal pay for equal work', it was explained that it is true that the principle of 'equal pay for equal work' is not expressly declared by our Constitution to be fundamental right, but it certainly is a constitutional goal. Article 39(d) of the Constitution of India proclaims' equal pay for equal work for both men and women' as Directive Principles of the State Policy.... means equal work for every one and as between the sexes.

In Sanjit Ray v. State of Rajasthan,[24] the Supreme Court delivered a monumental judgment holding that payment of wages less than that prescribed under the Minimum Wages Act, 1948 amounts to forced labour or beggar and no exemption by any other Statute can be allowed as Constitutional in view of the nature of the Minimum Wages Act. This case also represents a sort of socio-legal awakening amongst women workers engaged in drought or famine relief works or organised by the State.

In *T. Saritha v. Venkata Subbaiath*,[25] the Andhra Pradesh High Court extended the application of the principle of reasonableness to matrimonial matters and invalidated Section 9 of the Hindu Marriage Act, 1955 dealing with the restriction of conjugal rights and found that "the remedy of restitution of conjugal rights provided for by the Section is a savage and barbarous remedy, violating the right to privacy and human dignity guaranteed under Article 21 of the Constitution".

In *State of Maharashtra v. Madhukar Narain*,[26] the Supreme Court without referring Article 21, has held that even a woman of easy virtue is entitled to privacy and that no one can invade her privacy as and when he likes. In another case,[27] the Supreme Court had held that, the right to privacy of women would preclude such questions to be put to female candidates as modesty and self respect may preclude an answer. In the instant case, the petitioner, a probationer Assistant in LIC gave a false declaration regarding the last menstruation period, during her medical examination, since the clauses in declaration were indeed embarrassing if not humiliating like the regularity of menstrual cycle, the term therefore, the number of conceptions taken etc. The Supreme Court found that such embarrassing questions violate the right to privacy of the lady employees and further directed the Corporation to delete such columns in the declaration.

In *Gautam Kundu v. State*,[28] the woman refused the husband's application for a blood test to disprove paternity as it would be slanderous embarrassing and humiliating for the woman. In another important decision the Supreme Court rejected the plea of a husband in which he had prayed that his wife should undergo a medical examination to prove her virginity. The Court reject the plea and observed that allowing the medical examination of a woman for her virginity would certainly violate her right to privacy and personal liberty enshrined under Article 21 of the Constitution.[29] Such an order would amount to a roving enquiry against a female who are vulnerable otherwise. No Court shall order a roving enquiry and there has to be sufficient material before the Court to enable it to exercise such discretion.[30]

In accordance with the provisions of Article 243 D & T, the Supreme Court of India upheld the validity of reservation of certain posts exclusively for women.[31] In Kasambai F. Ghanchi v. Chandubhai D. Rajput,[32] the Supreme Court held that a Councilor of Municipality who belonged to a backward class but had been elected to the Municipality from an unreserved seat, could stand for election for the post of president of the Municipality which was reserved for a backward class candidate under the Gujarat Municipalities (Reservation of Scheduled Castes, Scheduled Tribes, Backward Class and Women for Office of President) Rules, 1994.

In *Lalitha Sundari v. R. Kethar Nathan*,[33] two vacancies in the Education Committee of a family trust were to be filled from the female descendants of the trustees. The Supreme Court which was the appointing authority, appointing two male members and observed that female descendants include male descendants and females who appeared in the interview lack practical experience. Setting aside the appointments of two males, the Madras High

Court held that the two petitioners were qualified and eligible to be appointed to Education Committee. It also observed that female descendants do not include males.

The era of globalization has heralded a new era for women's rights. The Supreme Court recently gave a new dimension to it by nullifying a provision in the Colonial piece of legislation.[34] Section 30 of Punjab Excise Act, 1914, prohibited employment of any man under the age of twenty five years or any woman in any part of premises in which liquor is served. The Court allowed the employment of such men and women in hotels and restaurants, who in large number taking hotel management courses. Everyone has autonomy to choose his/her profession. Right to equality has to be interpreted in view of the prevalent societal conditions and changed social psyche. Right to equality in employment cannot be taken away in the name of security of women. The State should develop new method of security and can not sacrifice the autonomy of women to choose their profession. Article 14 of the Constitution of India has to be interpreted in the light of international conventions, specifically CEDAW. This judgment of the Court has certainly opened up new avenues of employment for women but it also raises certain questions about public policy and cultural values.

The Supreme Court of India is heading towards a right direction in cases of gender equality. The Apex Court interprets Constitutional provision in favour of women. Whenever there is a anti-women legislation, rule or order of the Government or any other agency then the Court comes into picture to rescue the right of women. It is the helper of the last resort and fortunately, it is also working for the welfare of the women.

The judiciary in its own turn, helped in the process of equalization between men and women in the post independent period. However, the most sacred object 'The Constitutional mission of equalization' could not be achieved fully due to general ignorance of law; indifferent and hostile attitude of the law enforcing agency; economic backwardness and lack of community support for women seeking justice against discrimination; and ignoring the socio-economic implications of laws.

CONCLUSION AND SUGGESTIONS

In real sense liberation of women is not merely a sum of legal enactments and constitutional sanctions. While not denying the importance of an effective legislative policy, it was not possible to bring about a change in the status of women through legislation action alone. One must acknowledge that there is a large gap between the law and social attitudes and beliefs that act as barriers in the enforcement of laws for women's emancipation. The complex system of social institutions, norms of behaviour and religious prescriptions, some of which have congealed and hardened like statutory laws, come in the way of proper implementation of special protective legislation for women.

Though the Constitution provides for equality between the sexes with special protection for women and children, personal and religious laws that fail to give women their due have governed Indian, in their family life. Inspite of the medley of laws, women in India still continue to live under the stress and strain of male domination that manifests itself in the form of various kinds of cruelties to them.

Mere protective benevolent legislation is not enough. To bring social awareness women organizations should work more promptly and actively. The state must give priority to education to all. Education up to 12 standard must be made compulsory and free of cost for women. Such education system should compulsorily transmit primary legal education system should compulsorily transmit primary legal education to women. Various enactments relating to women for e.g. the Dowry Prohibition Act, 1961 must be taught to women. This should not only be the burden of the State, but women, political and other voluntary organizations should also work to change the attitude of the society towards women.

The status of women in society has also an important bearing on their participation in economic activity. In developing countries, the family incomes are by and large low and that can best be supplemented by requiring the female population to accept remunerative employments. There is a need for targeted efforts to ensure that rights of women in difficult circumstances who include women in extreme poverty, destitute women, women in conflict situations, women affected by natural calamities, women in less developed regions, the disabled widows, elderly women, single women in difficult circumstances women who are victims of marital violence, deserted women and prostitutes, etc.

In the words of Lord Denning:

A woman feels a keenly, thinks as clearly as a man. She in her sphere does work as useful as man does in his. She has as much right to her freedom - to develop her personality to the full-as a man. When she marries, she does not become the husband's servant but his equal partner. If his work is more important in the life of the community, her's is more important in the life of the family. Neither can do without the other. Neither is above the other or wider the other. They are equals.[35]

NOTES

1. M. P. Jain (2003), Indian Constitutional Law, New Delhi: Wadhwa and Company Nagpur, pp. 19-20.
2. Sreenivasulu N. S. (2008), Human Rights: Many Sides to a Coin, New Delhi: Regal Publication, p. 31.
3. M. Hidayatullah (1984), Constitutional Law of India, New Delhi, The Bar Council of India Trust and Arnold-Heinemann, p. 244.
4. Raj Kumar (2000), Encyclopaedia of Woman and Development Series: Women and Law, New Delhi, Anmol Publication Pvt. Ltd., p. 156.

5. VKS Chaudhary (2002), The Ivory Tower 51 Years of the Supreme Court of India, Delhi, Universal Law Publishing Co. Pvt. Ltd., p. 267.
6. *Ibid.*
7. K. C. Joshi (1996), "Law and Women: Problem and Prospects." In: R.K. Raizada (Ed.), Women and the Law: Problems and Prospects, Rohtak: The Bright Law House, p. 12.
8. Anjani Kant (1997), Women and the Law, New Delhi, A.P.H. Publishing Corporation, p. 77.
9. Raj Kumar (2000), p. 6.
10. P. Thomas (1964), Indian Women Through the Ages, Bombay: Asia Publishing House, p. 363.
11. Sujata V. Manohar (2001), "Gender Discrimination and the Indian Consitution", In: Venkat Iyer (Ed.): Constitutional Perspectives: Essays in Honour and Memory of H.M. Seervai, Delhi, Universal Law Publishing Co. Pvt. Ltd.; p. 107.
12. See, Charanjit Chowdhary v. Union of India AIR 1951 SC 41; State of Bombay v. F.N. Balsara, AIR 1951 SC 318; and Ram Krishan Dalmia v. S.R. Tendolkar AIR 1958 SC 538.
13. Narender Kumar (2004), Constitutional Law of India, Faridabad, Allahabad Law Agency, p. 609.
14. *Ibid.*, p. 620.
15. A. S. Anand (2003), Justice for Women Concern and Expressions, Delhi, Universal Law Publishing, p. 1c.
16. AIR 1954 SC 321.
17. Shadab v. Mohd. Abdulah, AIR 1967 J&K 120.
18. AIR 1972 P&H 117.
19. Kaur Singh v. Jaggar Singh, AIR 1961 Punj. 489.
20. (1981) 4 SCC 335.
21. C.B. Muthamma v. Union of India, AIR 1979 SC 1868.
22. Vijay Lakshmi v. Punjab University and Ors. AIR 2003 SC 3331.
23. AIR 1982 SC 877.
24. AIR 1983 SC 328.
25. AIR 1983 AP 356.
26. AIR 1991 SC 207.
27. Neera v. LIC, AIR 1992 SC 392.
28. AIR 1993 SC 2295.
29. Surjeet Singh v. Kamaljit Kaur, AIR 2003 P&H 354.
30. Sharda v. Dharampal, (2003) 3 JT (SC) 399.
31. Union of India v. V.P. Prabhakaran, (1997) 11 SCC 638.
32. AIR 1998 SC 815. In this case the Court Overruled Saraswati Devi v. Shanti Devi, AIR 1997 SC 347, decision wherein the apex Court had held that a woman candidate belonging of Scheduled Caste but elected from ward reserved for general category

of women, could not be elected to a seat of President from ward reserved for SC candidate.

33. AIR 2002 SC 17.
34. Anuj Garg v. Hotel Association of India, AIR 2008 663.
35. Lord Dennig (1981), Due Process of Law, London: Butterworths, pp. 194-95.

DOMESTIC VIOLENCE
AGAINST WOMEN AND GIRLS AND HUMAN RIGHTS

PUSHPA SINHA*

EDITORIAL

In recent years, there has been a greater understanding of the problem of domestic violence, its causes and consequences, and an international consensus has developed on the need to deal with the issue. The Convention on the Elimination of All Forms of Discrimination against women adopted by the United Nations General Assembly some 20 years ago, the decade-old Convention on the Rights of the Child, and the Platform for Action adopted at the Fourth International Conference on women in Beijing in 1995, all reflect this consensus. But progress has been slow because attitudes are deeply entrenched and, to some extent, because effective strategies to address domestic violence are still being defined. As a result, women worldwide continue to suffer, with estimates varying from 20 to 50 per cent from country to country. Violence against women is perpetrated when legislation, law enforcement and judicial systems condone or do not recognize domestic violence as a crime. One of the major challenges is to end impunity for perpetrators. So far, only 44 countries (approximately) have adopted specific legislation to address domestic violence.

Domestic violence is a health, legal, economic, educational, developmental and, above all, a human rights issue. Much has been done to create awareness and demonstrate that change is not only necessary, it is also possible. Now that strategies for dealing with it are becoming clearer, there is no excuse for inaction.

"Violence against women is a manifestation of historically unequal power relations between men and women, which have led to domination over and discrimination against women by men and to the prevention of the full advancement of women..." The United Nations Declaration on the Elimination of Violence against Women, General Assembly Resolution, December 1993.

* *Lecturer, Department of Economics, Patna Women's College, Patna-800001(Bihar).*

DEFINITIONS AND KEY CONCEPTS

There is no universally accepted definition of violence against women. Some human rights activists prefer a broad-based definition that includes "structural violence" such as poverty, and unequal access to health and education. Others have argued for a more limited definition in order not to lose the actual descriptive power of the term. In any case, the need to develop specific operational definitions has been acknowledged so that research and monitoring can become more specific and have greater cross-cultural applicability.

The United Nations Declaration on the Elimination of Violence against women (1993) defines violence against women as "any act of gender-based violence that results in, or is likely to result in, physical, sexual or psychological harm or suffering to women, including threats of such acts, coercion or arbitrary deprivation of liberty, whether occurring in public or in private life".

This definition refers to the gender-based roots of violence, recognizing that "violence against women is one of the crucial social mechanisms by which women are forced into a subordinate position compared with men." It broadens the definition of violence by including both the physical and psychological harm done towards women, and it includes acts in both private and public life. The declaration defines violence against women as encompassing, but not limited to, three areas: violence occurring in the family, within the general community, and violence perpetrated or condoned by the State.

Domestic violence includes violence perpetrated by intimate partners and other family members, and manifested through:

Physical abuse such as slapping, beating, arm twisting, stabbing, strangling, burning, choking, kicking, threats with an object or weapon, and murder. It also includes traditional practices harmful to women such as female genital mutilation and wife inheritance (the practice of passing a widow, and her property, to her dead husband' brother).

Sexual abuse such as coerced sex through threats, intimidation or physical force, forcing unwanted sexual acts or forcing sex with others.

Psychological abuse which includes behaviour that is intended to intimidated and persecute, and takes the form of threats of abandonment or abuse confinement to the home, surveillance, threats to take away custody of the children, destruction of objects, isolation, verbal aggression and constant humiliation.

Economic abuse includes acts such as the denial of funds, refusal to contribute financially, denial of food and basic needs, and controlling access to health care, employment, etc.

Acts of omission are also form of violence against women and girls. Gender bias that discriminates in terms of nutrition, education and access to health care amounts to a violation of women's rights. Although the categories above are listed separately, they are not mutually exclusive. Indeed, they often go hand in hand.

Violence against women and girls continues to be a global epidemic that kills, tortures, and maims-physically, psychologically, sexually and economically. It is one of the most pervasive of human rights violations, denying women and girls equality, security, dignity, self-worth, and their right to enjoy fundamental freedoms.

Violence against women is present in every country, cutting across boundaries of culture, class, education, income, ethnicity and age. Even though most societies proscribe violence against women, the reality is that violations against women's human rights are often sanctioned under the garb of cultural practices and norms, or through misinterpretation of religious tenets. Moreover, when the violation takes place within the home, as is very often the case, the abuse is effectively condoned by the tacit silence and the passivity displayed by the state and the law-enforcing machinery.

The global dimensions of this violence are alarming, as highlighted by studies on its incidence and prevalence. No society can claim to be free of such violence, the only variation is in the patterns and trends that exist in countries and regions. Specific groups of women are more vulnerable, including minority groups, indigenous and migrant women, refugee women and those in situations of armed conflict, women in institutions and detention, women with disabilities, female children and elderly women.

Table 1
Examples of Violence against Women Throughout the Life Cycle

Phase	*Type of Violence*
Pre-birth	Sex-selective abortion; effects of battering during pregnancy on birth outcomes.
Infancy	Female infanticide: physical, sexual and psychological abuse.
Girlhood	Child marriage; female genital mutilation; physical, sexual and psychological abuse; incest; child prostitution and pornography.
Adolescence and Adulthood	Dating and courtship violence (e.g. acid throwing and date rape) economically coerced sex (e.g. school girls having sex with "sugar daddies" in return for school fees); incest; sexual abuse in the workplace; rape; sexual harassment; forced prostitution and pornography; trafficking in women; partner violence; marital rape; dowry abuse and murder; partner homicide; psychological abuse; abuse of women with disabilities; forced pregnancy.
Elderly	Force "suicide" or homicide of widows for economic reasons; sexual, physical and psychological abuse.

Source: "Violence Against Women", WHO. FRH/WHD/97.8

Here we are focusing specifically on domestic violence-the most prevalent yet relatively hidden and ignored form of violence against women and girls. While reliable statistics are hard to come by, studies estimate that, from country to country, between 20 and 50 per cent of women have experienced physical violence at the hands of an intimate partner or family member.

The term "domestic violence" includes violence against women and girls by an intimate partner, including a cohabiting partner, and by other family members, whether this violence occurs within or beyond the confines of the home.

DOMESTIC VIOLENCE AND HIV/AIDS

Nearly 14 million women today are infected with HIV and the rate of female infection is rising. A forthcoming study from WHO finds that the greatest risk of HIV infection for many women comes from a regular partner, and is heightened by an unequal relationship that makes it difficult, if not impossible, to negotiate safe sex. For these women, sex is not a matter of choice.

A study of women aged 18 and over in one province in Zimbabwe found that 26 per cent of married women reported being forced to have sex when they did not want to. It is widely acknowledged that, even when a women is aware that her partner has other sexual partners, or is HIV infected, she may not be in apposition to insist on condom use or monogamy. Most HIV/AIDS prevention programmes, however, advocate both methods. Many women would feel that any attempt to discuss such measures would provoke yet more violence.

Other studies have found that the spread of HIV/AIDs in some parts of Africa is being exacerbated by practices that see women as the 'property' of men. The tradition of wife or widow inheritance, for example, is fairly common in eastern and southern Africa. When a women's husband dies, his wife and property are often inherited by his eldest brother. In western Kenya women have been forced to marry, even when their husbands have died of AIDS, when they themselves are infected, or when their future husband has AIDS. There are no laws to address this practice in Kenya.

Sexual cleansing is a more recent phenomena, resulting from, and contributing to, the spread of HIV/AIDS. Practised within extended families in western Kenya, Zimbabwe and parts of Ghana, it is based on the belief that a man can be cured of HIV/AIDS if he has sex with a young girl who is virgin. Girls as young as eight are selected to ensure their purity.

A new approach is required that acknowledges the links between violence against women and the spread of HIV/AIDS, and translates this into policies and programmes for HIV prevention and care.

CAUSES OF DOMESTIC VIOLENCE

There is no one single factor to account for violence perpetrated against women. Increasingly research has focused on the inter-relatedness of various factors that should improve our understanding of the problem within different cultural contexts.

Several complex and interconnected institutionalized social and cultural factors have kept women particularly vulnerable to the violence directed at them all of them manifestations of historically unequal power relations between men and women.

Table 2

Factors That Perpetuate Domestic Violence

Cultural	• Gender-specific socialization
	• Cultural definitions of appropriate sex roles
	• Expectations of roles within relationships
	• Belief in the inherent superiority of males
	• Values that give men proprietary rights over women and girls
	• Notion of the family as the private sphere and under male control
	• Customs of marriage (Bride price/dowry)
	• Acceptability of violence as a means to resolve conflict
Economic	• Women's economic dependence on men
	• Limited access to cash and credit
	• Discriminatory laws regarding inheritance, property rights, use of communal lands, and maintenance after divorce of widowhood
	• Limited access to employment in formal and informal sectors
	• Limited access to education and training for women
Legal	• Lesser legal status of women either by written law and/or by practice
	• Laws regarding divorce, child custody, maintenance and inheritance
	• Legal definitions of rape and domestic abuse
	• Low levels of legal literacy among women
	• Insensitive treatment of women and girls by police and judiciary
Political	• Under-representation of women in power, politics, the media and in the legal and medical professions
	• Domestic violence not taken seriously
	• Notions of family being private and beyond control of the state
	• Risk of challenge to status quo/religious laws
	• Limited organization of women as a political force
	• Limited participation of women in organized political system

MAGNITUDE OF THE PROBLEM

The extent, validity and reliability of the data available are critical in determining the magnitude of the problem and in identifying priority areas for intervention. Prevalence studies with samples of representative populations are relatively new in developing countries. Such studies were initially conducted in industrialized countries-the United States, Canada, and Europe. For example, one very influential survey conducted in Canada in 1993 under the auspices of the Canadian government was developed in consultation with women's organizations and ensured adequate support and services for women participating in the survey.

When designing research on violence against women, it is important that the research itself does not put women at risk. The World Health Organization (WHO) has developed specific ethical and safety recommendations that take into account, among other issues, the safety of respondents and the research team, protecting confidentiality to ensure both women's safety and data quality, and specialized training of interviewers.

Most of the data available on violence against women are believed to be not only conservative, but unreliable. Studies vary in the sample size of women chosen, and the ways in which questions have been posed. It is difficult to compare these studies because of inconsistency in the definition of domestic violence and in the para-meters used, which can range from physical abuse alone, to physical, sexual and psychological abuse.

Debate regarding the magnitude of the problem is also clouded by the fact that domestic violence is a crime that is under-recorded and under-reported. When women file a report or seek treatment, they may have to contend with police and health care officials who have not been trained to respond adequately or to keep consistent records. On the other hand, shame, fear of reprisal, lack of information about legal rights, lack or confidence in, or fear of, the legal system and the legal costs involved make women reluctant to report incidents of violence.

CONCLUSION

Women's groups have placed women's right firmly on the agenda of international human rights through their advocacy. The 1990s, in particular, witnessed concentrated efforts on the part of the world community to legitimize and mainstream the issue. The World Conference on Human Rights in Vienna (1993) accepted that the rights of women and girls are "an inalienable, integral and indivisible part of universal human rights." The United Nations General Assembly, in December 1993, adopted the Declaration on the Elimination of Violence against Women. It is the first international human rights instrument to deal exclusively with violence against women, a groundbreaking document that became the basis for many other parallel processes.

In 1994, the Commission on Human Rights appointed the first UN Special Rapporteur on Violence against Women, entrusting her with the task of analyzing and documenting the phenomenon, and holding governments accountable for violations against women. The Fourth World Conference on Women in Beijing (1995) included elimination of all forms of violence against women as one of its twelve strategic objectives, and listed concrete actions to be taken by governments, the United Nations, international and non-governmental organizations.

This growing momentum has compalled a better understanding of the causes and consequences of violence against women, and positive steps have been taken in some countries, including reforming and changing laws that deal with this issue. Some regions have developed their own conventions on violence against women, examples of which are the Inter-American Convention on the Prevention, Punishment and Eradication of Violence against Women, and the African Convention on 'Human and People's Rights, including its Additional Protocol on Women's Rights justice system (the police, judiciary and lawyers); the health care system; parliament and provincial legislative bodies; and the education sector. Women because their life and dignity are at stake, women have emerged as the most significant agents of change in the struggle against gender-based violence. While women's organizations have played a critical role the collective strength and courage of individual women has been notable in fighting many forms of violence. Poor and often illiterate, these women have man-aged to mobilize hundreds of other women, raised resources, designed strategies and forced policy-makers to revise laws and policies. A systematic effort has to be made to listen to the voices of grass-roots women and survivors of domestic violence, and to incorporate solutions they have to offer. Their perspectives will provide valuable lessons in making pro-grammes and services effective and targeted to their needs. Women need to be empowered through education, employment opportunities, legal literacy and right to inheritance. Human rights education and information regarding domestic violence should be provided to them because this is a matter of their absolute rights. Integrated supportive services, legal intervention and redress should be made available in situations of domestic violence. Assistance to help women rebuild and recover their lives after violence should be part of the intervention strategy, including counselling, relocation, credit sup-port, and employment.

Consistent support for women must be provided by all relevant sectors- the criminal justice system, health, welfare, and the private sector. Support must also be available to women via informal net-, works such as family, friends, neighbours, and local community groups.

Community groups and government institutions should be trained to identify women, men, adolescent boys and girls, and children at risk of domestic violence, and to refer them to confidential and accessible services. Where such services are riot available, communities must be helped to establish local culturally appropriate mechanisms to support women.

REFERENCES

World Health Organisation (1996), Violence Against Women' WHO Consultation, Genera; WHO.

Violence Against Women in the Family United Nations (ST/CSDHA/2) New York, 1989.

The World's Women 1995: Trends and statics. United Nations, 1995.

The U. S state Department's Annual Survey of Human Rights Published 25 February, 2000.

UNICEF (1999).

The Human Rights Watch Global Report on Women's Human Rights, New York, 1995.

W.W.W Unicef org.

Various News papers.

FEMINIST JURISPRUDENCE: THE ROLE OF WOMEN IN POLITICS IN NIGERIA

HAKEEM IJAIYA*

INTRODUCTION

There is good reason to believe that men and women have different perception of politics. Men's and Women's experience with their political systems have been substantially different in the past, and continue to vary today. The clearest evidence of difference is over-representation, in terms of population distribution, of men political elites. It is still the case that "women are the most underrepresented group in the political elites of the world. The world of high politics is almost, exclusively a man's world"[1] In addition, if, the world of politics is interpreted as government, "the experience women have ranges from total exclusion to selective inclusion, from discrimination to paternalism, from rejection to condescension"[2]. There has been little research about the role of women in politics in Nigeria. In this paper we intend to examine in some detail gender inequality and discrimination against women. The paper is for this purpose divided into four sections. The first section which is introductory examines the concept of feminism. The second section focuses on the position of women in the historical perspective. Assessment of women participation in democratic process in Nigeria are provided in the third section. The forth section contains suggestions and recommendations on the way forward.

FEMINISM-THE CONCEPT

A concept is an idea formulated to achieve certain objectives. As a concept, feminism emerged due to women's rejection of treatments met to them in the society. Women are construed as weaker vessels who are conterminous because of their physiological composition. The idea is that God created man, as the representative of the human race and the women as an after-thought or appendage. The cultural assumption that women are weak and intellectually inferior finds expression in sayings that discourages women's participation in politics and explain the prohibition of women from holding leadership positions[3].

---

* *M. Phil (Law) Lecturer, Faculty of Law, University of Ilorin, Nigeria.*

The political system has been thoroughly dominated by men, so too the social, economic and legal systems, with the consequence that they have reserved for themselves the most powerful public roles.

Feminist analysis begins with an exposure of the myths of patriarchy, the feminist term for the pervasive dominance, in and of society, by the male hierarchy. Feminism therefore seeks to make men and women aware of the ways in which patriarchy has distorted gender issues, and indeed, sees this as one of its main task.

The theories of jurisprudence are political theories. This is borne out by such political theories as liberalism, marxism and socialism which have generated jurisprudential theories to support and express them. The feminist call for liberation of women has a decidedly political agenda, and feminist jurisprudence has applied a number of political theories to the overt and convert discrimination against women in the law. Liberal feminists, for example, contend that liberal values should be as applicable to women as they are to men. Marxist feminists have transposed the Marxist theory of class to gender[4].

Feminism supports gender equality among the sexes and also encourages women participation in politics.

HISTORICAL PERSPECTIVE

The history of the participation of Nigerian women in politics, dates back to the pre-colonial period. However we shall limit our discussion to the situation after Nigerian independence in 1960.

A striking fact about the Nigerian state is that there has been no political space for women since independence. Women in Nigeria have been under domination, be it under civilian administration or military rule. Tokenism in politics has been the lot of Nigerian women.

Take for instance the first republic (i.e. the period 1969–1965). In northern Nigeria, the ruling party, the Northern People's Congress (NPC) did not allow women to participate in politics. Northern People's Congress (NPC) emotionally insisted that the domestic and not political space belonged to women. Additionally some evoked the injunction of Islamic religion and argued that women were supposed to be in seclusion and therefore could not participate in politics even as voters[5]. Others argued that politics was a dirty game and women as mothers of the nation needed not participate in politics.

The situation of women in the Southern regions was different but marginal. The difference can be appropriately accounted for within the context of ethnicity. The move to enfranchise women in the south was a political strategy in the wake of inter-ethnic competition for the national cake, the southern region (which had a smaller population than the northern region) decided to enfranchise their women so as to substantially push up the votes of southern candidates. As Mba, N put it:

In the South very few women contested the election and none won a seat in the House of Representatives. Therefore there were no women in the federal cabinet. One woman was appointed to the senate (each regional government nominated 12 members) and a second was appointed in 1964 in 1961 regional elections, three women were elected to the Eastern House of Assembly. There was no female minister in the regional government. The two Southern-based parties had women's wings but there was no women in the top positions of the party. Several women were elected to local government councils in the south[6].

In the second republic, women candidates were clearly more visible than the 1st republic, of the four women out of 475 candidates who contested for senate in 1979, none was successful. Three women were elected into the house of representatives, three female federal ministers were appointed Mrs. Janet Akinrinade, was federal Minister of Internal Affairs, Elezabeth Ivase was a junior minister of Education and Mrs. Oyagbola was for National Planning. Mrs. Stella Odesanya was also appointed the second female permanent secretary in 1980. There were also several women appointed on statutory boards of parastatals. There were obviously more women appointments in the Shagari government than its predecessors but women issues generally, were poorly treated. The United Nations call on member governments to consider the establishment of women commission to enhance the status of women was not adhered to or established by the Shagari Government, in spite of the agitation mounted by the National Council of Women Society (NCWS) and other women groups.[7]

In the third republic out of the total of 39 women who contested in the state House of Assembly election in 1999, only 12 of them were successful. In the federal House of Representatives 29 women contested but only 12 won. In the senate only five women contested but three won the election out of the 240 candidates for senate seates. In the 1979 and 1983 elections only one woman was elected into the senate in Nigeria. Whereas five woman contested for the position of deputy governor in 1979, two women contested for the position of deputy governor in 1970, two woman contested in 1999 and only in Lagos was a woman elected a deputy governor.

In the fourth republic i.e Obasanjo's administration, six women are appointed ministers and four special advisers to the president as the national level. But it is worthy to note that only six women out of 49 members represents to just 12% females constitute 20.5% of the executive arm of the federal government. Of the 774 Local Government Area Chairpersons in Nigeria, only nine are women representing 1.2%. only 1.6% (i.e n = 143) of local government councilors are women and 1.2% (i.e n-12) are in the state House of Assembly[8].

ASSESSMENT OF WOMEN PARTICIPATION IN POLITICS IN NIGERIA

Women representation in Nigeria's present democratic dispensation is put at 1.33%, far below the present world average of 11.75%. Nigeria has only 15 women out of 469 members of the federal legislation. This gives Nigeria a percentage of 3.2% far below the world average of 13%, at present Nigeria's figure is below Africa's average, which is 10% for women. Nigeria is even below the average for the Arab world put at 3.4%.[9]

There can be no doubt that women are disadvantaged in Nigeria. The Nigerian society is essentially a patriarchal one. This clearly manifests in the social categorization of women implicit in femininity as being inferior to men, and therefore not capable of or suitable for political leadership.

There can be no doubt that lack of political participation by women means denial of opportunities and platforms to articulate and defend their interests at the highest level of governance.

Among the factors that have militated against the participation of women in politics are low levels of literacy among women and negative cultural practices. In 1991, participation of females in higher education in Africa accounted for 31%. This is a serious obstacle to the integration of women into the political system. Knowledge is power and a crucial factor in the guest for political ascendancy.

The traditional/cultural stereotyped perceptions that politics is a male-domain is another constraining factor. Women are regarded as home-makers when they venture into politics, they are harassed by everyone for venturing into an arena meant for males.

Education is crucial to whatever plan of action that may be put in place to address the problem of low level of women participation in politics. Besides action plans to remove traditional gender-based subordination which limit women's access to and control over productive resources such as land and labour must be consolidated. We must also advocate for decentralization of political authority where it does not exist and intensify action for women participation. We must intensify lobby on affirmative action in the distribution of parliamentary seats and council seats in local government so that women can participate and influence decision which affect their daily lives. Civic education campaigns on the importance of women participation at all levels of government and women must use their votes to guarantee victory for women candidates.

We must also institute continuous dialogues not only with different arms of government including the chieftaincy institutions and political leaders but "gender dialogue in order to sensitize men to place greater emphasis on the human capabilities other than the sex and custom of the individual.[10]

CONCLUDING REMARKS

In this paper, attention has been focused on the gender problem of gender inequality and the specific problem of discrimination against women in the field of politics in the Nigeria. There can be little doubt that the status of women has been a cause for grave concern in every culture and in every clime. As Oputa observed "in some areas of the globe, it has passed the stage of sympathetic concern and has entered an era of aggressive feminism"[11]. In spite of the United National Charter which encourages equal participation of men and women in politics, the fact remains that women remain subject to distinctive and continuous form of political suppression by their men fold.

To address the problem of inequality in the level of women's participation in politics in Nigeria, three things must be done, viz liberating women, centering women and empowering women. To liberate and empower women to participate in politics, they must be properly educated. As Ake C rightly put it.

> *We have to do a great deal more of women because lack of education is by all indications the greatest obstacle to the development of women... lack of education is also arguably the major cause of the poor reproductive health of women. Illiterate women are likely to have too many children, poor spacing of births, high maternal morbidity and submissiveness to repressive values which oppress women*[12].

In addition to providing basic education by the government, the following deserves support.

(a) Organization of women's interest on the political level (political parties). Women should be motivated to participate actively in politics and be encouraged of form political parties of their own.

(b) Improving the socio status of women and support them in their domestic jobs so as to enhance their level of participation in politics.

(c) The NGOs and other regional and international organizations should intensify on sensitization of women to actively participate in politics. Enlighten the populace on the importance of integrating women into politics and removing all forms of traditional/cultural/religious barriers on women in the society through education/legislation. The NGOs should design capacity building programme to improve the skills of women politicians. They should also provide financial support to encourage effective participation of women in politics.

(d) A decentralized civil society network of institution, foundations and groups should be established to address gender issues and diverse cultural and regional requirements. The institutions should aim at sustaining and reforming political culture through workshops, seminars and recommending policies and advocating policy analysis through publications and workshops.

NOTES

1. Robert Putnam as quoted by Allan Kornberg et. al., Citizen Politicians–Canada (Durharm, North Carolina: Carolina Academic Press, 1979) p. 186. The word elite

is being employed here in a statistical sense to refer to those who enjoyed more than a proportionate share of the distribution of wealth, power and status. See also Ityaryar "Women in Leadership and Decision Making in Nigeria-1960 to Date" paper presented at Workshop on Gender, Violence and Family Poverty Organised by the Office of the Special Adviser to the President, July 2001 p. 3.

2. Thelma Mc. Carmack, "Toward a Nonsexist Perspective on Social and Political Change," in Another Voice, eds. Marcia Millman and Rosabeth Moss Kanter (Garden City, New York; Anchor Press/Doubleday, 1975), p. 25 see also Sandra Burt "Different Democracies? A Preliminary Examination of the Political Worlds of Canadian Men and Women" in Women and Politics, Sarah Slavin (ed). The Harworth Press Inc. pp. 57-58.

3. Feminism is a term coined in the 20th century to signify that the women's movement advocated revolutionary changes to the status of woman in society: see Leslie Bender "A Lawyer's Primer on Feminist Theory and Tort" (1988) 30 *Journal of Legal Education*, pp. 5-6 Ann C. Scales "The Emergence of Feminist Jurisprudence: An Essay" (1986) 95 *Yale Law Journal* 1375, 1379 Kate. Millett first linked the connotation of male domination with the concept of patriarchy in her feminist tract sexual politics (1970). Hussaina, Abdullahi," Wiefeism and Activism: The Nigerian Women's Movement" in Amrita Basu (ed) The Challenge of Local Feminisms, Women's Movements in Global perspective, Bailden Colo: Westiveiw Press, 1995, p. 209 Carol Smart Feminism and the Power of Law (1989) 66, 86.

4. Modern Feminists, including socialist feminists, have become disenchanted with the Marxist approach as it does not explain the oppression of women as women, but rather emphasizes the prejudice which attaches to women as workers. Furthermore the subjection of women in both the private and public sphere and an analysis of gender and patriarchy are overlooked: See Patricia Smith (ed). Feminist Jurisprudence (1993) 6, Adrienne E. Van Blerk "Feminism and the Law" Jurisprudence. An Introduction Lexienexis Butterworth's Durban, pp. 171-192. Carrie Menker-Meadow "Feminist Legal Theory, Critical Legal Studies, and Legal Education" or The Fem-Crits Go to Law School" (1988) 38 *Journal of Legal Education* 61,62, Janet Rifkin "Toward a Theory of Law and Patriarchy" (1988) 3 *Harvard Women's Law Journal.*

5. D. Ityauvar "Women in Leadership and decision making in Nigeria-1960 to date". Paper presented at workshop on Gender, Violence and Family poverty, organized by the office of the special adviser to the President on Women Affairs, Abuja held at Arewa Home Kaduna, Nigeria, July 2001 p. 4, see also Abubakar Sokoto Mohammed" The Working Class" in Yusufu Bala Usman (ed) Nigeria Since Independence: The First 25 Years Volume 1: The society. Ibadan: Hememann Educational Book Ltd., 1989, pp. 185-187.

6. See Mba, N. "Kabe and Khaki: Women and the Militarized State in Nigeria" in J. Parpart and K. Standt (eds). Women and the State in Africa. Lynne Reiner Publishers, Boulder and London, 1989, P. 71, See also Bolanle Awe (ed). Nigerian Women in Historical Perspective Sankore/Bookcaraft, 1992.

7. Ityanvar, *op cit.* p. 10. see also Isa Wali "The True Position of Women in Islam" in Women in the Transition to Democracy in Nigerian Politics (ed). By Kole Ahmed Settima Ibid, *et al* (1989) Wale Are Olaitan" Women in Politics in Nigeria" Chapter,

4 in Amadu Sesay and Adetunwa Odebiyi (eds) Nigerian Women in Society and Development, Dokun Publishing House, Ibadan, 1998.

8. *Ibid*, p. 22.
9. Awe, B. "Gender Issues in Democratic Transitions" paper presented at the first Nigeria-South Africa Dialogue, 12-13 February, 1999, Lagos, p. 3.
10. Popoola Ademola O, "Gender Equality, Political Participation and Leadership: The Past, Present and Future. See also Hon. Justice Chukwudifu Oputa" Women and Children as Disempowered Group" in Awe Kalu and Yemi Osinbanjo (eds) Women and Children Under Nigeria Law (Federal Ministry of Justice, Lagos 1998, Janat B. Mukwaya "Limitations faced by women in their Quest for Political Participation and Ascendancy" in Empowering Women for the 21st Century. The Challenges of Politics, Business development and Leadership edited by Ayodele Aderinwale, African Leadership Aminu 1997. Catherine Mackinnon "Feminist Discourse, Moral Values and the Law–A Conversation" (1985) 34 Buftalo Law Review 11 20-28 Joan C. Williams "Dissolving the sameness/Difference Debate: A Post Modern Path Beyond Essentialism in Feminist and Critical Race Theory" (1991) 199 *Duke Law Journal*, 296 p. 321.
11. Hon. JusticeChukwudifu Oputa "Women and Children as Disempowered Group" ibid. See also Azza Haram Women in Parliament by Number International IDEA 1998, Isabella Okagbus Women's Right Are Human Rights NIALS 1996, Chinweizu Anatomy of Female Power: A Matriarchy dissection of Matriarchy (1991), Akintunde O. Obilade (ed). Women in Law 1993. Mrs. Jeredine Williams Sarhu" Women and Political Participation in Africa: The Limitation of the Immediate Environment" in Empowering women for the 21st Century, The Challenges of Politics, Business" Development and Leadership Summary Re-book of the 9th Annual Conference of the Africa Leadership Forum Accra Ghana 27-29 January 1997 ALF Publications, p. 65.
12. Professor Claude Ake as quoted in Ali A Mazrui. The Black Women and the Problem of Gender: Trial, Triumphs and Challenges, the 1991 Guardian Lecture, see also Olajubu O. Feminism in Christianity: An Issue of Reconceptualization or Recontextualization? *Gender Discourse A Journal of the University of Ilorin Women Academics*, Vol. 1 No 1, 2004, Steady, F. (1994) The Black Women Cross-Culturally. Cambridge: Schenkam Publishers, Surdakasa, N. (1996). The Strength of our Mother New Jersey: African World Press.

GENDER INEQUALITY IN EDUCATION AND ECONOMIC DEVELOPMENT: AN EMPIRICAL ANALYSIS OF DISTRICT LEVEL DATA IN KARNATAKA

K. B. Rangappa*, S. Suchitra* & N. Geetha**

INTRODUCTION

Education is one of the fundamental factors of economic development. It stimulates economic development and improves people's lives through many channels: by increasing the efficiency of the labour force, by fostering democracy and thus creating better conditions for good governance, by improving health, and so on (Thorvaldur, 2000). Education also raises people's productivity and creativity and promotes entrepreneurship and technological advances. The new growth theories in economics, therefore, place education and human resource development at the centre of their explanation for long-term economic development. In recent decades women's education is considered as of greater importance than that of men's education. Research world-wide shows that, in general, the economic benefits from women's education-calculated as the economic rate of return to education-are comparable to those from men's education whereas the social benefits from investing in females' education are far greater than those from investing in males' education (Kingdon, 2002). Specifically, female education has powerful effects on the total fertility rate and hence on population growth, the infant mortality rate, the female disadvantage in child survival, and on child health and nutrition. Girls' education and the promotion of gender equality in education are critical to development, and policies and actions that do not address gender disparities miss critical development opportunities (World Bank, 2006).

The existing theoretical literature reported that the gender inequality reduces the average amount of human capital in a society and thus hampers economic performance. It does so as by artificially restricting the pool of talent from which to draw for education and thereby excluding highly qualified girls and taking less qualified boys instead (Stephan and Francesca, 2003).

* *Senior Scale Lecturers, Department of Studies in Economics, Kuvempu University, P.G.Centre, Shivagangothri Campus.*

** *Guest lecturer, A.V.K College, Davangere, Karnataka-577 002.*

Moreover, if there are declining marginal returns to education, restricting the education of girls to lower levels while taking the education of boys to higher levels means that the marginal return to educating girls is higher than that of boys and thus would boost overall economic performance (Knowles *et al.*, 2002). The researches conducted in different parts of the World (For example, Subbarao and Raney (1995), Knowles *et al.*, (2002)) have also reported the impact of gender difference in the education on socio economic indicators like fertility rates, infant and child mortality rates, maternal mortality rates, protecting against HIV/AIDS infection, women's labour force participation rates and earnings and creating intergenerational education benefits.

Though, the women's disadvantage in education is economically inefficient it prevails in most part of the world at varying degree. Female deprivation of education is particularly acute in the developing countries like India with high levels of poverty. Against this backdrop, this study has been undertaken with the objective of analysing the impact of gender inequality in education on economic development in Karnataka. Accordingly, two hypotheses have been formulated for the empirical verification. Firstly, some select economic development indicators are being influenced more by the female education than by the education of the male. Secondly, Gender inequality in education affects the economic development.

DATA AND METHODOLOGY

This paper has been prepared based on the district level secondary data collected from the secondary sources. Three economic development indicators viz. per capita income, Human Development Index (HDI), and Gender Development Index (GDI) have been considered for this study. District level data on these variables have been collected from the Karnataka state at a Glance and Human Development Report of Karnataka, 2005. There is no single variable, which reflects a state's relative achievement in the education. Gross enrolment ratio and adult literacy ratio were considered for this purpose. Gross enrolment ratio for class I-XII refers to the number of students enrolled in these levels of education, regardless of age, as a percentage of the population of official school age for these levels. The district level data on the gross enrolment ratio and adult literacy ratio are obtained from Human Development Report of Karnataka, 2005. The simple average of adult literacy ratio and combined gross enrolment ratio is considered as *the education level.* The education level was computed separately for males and females of all the districts of the district.

Gender Inequality in Education (GIE) was worked out as the difference between education level of males and females i.e. education level of males-education level of females. Index of Gender Inequality in Education (IGIE) was computed as follows:

$$\text{IGIE of } X_i \text{ district} = \frac{\text{GIE of } X_i \text{ district-Minimum Value}}{\text{Maximum Value-Minimum Value}} \times 100 \quad (1)$$

Where, minimum and maximum values refer to the lowest and the highest level of GIE among all the districts of the State. The IGIE in the year 1990-91 was calculated for all the district of the state. Education may not influence the socio economic development immediately. It's impact on the economic development may reflect after some time gap. Similar rationality was used by Subbarao and Raney (1995) to estimate the impact of education on the total fertility rate and infant mortality rate. Therefore, In order to compare the effect of males and females education on the economic development indicators regression equations of the following type were estimated:

$$Dij_{(t)} = a + bEsj_{(t-n)} \quad (2)$$

Where, Dij refers to i^{th} economic development indicators with respect to j^{th} district, Esj refers to the education level of sth sex (male or female) with respect to j^{th} district, t and (t-n) refers to t^{th} and $(t-n)^{th}$ year respectively. Intercept and coefficient of the regression function indicated by a and b respectively. This equation regress the economic development indicators selected for this study on the education index of males and females lagged by 'n' number of years. For example, it regress the HDI, transformed to 0 to 100 scale, of the year 2001 on the female education level lagged by 10 year i.e. education level of 1991. Here, the value of 'n' is 10 because 2001-1991=10. Since, there are three economic development indicators (i.e. dependent variables) three regression equations of this type were estimated separately for males and females by taking the education level of respective sex pertaining to the year 1991 as independent variables.

The effect of gender inequality in education on the socio economic development indicator is assessed by estimating the parameters of the following type of regression equation.

$$Dij_{(t)} = a + bGj_{(t-n)} \quad (3)$$

Where, Dij, (t), (t-n), a and b are the same as explained in equation 2. Gj refers to the IGIE with respect to the jth district. IGIE in the year 1991 was estimated for each district by using the formula 1. The equation 3 regress the economic development indicators selected for this study on the IGIE lagged by 'n' number of years.

RESULTS AND DISCUSSION

The economic development indicators selected for the study were separately regressed on the males and females' education level for the year 1991 by using the equation 2 and the results are summarised in the table 1. The overall significance of the estimated regression equations was tested by the F test. The equations, which regress the per capita income, HDI, and GDI on both females' and males' education level, as per the 'F' test results, were found to be statistically significant. Females' education level explains the 88.1 and 86.7 per cent (R^2) of variation in GDI and HDI respectively. The linear regression model, thus, is a good fit to these variables. Though, the regression model fitted to HDI and GDI on males' education level is good fit it is not the extent of males' education level. The equation which regress the per capita income on males' education level is not a good fit (R^2 = 0.179) almost similar is the case with females' education level.

Table 1

Effect of Males' and Females' Education on the Economic Development

Dependent Variable	*Particulars of Regression*	*Independent Variables*	
		Females' Education Index	*Males' Education Index*
Per Capita Income	Intercept	-3185.48	-1343.55
		(-0.511)	(-0.137)
	Coefficient	458.78	319.87
		(4.01)*	(2.332)**
	R^2 Value	0.392	0.179
	F Value	16.115*	5.440**
	Observations	27	27
Human Development Index	Intercept	44.29	40.925
		(28.996)*	(12.028)*
	Coefficient	0.358	0.318
		(12.798)*	(6.679)*
	R^2 Value	0.867	0.641
	F Value	163.804*	44.615*
	Observations	27	27
Gender Development Index	Intercept	41.802	38.229
		(27.512)*	(10.883)*
	Coefficient	0.379	0.336
		(13.590)*	(6.839)*
	R^2 Value	0.881	0.652
	F Value	184.680*	46.780*
	Observations	27	27

* and ** indicate significance at 1 and 5 per cent probability levels respectively.

The regression coefficients were found to be statistically significant in all the six regression models. It clearly shows that education significantly influence all the selected development variables. R^2 and F values are found to be relatively more in all the regression models which have fitted on females education level compared to the models fitted on males' education level. Regression coefficients are also relatively more in the models fitted on females' education level compared to males' education level. Per capita income, HDI and GDI increase by RS.458.58, 0.204 and 0.216 points respectively for every one point increase in the education level of females' whereas it is only Rs.319.87, 0.185 and 0.196 with respect to males' education level. It shows that the responsiveness of per capita income, HDI and GDI is relatively more with females' education compared to the males' education.

The impact of gender inequality in education on the economic development indicators was estimated by using the equation number 3 and the results are documented in the table 2. IGIE was used as independent variable to explain the variations in the economic development indicators. The regression equations which estimate the impact of IGIE on the per capita income, HDI and GDI were found to be statistically significant as proved by the F test. However, the extent of risk in this inference is 10 per cent with respect to the model which regress GDI on IGIE. The models which regress per capita income, HDI and GDI are not so good fit. However, the impact of IGIE on per capita income, HDI and GDI is found to be statistically significant. Every one point higher IGIE is associated with Rs.192.437 lower Value of per capita income as well as 0.076 and 0.073 lower points of GDI and HDI respectively. Thus, gender discrimination in education negatively affects these development indicators.

Table 2
Effect of IGIE on the Socio Economic Development

Dependent Variables	*Particulars of Regression*	*IGIE (Independent Variable)*
Per Capita Income	Intercept	28676.04
		(9.231)*
	Coefficient	-192.437
		(-2.797)*
	R^2 Value	0.238
	F Value	7.823*
	Observations	27
Human Development Index	Intercept	66.168
		(37.809)*
	Coefficient	-0.073
		(-1.979)**
	R^2 Value	0.132
	F Value	4.534**
	Observations	27
Gender Development Index	Intercept	64.900
		(35.391)*
	Coefficient	-0.076
		(-1.986)**
	R^2 Value	0.142
	F Value	3.559***
	Observations	27

* , ** and *** indicate significance at 1, 5 and 10 per cent probability levels respectively.

CONCLUSION

The education level that shows the relative achievement of a district in both adult literacy and combined gross enrolment ratio was computed separately for males and females. Select economic development indicators were separately regressed on males and females education level. The per capita income, HDI and GDI were found to be influenced by males' and females' education level. However the extent of influence was more by females' education level than by the males' education. In another regression equation IGIE was used as the independent variable to estimate its influence on the economic development indicators. The results of this equation revealed the negative influence of IGIE on the per capita income HDI and GDI. The regression coefficients of these variables were found to be statistically significant. Thus, it could be inferred that education in general woman' education in particular play a vital role in economic development.

REFERENCES

Kingdon, G. (1997), "Education of Women and Socio-Economic Development" *Baha'i Studies Review,* Vol. 7.

Government of India (2002), *National Human Development Report 2001*, Planning Commission.

Government of India (2006), *Economic Survey 2005-06*, Ministry of Finance and Company Affairs, Economic Division, New Delhi.

Knowles, S., Lorgelly P. K. and Owen P.D. (2002), "Are Educational Gender Gaps a Brake on Economic Development? Some Cross-Country Empirical Evidence." *Oxford Economic Papers,* 54: 118-149.

Stephan Klasen and Francesca Lamanna (2003), "The Impact of Gender Inequality in Education and Employment on Economic Growth in the Middle East and North Africa", *Background Paper for a Report on Gender in the MENA Region*, World Bank.

Subbarao, K. and L. Raney (1995), "Social Gains from Female Education: A Cross-National Study," *Economic Development and Cultural Change,* Vol. 44 (1): 105-128.

Thorvaldur Gylfason (2000), "Natural Resources, Education, and Economic Development", 15th Annual Congress of the European Economic Association, Bolzano, 30 August–2 September 2000.

World Bank (2006), *"Girls' Education: A World Bank Priority"*, *http://www.worldbank.org/.*

EMPOWERMENT OF WOMEN THROUGH RIGHTS; IDEAS AND INITIATIVES

HIMANI VAID* & AJAY KUMAR**

ACTS FOR EMPOWERMENT OF WOMEN

At present women's empowerment not only the most popular slogan of the contemporary age but also the need of the hour. This slogan is the outcome of several years' consistent efforts in the direction of gender equality and gender justice. Some efforts yielded results while some could not. Year 1611 is considered as the pioneer year in the direction of women's empowerment. This year in witnessed the provision of the right to the women lip the American state of Massachusetts. This is another issue that the right to vote was taken back in the year 1780 but the step was certainly a milestone in the direction of gender equality. Another milestone came when on March 8, 1857 women workers of the garment and tailoring factories of America went on a strike with the demands of fixation of working hours and equal remuneration. Their echoes of their voices were heard in the entire world. They succeeded after a long struggle. Since than 8th March is observed as International Women's Day in order to salute the courage and efforts of women to challenge the gender in equality. Then came the year 1975' which was declared as International women's year and the decade of 1975-85 as women's decade by UNO.

In India, the conspicuous efforts in the direction of gender equality began in the year 1974 with the formation of Women's Committee to study the status of women in India. The committee had the eminent personalities like Ila Bhatt, Mrinal Pandey, Veena Mazumdar and Phulkin Guha. The members conducted their study on the basis of different variables pertaining to the conditions of women. Their report presented in the parliament in the year 1915. It brought out some alarming findings like:

- Continuously decreasing gender ratio (number of females per thousand males).

* *Academic Counsellor, Public Administration, IGNOU Centre, Govt. Post Graduate Degree College, Chamba, Himachal Pradesh.*

** *Research Scholar, Deptt. of Public Administration, H.P. University, Summer Hill, Shimla-5.*

- Increasing gender disparities in prominent sectors like health, education, employment.
- Women's, negligible participation in the decision- making process.
- Increasing rate of crime against women.

New Acts have been passed and some existing acts amended during the X Plan period. The Protection of Women from Domestic Violence Act. 2005 is first of its kind in the country and gets Into the private sphere of a household. For the first time the term 'domestic violence' has been widened in meaning and scope from the culture specific restriction of 'dowry deaths' and penal provisions to positive civil rights of protection and Injunction; The Hindu Succession Act has been amended to give daughters equal rights as sons in ancestral property. Property here includes agricultural land as well. Tile National Rural Employment Guarantee Act seeks to provide for the enhancement of livelihood of the households in rural areas of the country by providing at least one hundred days of guaranteed wage employment in a financial year to every household whose adult members volunteer to do unskilled manual work. Specifically, the Act seeks the creation of durable assets and strengthening the livelihood resource base of the rural pool. Priority is being given to women by reserving at least one-third of the jobs for women' who have registered requested for work under this Act. The Immoral Traffic Prevention Act is being amended to strengthen its provisions, enforce more stringent punishment for traffickers and prevent revitalization of victims. States are being requested to set up anti human trafficking units.

These efforts marked the beginning of the efforts for gender equality in India. The efforts got a tempo with the establishment of a separate department-Women and Child Development at union and state levels. The department gradually took the shape of a full-fledged Ministry of Women and Child Development. The Ministry at the Union level came into being on January 30, 2006 and since then has been catering to the development needs of both of these prominent sections of the society.

IMPROVEMENT IN WOMEN STATUS

The Impact of the various developmental policies, plans and programmes implemented by the government over the last years has brought forth a perceptible improvement in the socio-economic status of women. Expectation of life at birth has increased over the years. While it is 62.79 years for males, it is slightly higher for females at 65 years. Sex ratio has registered marginal improvement from 927 in the year 1991 to 933 in 2001. There has been a decline in the infant and maternal mortality rates. Infant Mortality Rate has declined from 80 in 1990 to 64 in 2002 and further to 58 in 2005. The corresponding rate for women has decreased from 81 to 65 and further to 61 during the same period. The Maternal Mortality Rate (MMR) has declined from 407 per 100,000 live births in 1998 to 301 in 2001-03. The work force participation rate for women has increased from 14.2 in 1991 to 25.7 in 2001.

NEW INITIATIVES

The Ministry of Women and Child Development has been implementing a number of schemes, which strive towards both economic and social empowerment. Swayamsiddha is the flagship scheme of the Ministry for women. It aims at holistic economic empowerment. The schemes for economic empowerment also include the Support for Training and Employment Programme (STEP), which aims to holistic the incomes of rural women by updating their skills in the traditional sectors. The Ministry has also set up support systems like Working women hostels and creches to help women in their struggle towards economic empowerment. Swadhar and short stay homes have been set up to provide shelter and care services for women in distress. The Ministry also implements laws and legislations for women including Sati Prevention Act, Dowry Prohibition Act protection from Domestic Violence Act, ITPA etc.

Rashtriya Mahila Kosh provides micro-credit in a quasi-informal manner, whereby it lends to intermediate micro-credit organizations (IMO's) such as NGO's and voluntary Organisations women development corporations, women co-operative societies, suitable Govt./local bodies etc. RMK has 36 nodal agencies.

In the XI Plan, the Ministry proposes to take up the second Phase of Swayamsiddha. This phase would be a countrywide programme with larger coverage in states lagging behind on women development indices. The lessons learnt in Swayamsiddha, Phase-I and Swa-Shakti would be incorporated in the next phase giving an integrated set of training inputs relating to social and economic empowerment, including skill development and training in traditional and non-traditional sectors. The scheme for construction of working women's hostel is being revamped.

Considering the increasing need of shelter names, it is proposed to set up one Swadhar home per district. A new scheme for rehabilitation of rape victims has been launched.

EMPOWERING THE ADOLESCENT GIRLS

The approach for holistic child development remains unaddressed if adolescent girls are excluded from the developmental programmes. Adolescence is a crucial please between childhood and womanhood. This Intermediary stage is the mast eventful for mental, emotional and psychological well being. Various surveys clearly reveal that the health, nutrition education and social status of adolescent girls are at sub optimal level and the adolescent girls do not have adequate access to vital health and nutrition information or services.

The Integrated Child Development Services (ICDS), with its opportunities for early childhood development, seeks to reduce both socio-economic and gender inequities. To better address concerns for women and the girl child, it was necessary to design interventions for adolescent girls which addressed their needs of self development, nutrition and health status, literacy and numerical skill vocational skills etc.

The epeeist Intervention Kishori Shakti Yajana (KSY) and Nutrition Programme for Adolescent Girls (NPAG) are being implemented for adolescent girls, using the ICDS infrastructure. These interventions focus on school dropouts, girls in the age group of 11-18 years, to meet their needs of self-development, nutrition, health, education, literacy and recreational skill formation.

KISHORI SHAKTI YOJANA (KSY)

Kishori Shakti Yojana (KSY) seeks to empower adolescent girls, so as to enable them to take charge of their lives. It is viewed as a holistic initiative far the development of adolescent girls. The pragramme through its interventions aims at bringing about a difference in the lives of the adolescent girls. It seeks to provide them with an opportunity to realize their full potential.

This scheme is a redesign of the already existing Adolescent Girls (AG) Scheme being implemented as a component under the centrally sponsored integrated Child Development Services (ICDS) Scheme. The new scheme dramatically extends the coverage of the earlier scheme with significant content enrichment, strengthens the training component, particularly in skill development, aspects aimed at empowerment and enhanced self-perception. It also fosters convergence with other sectoral programme, addressing the interrelated needs of adolescent girls and women.

The broad objectives of the scheme are to improve the nutritional, health and development status of adolescent girls, promote awareness of health, hygiene nutrition and family care, link them to opportunities for learning life skills, going back to school, help them gain a better understanding of their social environment and take initiatives to become productive members of the society.

NUTRITION PROGRAMME FOR ADOLESCENT GIRLS

To address the problem of under-nutrition among adolescent girls and pregnant women and lactating mothers, the Planning Commission, in the year 2002-03 launched the Nutrition Programme for Adolescent Girls (NPAG), on a Pilot Project basic in 51 districts in the country. Under this scheme, 6 kg of food-grains were given to under flourished adolescent girls, pregnant women and lactating mothers. Eligibility was determined on the basis of their weight. The Pilot Project was continued in the year 2003-04 also. It, however, could not be continued In the year 2004-05. The Government approved the implementation of NPAG, through the Department of Women and Child Development, in 51 backward districts identified by the Planning Commission in the year 2005-06 to provide 6 kg of free food-grains to undernourished adolescent girls only (pregnant women & lactating mothers are not covered as these are targeted under ICDS). The scheme is being continued for the Annual Plan 2006-07 on pilot project basis.

The funds are given as 100% grant to States/UTs so that they can provide food grains through the Public Distribution System free of cost to the families of identified undernourished persons.

A comprehensive sustainable progressive policy measure for the women is the need of the hour. However, initiatives that have been taken till now should get unnoticed. In India the National Commission for Women (NCW) was set up as statutory body in January 1992 under the National Commission for Women Act, 1990 to review the Constitutional and Legal safeguards for women; recommend remedial legislative measures; facilitate redressal of grievances and advise the Government on all policy matters affecting women. Some important issues taken up by the Commission include:- Gender and Law Enforcement Impact of Displacement of Women Sexual Harassment at Workplace Women in Detention Anti-Arrack Movement Issues concerning Prostitution Political Empowerment of Women and Technological Empowerment or Women in Women in Agriculture, A number of new bills and laws has been proposed by the NCW. These Include bills and laws related to NRI Marriage, Older persons maintenance Bill, Mental health, Recommendations or amendments, to the laws relating to rape and related provisions.

The NCW initiated various, steps to improve the status of women and worked for their economic empowerment. The commission completed its visits to all the States/UTs except Lakshadweep and prepared Gender Profiles to assess the status of women and their empowerment. It receives complaints and acts suo-moto in several cases to provide speedy Justice. Till now, it took up the issue of child marriage, sponsored legal awareness programmes, Parivarik Mnhila Lok Adelats and reviewed laws such as Dowry Prohibition Act, 1961, PNDT Act 1994, Indian, Penal Code 1860 and the National Commission for Women Act, 1990 to make them more stringent and effective. It organized workshops/consultations, constituted expert committee's on economic empowerment of women, conducted workshop seminars for gender awareness and took up publicity campaign against female foeticide, violence against women, etc. in order to generate awareness in the society against these social evils.

In India the Domestic Violence act, 2005 can prove to be life saver for the aggrieved women of the country. This is an act which provides for more effective protection of the rights of women guaranteed under the Constitution who are victims at violence of any kind occurring within the family and for matters connected therewith or incidental thereto. Specialized training for law enforcement authorities as well as medical and legal professionals and the establishment of community support services for victims, including access to information and shelters should stressed upon for the act to give the expected results.

At the global level similar activities are going on related to the issue of women empowerment. The United Nations Commission on the Status of Woman have finalized the theme: "Financing for gender equality and the empowerment of women" for its 52nd session at United Nations Headquarters in New York from 25 February to 7 March 2008. The Women's participation in conflict prevention, management, conflict resolution and in post-conflict peace-building will be emphasized in this formal meet.

WOMEN AND THE FIVE YEAR PLANS

The concept of women's development in the First Five Year Plan (1951-56) was mainly welfare oriented. The Central Social Welfare Board (CSWB), sat up in 1953, undertook a number of welfare measures through the voluntary sector. In the Second Five Year Plan (1956-61) women were organized into Mahila Mandals to act as focal points at the grass-root levels for the development of women. The Third, Fourth and other Interim Plans (1961-74) accorded high priority to education of women. Measures to improve maternal and child health services,' supplementary feeding for children and nursing and expectant mothers were also introduced. In the Fifth Plan (1974-78), there was a shift in the approach for women's development from 'welfare' to 'development'. The new approach aimed at an integration of welfare with developmental services. The Sixth Five Year Plan (1080-85) was a landmark in the history of women's development as it received recognition as one of the developmental sectors and was included, in the, Sixth Plan Document as a separate chapter for the first time in the history of developmental planning. The Sixth Plan adopted a multi-disciplinary approach with a three pronged thrust un health, education and employment. In the Seventh Plan (1985-90), the developmental programmes for women continued with the major objectives of raising their economic and social status and to bring them into the mainstream of national development. A significant step in this direction was to identify/promote the 'beneficiary-oriented programmes' for women ill different developmental sectors which extend direct benefits to women. The Eighth Five Year Plan (1992-97), which was launched in 1992, promises ensure that the benefits of development from different sectors do not bypass women and special programmes will be implemented to complement the general development programmes. Therefore, the flow of benefits to women in the three core sectors of education health and employment will be monitored with a greater vigil. Women must be enabled to function as equal partners and participants in the developmental process. This approach to the Eighth Plan marks a further shift from 'development' to 'empowerment' of women. In order to meet both the increasing and challenging needs of women and children, there has been a progressive increase in the Plan outlays over the period of last four developmental decades, The outlay of As. 4 crores in the First Plan (1951-56) has gone upto As. 2000 crores in the Eighth Five Year Plan (1992-97).

Empowerment of Women as agents of socio-economic change and development became one of the nine specific objectives of the Ninth Plan (1997-2002). The Plan envisaged primarily to ensure that benefits flow to women from all the general development sectors and emphasized on (i) reservation of not less than 1/3rd seats for women in the Parliament and State Assemblies (ii) convergence of existing services, resources, infrastructure and manpower in women specific and women-related sectors; (iii) adoption of special strategy of Women Component Plan (WCP) to ensure that not less than 30% of funds/ benefits flow to woman from other development sectors; (iv) organizing women Self Help Groups as a major process of empowering women; (v) high priority to reproductive child health care; (vi) universalizing on-going supplementary feeding programme; (vii) ensuring easy and equal access to education for women and girls; (viii) elimination of gender bias in all educational programmes; (ix) free education for girls up to college level including professional courses; (x) promoting skill development amongst women in modern upcoming trades etc. Some special initiatives taken during Ninth Plan including launching of an externally aided scheme of Swashakti (1998) for socio-economic empowerment of women through self reliant self help groups, instituting Stree Shakti Puraskars (1999), setting up of a Task Force under the Chairpersonship of Deputy Chairman, Planning Commission to review existing women-specific and women-related legislations (2000), adoption of National Policy for Empowerment of Women (2001), celebration of the year 2001 as Women's Empowerment Year, recasting of Indira Mahila Yojana as Swayarnsidha (2001), launching of Swadhar (2001) to extend rehabilitation services for women in difficult circumstances etc. Tenth Five Year Plan 'Empowerment of Women' as Agents of Social Change and Development was continued in the Tenth Plan. Towards this a Sector-specific 3-Fold Strategy was adopted based on the National Policy for Empowerment of Women (2001).

In the context of the preparations of the 11th Five Year Plan (2007-2012), the Planning Commission constituted a Steering Committee on the 'Empowerment of Women and Development of Children' under the Chairmanship of Dr. Syeda Hameed, Member, Planning Commission with the following Terms of Reference. The female population of the country rose marginally from 48.1 per cent of the total population in 1991 to 48.3 per cent of the total population in 2001. In absolute numbers, this implies an increase by 89.4 million from 407.1 million in 1991 to 496 million In 2001. The growth rate of female population for the 1991-2001 decade was 23.08, slightly higher than the male population decennial growth rate of 22.26. The expectancy of life at birth has been rising steadily for women. It increased from 58.6 in 1987-91 to 66.91 in 2001.06, and is higher than the male life expectancy of 63.87. However, demographic imbalances between men and women continue to exist, even worsen, in certain regions. As revealed by the Sachar Committee Report (Social economic and Educational Status of the Muslim Community of India - A Report - November 2006), the educational status of Muslim and SC/ST women in particular is a major cause of concern. The literacy rate figures for Muslim, SC and ST women are 50%, 47.1% and 34.8'% respectively. At the bottom of the rung are Muslim arid SC/ST women in rural areas whose literacy rates are 43% and 36% respectively. It should also be noted that disparities increase with the level of schooling. At the basic level of literacy, Muslim women were 11 % worse off than non-Muslims. However, the difference widened to 9% at the middle school level, 35% at Class- X, 45% at Class-12 and 63% for graduates and above as per Census 2001.

The National Policy on women 2001, which informed the 10th Five Year Plan, articulated a series of goals towards women's empowerment. The objectives of this policy include, (i) Creating an environment through positive and social policies for development of women; to enable them to realize their full potential (ii) The de-jure and de-facto enjoyment of all human rights and fundamental freedoms by women on equal basis with men in all spheres -political, economic, social, cultural find civil (iii) Equal access to participation and decision making of women in social, political and economic life of the nation (iv) Equal access to women to health care, quality education at all levels, career and vocational guidance, employment, equal remuneration, occupational health and safety, social security and public office etc: (v) Strengthening legal systems aimed at elimination of all forms of discrimination against women (vi) Changing societal attitudes and community practices by active participation and involvement of both men and women, (vii) Mainstreaming a gender perspective in the development process. (viii) Elimination of discrimination and all forms of violence against women and the girl child; and (ix) Building and strengthening partnerships with civil society, particularly women's organizations. The 11th plan approach to gender equity has FIVE key elements:

(1) The recognition that women are not a homogenous category for planned intervention–that they belong to diverse castes, classes, communities, economic groups, and are located at a range of geographic and development zones, and that mapping and acknowledging the specific deprivations which arise from these multiple locations can alone determine the success of planned interventions. In order to operationalize this understanding official directives must be issued to WOD programmes as well as women-related programmes in other ministries to teach women across multiple axis of deprivation (gender, class, caste, community, marital status, geographic location etc.), to monitor implementation and collect disaggregated data along these multiple axis. The double deprivation

of particular categories of women (SC, ST women, Muslim women, single women/widows, and women in conflict .zones like the north-east and J&K), in addition to being addressed through general programme interventions, have to also be addressed through a range of special, targeted and/or pilot interventions for those particular categories of women.

(2) The recognition that only inclusive development of all categories of women can ensure holistic national development toward the millennium development goals.

(3) The recognition that both inter-sectoral convergence as well as targeted exclusive women focused planning (through the Ministry of WCD) are necessary to achieve inclusive development towards the social, economic and political empowerment of women.

(4) The recognition that for interventions in favour of women to have a sustained, long term, incremental impact beyond individual five year plan periods, they have to be four-pronged, (i) to provide women with basic entitlements such as food security, health and education, (ii) to address the reality of globalization and its impact on women by prioritizing economic empowerment and mainstreaming women in new and emerging areas of the economy, (iii) ensure an environment free from all forms bf violence against women physical, economic, social, psychological, and (iv) ensure the participation and adequate representation of women at the highest policy levels, particularly ill Parliament and Assemblies. Even a State like Kerala, with high female literacy, has only 7 women in a 141 member State Legislative Assembly. This situation must not continue beyond the 11th plan.

(5) The recognition that permanent institutional mechanisms such as a Women's, Knowledge Commission or alternatively a permanent (Inter-Ministerial) Standing Committee on Gender, with 50% participation of civil society gender experts, must be put in place to include women's participation, experiences capacities and knowledge into the process of development planning formulation and administration across all sectors. There must be mandatory representation of qualified women in all Planning Commission Steering Committees.

The feminization of poverty in India has been well documented in recent years, demonstrating the rising levels and differential gender impacts of poverty on women. Liberalization of the economy has led to a paradigm shift in the country's economy towards technology dominated sectors rendering women dominated sectors like agriculture unviable and without any security cover. Liberalization has increased wage differentials job vulnerability and unpaid work burden for women, while lowering their social safety nets. Unequal access for women to schooling, land credit facilities, alternate employment, skill, training and technology also undermines their prospects for poverty reduction. 11th Plan has to address the issues relating to feminization of poverty especially that of large gender differential in wage rates, exploitation of women.

In addition to prioritizing the key focus areas listed above, the 11th plan will follow the following five-fold strategy:

Economic empowerment, with special focus on women in agriculture and on the effects of globalization; Social empowerment and engendering social change;

Political Empowerment-to facilitate entry and effective functioning of women in Parliament, PRIs and in premier government services;

Strengthening mechanism for effective implementation of women related legislations;

Creating institutional mechanisms for gender mainstreaming and strengthening delivery mechanisms for effective implementation of women-related programmes.

Government run rural development projects, as practiced today are unlikely to improve the social and economic status of women in the foreseeable future. The first step has bean taken with the unprecedented 73rd amendment to India's constitution. This amendment mandates the transfer of decision-making power and resources in the rural areas to local democratic councils known as panchayats. Most, revolutionary of all, one-third of all panchayat seats are to be reserved for women-guaranteeing them a role in determining he future of their communities. If fully implemented, Women will, for the first time in India's history, have a voice in the decisions that affect their lives.

Women are changing governance in India. They are being elected to local councils in unprecedented numbers as a result of amendments to the Constitution which mandate the reservation of seats for women in local government. Some of the ways in which women, through PRI, are changing governance are evident ill the issues they choose to tackle; water, alcohol abuse, education, health and domestic violence. Since Independence, the Government of, India has enacted a constitutional and legal framework and has developed institutional mechanisms to enable improvement in the living conditions of women and children in India. The basic provisions of the Indian Constitution that guarantee justice liberty and equality to all citizens. and the specific articles and amendments that have been enacted to ensure that women enjoy the constitutional rights that assure their participation in society as equal partners provide the framework for women development in India. But mere legislation and constitutional provision are not enough; true emancipation is required at individual levels. Legislation means can however, be a short term remedy or fascinator. It is only through empowerment of woman that development of a society and the nation is possible. Not only the removed of inequality and

Table 1
Views of Different Five Year Plans on Women

Five Year Plans	*Views on Women*
First Plan (1951-56)	Sets up the Central Social welfare board in 1953 to promote welfare work through voluntary organizations, charitable trusts etc.
Second Plan (1956-61)	Supported the Development of Mahila Mandals to work at the grassroots.
Third, Fourth & Interim (Plan 74) mothers	Had provisions for Women's Education, pre-natal and child health (1961 services, Supplernentary feeding for children, nursing and expectant.
Fifth Plan (1974-78)	A major shift in the approach towards women from Welfare to Development.
Sixth Plan (1980-85)	Accepted Women's Development as a separate Economic Agenda. Took a multi-displinary approach with a three-pronged thrust on health, education and employment.
Seventh Plan (1985-90)	Had the objective of bringing women into the mainstream of National Development.
Eighth Plan (1992-97)	Saw a paradigm shift from development to Empowerment and benefits to women in the core sector of education, health, and employment. Outlay for women rose from Rs. 4 crore in the first plant to Rs. 2,000 crore in the Eight.
Ninth Plan (1997-02)	Had Empowerment of Women as its Strategic Objective. Accepted the concept of a Women's component plan to assure that at least 30% of funds/benefits from all development sector flow to women.
Tenth Plan (2002-07)	Suggests specific Strategies, Policies and Programmes for the Empowerment of Women.

imbalance but improvement in the quality and standard of the women should be our goal. We can quote Mahatma Gandhi, "As long as women of India do not take part in public life, there can be to salvation for the country." So every effort should be made for women empowerment in the various administration political and economic perspectives in this era of feminism.

CONCLUSION

In our country the Government have a decisive role to play in strengthening the women capacity to undertake boarder decision making and representative roles. Government should take initiative in improving the rural women's access to leadership development opportunities and initiatives and thus support their leadership aspirations by way of different scholarship, fellowship and exchange programme in collaboration with other countries or international agencies. Grants provided by government will help to self reliant. Government with the due cooperation from other voluntary organization and population at large should be keen to face the challenge of offering workable solutions to these serious problems.

India's traditional inheritance and land tenure laws limit the women's ownership and land rights. In today's developing world, banks and credit institutions are less reluctant to give credit to women because without land and property they lack the collateral security to acquire loan. However, inheritance on part of the government like implementation of institution like Rashtrlya Mahila Kosh implemented to facilitate credit support to poor women which is totally security free is giving some relief. Breaking the cycle of abuse will require concerted collaboration and action between governmental and non-governmental actors, including educators, health-care authorities, legislators, the judiciary and the mass media. In Indian context the patriarchal structure of the society over the centuries have gradually lead to gender inequality. The plethora of government schemes aimed at rural development met with only partial success, without much improvement in the overall situation. The government should come out schemes that provide an opportunity for brothers and sisters of every part of the country to get to know each other better and in turn share their experience and expectation in terms of what they can do for their counterparts. Women equipped with education will surely demonstrate beyond doubt that given the right type of orientation and opportunities and support for building up their skills and thus they can rise to any occasion in order to contribute towards their self empowerment.

REFERENCES

Deepti Agarwal (2001), "Empowerment of Rural Women", Intensive Agriculture, March.

Kurukshetra, A Journal on Rural Development, Empowering Rural Women, Sep. 2008.

The Hindu, Daily Newspaper, Feb. 25, 2007.

Vijay Kaushik (1997), "Womens Movements and Human Rights", Pointer Publishers, Jaipur.

Yojana, A Development Monthly, Vol. 51, Feb. 2007.

Yojana, A Development Monthly, Vol. 51, May 2007.

PLURAL LEGALITIES, HUMAN RIGHTS AND GENDER JUSTICE IN INDIA: ISSUES AND PROSPECTS

YOGETHA KUNVER* & NANJUNDA D C**

INTRODUCTION

A look at the status of women in India today is a cause for concern. Right from female foeticide, infanticide, child marriage, domestic violence, sexual violence, sexual harassment at the work place to the treatment meted out to elderly women makes any thinking person to wonder at the nature of the society. Participation of women in the decision making bodies be they within the home, workplace or community is marginal, never reaching even 25% of the total population of women in India. At the same time women are seen as the bearers of Indian tradition and culture. Without enabling women to exist as citizens with political and economic power is it possible for them to safeguard the tradition and culture of this country. The status of women in British India and the princely States was worse and the various practices like sati, widowhood, child marriage, female infanticide were all seen as reflective of the backwardness of Indian society and were therefore targeted for change. The role of women in the National Movement and the rise of the womens movement during the pre-independence days ensured that the Constitution of India and Independent India? would see a change for the better in the status of women

Women were considered to be devoid of intellect and consciously denied any learning. They were denied right to property and were forbidden from performing sacrifices, religion also contributed in a substantial measure to aggravate these inequalities.

Rig Veda is the only scripture among those of all religions in which the Divine truth are revealed to women sages. There are more than 30 women sages in Rig-Veda with specific hymns associated with them. There are numerous hymns in the Rig-Veda indicating the high status to women in the

* *Independent Researcher, Capetown, South Africa.*

** *Correspondence Author: Project Director, Center for Advanced Rural and Tribal Policy Innovation and Management, Kushalnager-34, Kodagu Dist, Karnataka State, India, E-mail: ajdmeditor@yahoo.co.in).*

Vedic society. Fro instance the hymn 10.85, the so called marriage hymn explicitly states that the daughter in law should be treated in the family as a queen, smrajni by all members especially the mother-in-law, husband, father-in-law etc. (Ali, 2000).

INDIAN CONSTITUTION AND GENDER EQUALITY

The founding fathers of Indian constitution really wanted to eliminate gender inequality in India. Our constitution forbids sexual discrimination and guarantees social and economic justice to women.

The Constitution in its preamble guarantees:

(a) Social economic and political/justice.

(b) Freedom of thought, expression, belief, faith and worship.

(c) equality of status and opportunity.

(d) Fraternity assuring the dignity of the individual and national unity to all the citizens of India without any discrimination of caste, creed or sex.

Articles in the Constitution which helped the women to improve their status and to compete with their male counterpart:

1. Article 14 the State guarantees the state guarantees equality before law ana equal protection of all its citizen within Indian terrority.
2. Article 16 provides that there shall be equality of opportunity for all citizens in matters relating to employment or appointment to any office under the State. There shall be no discrimination based on religion race, caste, sex, place of birth against any employment or office under the State.
3. Article 21 provides that no person shall be deprived or his life or personal liberty except according to procedure established by law.
4. Article 39 the State grants to all the citizens both men and eaual work rights to have adequate means of livelihood and Article 39(b) states that there is equal pay for equal work for both women and men.
5. Article 41 the State shall guarantee within ite sconomic limits to all the citizens the right to work education and public assistance in certain cases.
6. Article 42 the State makes provision for just and human conditions of work and maternity relief.
7. Article 44, the State provides a Uniform Civil Code to all the citizens throughout the territory the India.
8. Article 51-(c) caste Fundamental duties on every citizen of India to promote harmony and the spirit of common brotherhood amongst all

> the people of India transcending religious linguistic and regional or sectional diversities to renounce practices derogatory to the dignity of women.

In its judgment the Supreme Court of India pointed out that it is the responsibility of the legislature and of the executive government to ensure that the working women could live with dignity and carry on their respective vocations in a safe environment. This requires, suitable legislation and the creation of a mechanism for the enforcement of the rights of women. If the legislature and the executive failed to perform their duties the Court said that it had to assume an active role to administer gender justice when required. In this context, the SCI looked for inspiration to the Beijing Statement of Principles of the Independence of the judiciary in the LAWASIA region. These principles were accepted by the Chief Justices of Asia and the Pacific at Beijing in 1995 as the minimum standards necessary to maintain the independence and effective functioning of the judiciary. According to the Court , the Objectives of the judiciary as mentioned in that Statement include: (a) ensuring that all persons are able to live securely under the rule of law (b) promoting within the proper limits of judicial function, the observance and attainment of human rights and (c) administering law impartially among persons and between persons and the State. Court also adverted to the provisions of 'Convention on Elimination of All forms of Discrimination against Women' (CEDAW) which required the States Parties to take all appropriate measures to eliminate discrimination against women in the field of employment, as the right to workis an inalienable right of all human beings. Under the Convention, equality in employment can be seriously impaired when women are subjected to gender specific violence, such as sexual harassment in the workplace. CEDAW defines sexual harassment in comprehensive terms: it includes unwelcome sexually-determined behavior, sexually-colored remarks etc. Such conduct can be humiliating for the working women and may constitute a health and safety problem (Tsanga, A. 2007). It is discriminatory when the woman has reasonable ground to believe that her objection would disadvantage her in connection with her employment, or when it creates a hostile working environment. The Government of India ratified the CEDAW Resolution on 25th June 1993 and had also made an official commitment at the Fourth World Conference on Women in Beijing undertaking to formulate and put into operation a national policy on women and to take other measures as required under the said instrument. At the time of Vishaka, however, the legislature had not made any law to give effect to CEDAW Resolution and as such there was a void in domestic law, said the Supreme Court . Against this background the SCI declared, "It is now an accepted rule of judicial construction that regard must be had to the international conventions and norms when construing domestic laws when there is no inconsistent (Griffiths, 2002).

UNIFORM CIVIL CODE AND GENDER

The heated debate on Common Civil Code that one comes across today makes it appear that the greatest problem faced by India is nothing but the lack of a Common Civil Code. Political propaganda has obscured the fact that the rest 99% of the laws in the country is 'common' for all and it hasn't made any difference. Rajeev Dhawan, leading Supreme Court lawyer has pointed out 'India already has a 'uniform civil code'-reputedly the best in the world. The Contract Act, Transfer of Property Act, Evidence Act and the Civil Procedure Code and the laws relating to torts are common for all citizens. The controversy as rightly pointed about by Rajeev Dhawan is about 'codification of personal laws'. Personal laws imply laws relating to family like marriage, divorce, inheritance, adoption etc. As far as marriage is concerned ,any Indian citizen is free to get married under the Special Marriage Act which removes many of the restraints under the personal laws. Even those who make the biggest noises about the Common Civil Code have not opted to undergo a marriage under this law. India being a country with diverse religions, cultures, castes and myriad other social formations and affiliations, people prefer to stick on to their traditions and practices when it comes to their private lives. People continue to marry from their own group. Ironically those who speak of the Common Civil Code have not been honest about gender justice. No one is really interested in the Women's Reservation Bill. The Hindutva forces have been making a lot of hue and cry about Uniform Civil Code. However they have been seen promoting the Sati-Savithri imagery. Some of the statements from the Sangh parivar leaders have been relegating women to a secondary role. Some of the BJP leaders have been seen glorifying Sati (Sevenhuijsen, 1998).

The concentration ought to have been on the empowerment of women, enforcement of equal educational and employment opportunities and so on. The atrocities against the women are increasing by the day. The Gujarat episode showed the Hindutva forces using assault and rape as a weapons against women of the minority communities. It is surprising that people don't want to see these as the real threat to 'national integration'. Technically speaking ,are all the criminal laws uniform all over the country for that matter? The answer is a big no, especially when it comes to the minor laws. For example the possession or consumption of alcohol or beef may be an offence in one state but not in another. If the people of India were all devoid of religions and their attached customs and traditions then uniform laws related to marriage, divorce or divorce would have been easier. What the legislators could do is to make laws like Special Marriage Act where the parties could make the choice. The courts have ample power to strike down any element of the current personal law which they feel is discriminatory. The Christian laws have indeed been changed drastically by judicial legislation. Thus the Christian divorce laws, property rights of women and laws relating to wills have been made non-discriminatory. The adoption laws are also expected to be changed in this manner soon (Charlesworth, H. & Chinkin, 2000).

In Gita Hariharan vs Reserve Bank Of India (1999) 2 SCC 228 the gender justice question arose as to whether the mother of a minor child could be regarded under the Guardianship statute, as the 'natural guardian' of the child when the father was alive. The statute law on the subject was to the effect that the natural guardian of a minor is the 'father and after him the mother'. This was always taken to mean that if the father was alive, he would be the natural guardian, and only after his death the mother can be the natural guardian. But Supreme Court felt that such an interpretation would lead to unfair discrimination against the mother and would amount to a breach of gender equality as guaranteed by the Constitution and international instruments. The Court therefore read down the provision of the statute, and construed the words "after him" following the word "father" to mean, that the mother would be the natural guardian even during the life time of the father, if the father was absent from of the scene of the minor either due to his own indifference or by choice or when he was physically absent or when he is unable to perform the duties of guardianship for any disability or did not want to, due to an understanding with the mother, or when he had no objection to the mother being the guardian.

EDUCATION

It has long been recognized that present day lawyers and judges are insensitive and unaware of the problems and perspectives of women resulting in grave injustice to them in various ways Orientation and in-service refresher training programmes for lawyers and judges have been suggested by all concerned with the problem and indeed such training programmes are being organised too. Law Faculties in this scenario have the important obligation to generate awareness of the gender bias operating in society and legal system in India. Education should familiarises the students with the real facts relating to the status of women in India and nature, extent and kind of gender bias in the extant law and judicial decisions. It should also explores the jurisprudential explanations for the existing state of affairs. It focuses on the patriarchal nature of state and family and contemporary feminist debates. The course consciously has excluded familiar areas of discrimination, like family law, criminal law and labour law, as it is believed that discriminatory aspects of those laws should be focused in those courses.

PREJUDICE ABOUT GIRL CHILD IN INDIA

In its campaign against SD (Sex-determination), Forum Against Sex-Determination and Sex-preselection (FASDSP) deliberately used the terms 'female foeticide' and 'femicide' to signify murderous attack by the patriarchal value system to annihilate the females among the human species. FASDSP finds an ideological continuity in the four types of 9 acts of gender violence:

pre-conceptional sex-selection, selective abortion of female foetus, female infanticide and systematic neglect and ill-treatment of daughters, wives and mothers. We don't subscribe to the myopic world-view of the liberal school of thought which glorifies 'value-neutrality' and 'non-partisanship'. Our first-hand knowledge of the bleak reality of unequal gender relations in our society and our faith in humanism motivated us to demand affirmative action from the state to stop scientifically approved slaughter of daughters. As a result of a decade- long advocacy based on field research, acquisition of scientific knowledge, collection of anthropological evidence, development of legal expertise, use of media coverage, public debate, personal zeal and political will; we have a law regulating SD tests in India.

The number of professionally competent and employed daughters (married or otherwise) who are supporting their ageing parents is increasing progressively. Over the past decade and a half, action against dowry harassment has made parents and daughters precocious. Parents make conscious efforts to see that their daughters are emotionally and economically self-sufficient. Women facing dowry-harassment after their marriage refuse to suffer in silence. They have not only got out of the oppressive situation but have helped other women in similar predicaments.

These brave women who are courageous, confident and economically independent have proved to be role models to thousands of girls to fight anti-women customs and traditions. Weeping and wailing about dowry- harassment has its place only in the dustbin of history. Instead of victim- baiting we prefer to empower the forces within the state apparatus and society which are helping women's development (Molyneux, M. & Razavi, 2002).

However, it must be remembered that guaranteeing a right in law does not ensure the ability to access the right in reality. The fact that the historical subjection of women has not been ended is constantly before us in the form of the reducing number of women in each census. It is falling at an alarming rate which is a matter of concern. Similarly crimes against women have been on the increase. Incidents of rape, sexual assault, sexual harassment, domestic violence, cheating etc have been growing not only in numbers but also in intensity and brutality. The statistics provided by the Crime Bureau of India brings this before us every year. These statistics only reveal the numbers of reported cases. One can easily imagine how much bigger the numbers would be if one were to take into account the numerous unreported cases. In addition, in the context of an expanding market economy, there has been the increasing objectification of women in the advertisements and the media. Parliament has from time to time either made amendments to the existing law or enacted new laws to address these various concerns. Women have huge responsibilities in relation to their families as the carers and nurturers but have low negotiating power at the same time. This results in neglect of their health and nutrition and access to health care is also restricted as women are most often unable to go to the primary health centres and hospitals leaving their responsibilities at home. It is, however, very important to realize that gender justice can not be secured merely through laws and the legal system. Enacting gender just laws will not mean an end to the exploitation of and discrimination against women. Using law and the legal system can only be one of the many remedies to be used to change the unequal status of women. Law is one of the means of empowerment of women but it is very essential that we realize the limitations of law and not just hope that since we have a Constitution that guarantees equality and various laws to address the different kinds of atrocities against women that women now are enjoying equality. Society has to be changed, attitudes of people in society have to be altered before equality can become real for women.

CONCLUSION

The legislative framework provided in the Constitution provides for equality in society between men and women. In order to fulfil this constitutional mandate the Parliament and the Judiciary have from time to time made laws and interpreted the existing ones that would guarantee gender justice. However since law, the legal system and society are closely interlinked it is not possible to enforce the rights provided in law without changes in social institutions, values and attitudes. Social change cannot be brought about through law. It is only through the process of sensitizing various branches of the government and more importantly the members of society to the rights and concerns of women can gender justice become a reality. Law is only one method by which the various problems of women can be resolved. While law can empower women at one level it is not possible to completely the subordination of women or the discriminatory practices merely through the legal system.? If it had been otherwise we should not have to worry about the falling numbers of women in the year 2004. After all we have the Constitution that guarantees various rights to women and enactments since then which have attempted to address various crimes against women. We have to recognize the limitation of law in bringing about change in society and in ending oppression of women.

At national level, legal policy makers, women's ministries and equality and human rights commissions struggle with difficulties relating to gendered access to labour markets and confront the complex issues relating to gender justice within plural/multicultural societies particularly in relation to family relations. Measures to tackle violence against women within households and communities are emerging across the world. In a range of countries judges are recognising that gender justice is an essential ingredient to developing and maintaining legitimacy within the legal system. At a grassroots (or civil society) level legal strategies are an important focus for many activists who have campaigned for greater equality between men and women in a wide range of contexts including improved labour rights, more equal inheritance laws, and violence against women.

REFERENCES

Ali, S. S. (2000), *Gender and Human Rights in Islam and International Law: Unequal Before Allah, Unequal Before Man*, The Hague: Kluwer Law International.

Charlesworth, H. & Chinkin, C. (2000), *The Boundaries of International Law: A Feminist Analysis*, Manchester: Manchester University Press.

Griffiths, A. (2002), 'Legal Pluralism' in R. Banakar & M. Travers (eds) *An Introduction to Law and Social Theory*, Oxford: Hart Publishing.

Molyneux, M. & Razavi, S. (eds.,) (2002), *Gender Justice, Development and Rights*, Oxford: Oxford University Press.

Sevenhuijsen, S. *et al* (2003), 'South African Social Welfare Policy: An Analysis Using the Ethic of Care' in *Critical Social Policy*, 23(3) 299-321.

Stewart, A. (1996), 'Should Women Give Up on the State? The African Experience' in S. Rai and G. Lievesly (eds) *Women and the State: International Perspectives*, London: Taylor and Francis.

Sevenhuijsen, S. (1998), *Citizenship and the Ethics of Care: Feminist Considerations on Justice, Morality and Politics*, London: Routledge.

Tsanga, A. (2007), 'Reconceptualising the Role of Legal Information Dissemination in the Context of Legal Pluralism in African Settings' in.

GENDER AND BIO-DIVERSITY MANAGEMENT IN A FOOD-GATHERING SOCIETY OF KERALA

Bindu Ramachandran*

Role of ecology in shaping the culture of a particular society has been a significant theme in anthropological literature since the contributions of Daryll Ford and Julian Steward. Ecology influences, supports, maintain and help in the growth of cultures and its survival. When we take the case of primitive societies it is seen that ecology is the part and parcel of their culture protected by adaptive cultural adjustments.

In Indian philosophy and culture, both men and women are seen as indispensable part of nature. Earth is equated with 'mother', a concept widely used in Indian literature. The role of gender in maintaining and determining the subsistence and other related eco-cultural and economic scenario has been the subject of growing anthropological and sociological interest today. When we analyses the role of women in the management of bio-diversity and environmental protection it is clear that ecological commitment cannot be replaced by any other factor as their participation is active in the rehabilitation of degraded land, replantation of endangering plant species and a strategy of conservation in collective initiation. They have a wide range of traditional knowledge in the manipulation of biological resources. Conservation of the ecosystem is now recognized as valuable information, which can be collected and used for ecosystem based development programmes.

In analyzing the role of tribal women in the forest economy of gathering, it should be noted that women perform a major part of labour of gathering. They also play a more active role in household activities and manage most of the basic means of sustenance. In a food-gathering society the division of labour is responsible for the environmental commitments. This paper is an attempt to explain the role of gender in the management of bio-diversity in Kattunaicken society, one of the food gathering societies of Kerala.

II

Kattunaicken are the primitive food gatherers of Kerala distributed mainly in Wayanad district. The natural vegetation surrounding Kattunaicken hamlets

* *Lecturer, Department of Anthropology, Kannur University, Kerala.*

is the forests especially the reserve forests. They dwell in the lap of nature, and hence they have ample source of forest products. Their settlements are found clustered inside the forest or in the village borders. The cluster of houses in a settlement is composed of a number of independent families. Nuclear family is the minimum social and economic unit. Traditionally Kattunaicken huts are distributed far from each other. This may be because of the territorial concept of collecting minor forest produces from the forests. The economic activities of Kattunaicken are a true reflection of the relationship of their culture with ecosystem. They are engaged in various activities such as gathering for consumption, collection of MFP for trade, honey collection, plantation labour and as mahouts. Food gathering is one of the oldest means of their livelihood. They gather wild natural produce like edible fruits, leaves and roots which varies with season.

Division of labour plays an important role in the management of bio-diversity. In Kattunaicken society it is mainly based on age and sex. Men usually do the arduous and tough tasks themselves and leave the monotonous and comparatively light work to their women. Women are forbidden to take up those tasks which require climbing on the roof or trees for honey collection. Household duties such as preparing food, fetching water, taking care of children, washing clothes are performed by women. Customarily women are not sent to watch the crops in the fields during night. Men take up ploughing,cutting of heavy logs, collection of minor forest produces, honey, indigenous medicines, herbs...etc. The women held the family by gathering fruits, leaves, and tubers.

III

Kattunaicken have a close interaction with ecology as part of their life activities revolve around the ecosystem they live in. The ecological equilibrium plays a vital role in the socio-cultural stability of Kattunaicken. In the case of technologically less developed group like Kattunaicken, food habits and subsistence pattern are mainly centered around food gathering, MFP collection and fishing. Subsistence through hunting has almost disappeared. As in any other food gathering community, Kattunaicken have developed techniques of food gathering as an adaptation to the surrounding ecosystem. When the environment is rich and resourceful, the food procurement technologies become simple, easy and less time consuming. Where as when it is deficient in resources, the inhabitants will have to find different and complex ways of food procurement strategies for a minimum survival.

Traditional food of Kattunaicken consists of wild fruits, tubers and roots available in the local ecosystem. Even now tubers constitute important item of food though there are seasonal variations in obtaining them. Kattunaicken collects different varieties of mushrooms from the surrounding ecosystem during the monsoon season. Usually women do this collection. They also use plenty of leafy vegetables obtained from the forest. The tender stem of bamboo, available in plenty in their habitat, is boiled in water. Excess water filtered off and the residual material is used for making curries.

Honey is a major item of collection for self-consumption. They have classified honey into many types according to its location. Women mainly do the preliminary works for honey collection. Honey is separated from the wax in the forest itself. As a preliminary step of honey collection, the kattunaicken women collect and dry the leaves and branches of two types of plants. This is used for making a traditional type of torch. When honey is located in a tree, male people collect long bamboo stems and prepare ladders by placing one after another. With the help of traditional torch (dried leaves tied together and put fire on the end), the bees are chased and the beehives are collected in the basket. In former days large bamboo vessels were used for storing honey. The honey obtained from a comb depends on its size, but generally they are able to obtain 5-6 liters of honey from a comb.

Fishing is leisure time activity of kattunaicken and is seasonal also. Those who live on the banks of rivers and paddy fields spend considerable time in fishing. They use eco-friendly techniques for fishing so that the bio-diversity in water will not be affected.

Kattunaicken not only identify the roots and tubers but also have adequate knowledge of the habitat and depth at which these are found. The digging stick and collecting basket are the main equipments used by them in gathering forest produces. When we go through the role of Kattunaicken women in the economy of gathering, it is clear that women perform a major part of the labour of gathering. Men also participate in gathering but they are more interested to do other jobs, which bring money directly. As far as men are concerned, gathering is only a leisure time activity or an activity they do on days without any other labour. Moreover it requires more patience and local environmental knowledge. If men dugout a root or tuber they take it carelessly and discard the remaining portions. But women after taking the product replant it and put a mark for future identification.

Location of the edible varieties and replantation of the same after harvest are usually done by women. The continuous interaction with the local ecosystem helps the Kattunaicken women to achieve an in-depth knowledge of the seasons and available varieties and naturally it became her duty to preserve it. In most instances it is women who locate the roots and tubers and men help them only when it is in long depth. Kattunaicken used to collect what they required enough for the day. Then they relaxed till the supply of food was finished, before going out foraging again. Children dig up a tuber from the forest and then cutting out the eyes delicately and replanting them with great care. They take from the earth just what they need. But they nurture it because they respect it.

The pattern of distribution is very interesting and it is in tune with the availability of the bio-diversity and settlement life. In olden days whenever an animal is hunted, it was divided into many portions. The important portions like heart, liver, and thigh were kept for gods. The rest of the portion was divided among the members. One portion was set apart for the chief. The portion set aside for the god was also taken by the chief later. One portion was set aside for the old and disabled men and women of the settlement. The portions of the god and the chief were cooked by the chief's wife separately and were kept on a plantain leaf together with rice in their sacred house. This was kept there for an hour propitiating their deity and the ancestral spirits. After that the food was served to the members of the family. The gathered surplus roots and tubers were also distributed. This type of distribution system is an adaptive strategy for managing a situation of food scarcity.

IV

As food gatherers they developed base and skills for natural resource management. Technology plays a major role in the utilization of ecosystem through skills. Major technology of Kattunaicken includes simple implements like digging sticks, small axe, knife...etc. that will never hurt the ecosystem while in use. One of the main naturefacts used by the Kattunaicken is plant and its products. In addition to the collection of logs, twigs and creepers for various purposes, most of their implements and equipment for food procurement are manufactured with wood as one item. When we examine each of their devices it is understood that wood is an indispensable item of their technology especially bamboo.

In the past Kattunaicken did not produce anything. They have completely depended on the resources of nature for their livelihood. Today, hunting and trapping of birds and animals for food procurement was relatively little owing to the restrictions imposed by the state forest department and also shortage of games in the forest. The collection of MFP has also reduced owing to the degradation of the forests. Ladies used to carry their children when they go out for collection and a child from its childhood itself learn to use the implements and the identification of edibles through an informal method. Here Kattunaicken ladies act as a medium of compromise between nature and culture and will automatically become better managers of natural resources.

REFERENCES

Bindu, B. (1998), Socio-economic Change among three Wayanad Tribes. A Study of Adiyan, Kattunaicken and Mullukuruman in Eco-cultural Context. (Unpublished Ph.D Thesis submitted to Calicut University.

———(1996), Social Structure and Kinship of an Ex-bonded Labourer Community, *Man and Life*, Vol. 22, July.

Iyer, Krishna, L. A. (1937), *The Travancore Tribes and Castes.*, Govt. Press Trivandrum.

Kunhaman, M. (1983), *Understanding Tribal Life. The Kerala Dossier*, State and Society Vol. 4, No. 2.

Kurup, K. K. N. (1989), *Agrarian Struggles in Kerala*, ABH Publications, Trivandrum.

Logan,William, (1887), *Malabar*, Vol.1, Madras Govt. Press (Reprinted 1951) New Delhi. Asian Educational Services.

Luiz, A. A. D. (1962), *Tribes of Kerala*, Bharatiya Adimjathi SevakSang, New Delhi.

Mathur, P. R. G. (1977), *Tribal Situation in Kerala*, Kerala Historical, Society, Trivandrum.

Rajalakshmi Misra (1971), *Mullukurumbas of Kappala*, Calcutta. Anthropological Survey of India.

Thurston, E. (1909), *Castes and Tribes of Southern India*. Madras Govt. Press.

Vidyarthi, L. P. (1976), *The Tribal Culture of India*, New Delhi, Concept Publishing Co.

HUMAN RIGHTS: GENDER DISCRIMINATION AGAINST FEMALE CHILDREN IN NIGERIA

HAKEEM IJAIYA*

INTRODUCTION

Section 42 of the Constitution of the Federal Republic of Nigeria, 1999[1] provides for freedom from discrimination on the grounds of ethnic group, origin, gender, religion, circumstances of birth, disability, or political opinion[2]. Female children in Nigeria are subjected to all forms of gender discrimination such as early marriages, female genital mutilation and other forms of discrimination. Discrimination also affects other groups of children like male children, orphans, street children, disabled children or children born out of wedlock. The paper will discuss gender discrimination against female children in Nigeria and make recommendations on how to solve the problem.

GENDER DISCRIMINATION

Section 42 (1) (2) of the Constitution of Nigeria makes provision for gender equality among male and female children. But as a result of culture and religious beliefs in the country, female children are often deprived of their fundamental rights to basic education, good nutrition, essential health care and all other basic needs, as well as protection against abuses, neglect, exploitation and slavery. Traditional practices such as early marriages and female genital mutilation are responsible for the discrimination against female children in Nigeria. These traditional practices have negative impact on the reproductive and health rights of the female children in Nigeria. Most of these practices have their roots in long-standing customs of particular communities in the country and they are often formulated ostensibly to achieve particular goals. While some of these practices may have noble goals and premised on sound moral principles[3], they nevertheless have adverse effects not only on the health of female children but their overall status in society[4]. They also have defective medical grounds and validity, understandably because at the time they are

* M. Phil (Law) Lecturer, University of Ilorin, Faculty of Law, Kwara State, Nigeria, E-mail hakeemijaiya@yahoo.com

formulated and adopted, these communities either did not have access at all to orthodox medical services or these were too remote for them[5].

EARLY MARRIAGES

One of the traditional practices common to many parts of Nigeria is early or child marriage. It is common in Nigeria to find girls under the age of 12 years been betrothed to adult males. Many pre-pubescent and adolescent girls are given away in marriage without their consent. Although it is a practice in vogue in several parts of the country, it is more prevalent among the Moslems of Northern Nigeria[6]. While the problem associated with child marriage are enormours[7], the existing legal rules have not provided any reasonable assistance in the matter. This is because there is no definite age specified in the relevant enactments as the marriageable age for girls in Nigeria.

The age of marriage is a highly controversial issue and varies from place to place. For instance, in the North West and North Central parts of Nigeria, 14 years is the age of marriage. While in the Northern and Central parts of Nigeria, the age of marriage is between the 2nd and 3rd menstruation, whereas in the Southern part of the country, the marriage age varies from between 16 to 18 years. Section 18 of the Marriage Act[8] allows persons under the age of 21 years to get married, provided that parental consent is given. The Matrimonial Causes Act[9] provides that one of the grounds upon which a marriage shall be void is when "either of the parents is not of marriageable age"[10] it does not go further to define the marriageable age. However, the Child Rights Act[11] attempts to infer the prescription of a marriageable age[12], Section 277 of the Act defines a child as a person under the age of 18 years.

The inconsistencies in the marriage age in Nigeria have negatively affected the rights of the female children. It limits the opportunities for them to accede to education, putting them in a disadvantaged position[13]. 36 million Nigerian female children are not educated.

Early marriage can be detrimental to physical, mental and emotional health. Apart from the fact that it deprives the female children from their rights to have control over their body and reproduction health, it puts them in position of complete dependency from their husband.

In the Northern part of Nigeria, where the majority of female children face the prospect of early marriage, there are reported cases of vesico-vaginal fistula, a condition caused by giving birth when the cervix is not well developed, because the pelvic bones have had insufficient time to develop to cope with child-birth[14]. Corrective operations often require the consent of the spouse, and more often then not the female children are abandoned or divorced by their husbands and ostracized by their communities[15]. 22 per cent of the teenage female children in Nigeria had at least one unwanted pregnancy. This situation is disastrous to the female children because it leads to severe discrimination within their own community or family. They are often punished for being pregnant or are excluded from school. Sociologically, early marriage creates enormous problems for the society. This is because upon the attainments of majority, such girl-wives may realize that they never really married their husbands on the basis of love and this could lead to breakdown of the marriage with the attendant social problems.[16]

FEMALE GENITAL MUTILATION

Female Genital Mutilation (FGM) refers to the surgical operation carried out traditionally on the female genitalia. It is often incorrectly referred to as female circumcision[17]. As Thomas[18] described it:

> *Female Genital Mutilation is now a universally accepted term used to describe any interference with natural appearance of the female external genitalia using a blade, knife or any sharp instrument in order to bring about either a reduction in size of the clitoris or a complete removal of the vulva.*

The World Health Organization (WHO) adopts a fairly more general definition by stating that:

> *Female Genital Mutilation comprises all procedures that involve partial or total removal of the female external genitalia and/or injury to the female genital organs for cultural or any other non-therapeutic*[19].

Female Genital Mutilation is practiced in the Southern and Eastern parts of Nigeria. The age of mutilation varies from 3 months to 17 years or just above the first pregnancy. Many female children faces health risks through mutilation, this include, HIV infection due to unhygienic methods that accompany the practice which in itself is a pubic health issue. One distressing feature of this practices is that crude instruments such as razor blades, knives, broken bottles and other sharp objects are mostly used for the operations which are often carried out by aged non-medical persons, intent on sustaining such practices in line with long-standing customs[20]. These instruments are invariably non-sterilized and the operations often carried out in unhygienic conditions with attendant health risks to the victim[21].

A number of reasons have been advanced for the practice of female genital mutilation in Nigeria. Prominent among these, is the belief that it helps to curb promiscuity among females[22]. This is predicated on the assumption that an uncircumcised woman is unduly sexually active which makes her sexual desires uncontrollable. However, not only is there no scientific validation of the assumption, there has not been any proper assessment of the comparative levels of promiscuity between circumcised and uncircumcised females. Indeed, the point must be made that female promiscuity is not necessarily dependent on the condition of the female genitalia but the result of a complex of social factors[23]. These include the social and family background of the female victim, her perception of the socialization process as well as other environmental conditions.

Furthermore, it is also said that the purpose of the exercise is to clean up the female genitalia which, in its naturally state is considered unsightly and dirty and so promote hygiene and provide aesthetic appeal[24]. However, such concern for purity and decency can only be legitimate if it is founded on sound medical reasons, which is manifestly lacking in this case.

In addition, the belief is rife among several communities that circumcision makes for easy and safe delivery of babies. The belief is that the presence of uncircumcised clitoris would greatly interfere with the child delivery process as it is capable of causing serious obstruction to the process. Again, medical evidence completely disproves this assertion as the clitoris is not known to be involved at all in the delivery process, since it has its own patently different function in the female body constitution[25].

The obnoxious practice of female genital mutilation and scarification which have the objective of suppressing female sexuality affect girls physically, psychologically and socially. Physically, the girl is in constant pain and torture, and there is excessive bleeding which sometimes leads to death after the genitals have been mutiliated[26]. At times, infection sets in, either due to the unsterilized instrument used or lack of care of the affected area. Socially, the practice rather than discouraging promiscuity has been the source of increased promiscuity as circumcised female are impelled by the spirit of adventure to have sexual relations with several men all in a bid to gain sexual pleasure[27].

Female genital mutilation has been outlawed in Edo[28], Delta and Cross River States[29] of Nigeria. Also as a result of public enlightenment and mobilization by the Federal Government and its agencies, FGM are diminishing in other states in Nigeria. But the practice of FGM remains widespread in the country and the proportion of the female population having undergone genital mutilation is high.

OTHER FORMS OF DISCRIMINATION

The other forms of discrimination against female children in Nigeria are protection from abuse and access to education.

PROTECTION FROM ABUSE

There is clear disparity in the severity of sanctions for children abuse, depending on both, the age and the gender of the children victim.

In the Northern part of Nigeria for instance Section 216 of the Criminal Code Act[30] States that:

> *Any persons who unlawfully and in decency deals with a boy under the age of fourteen years is guilty of a felony, and is liable to imprisonment for seven years*

While Section 222 of the Criminal Code Act reads:

Any person who unlawfully and indecently deals with a girl under the age of sixteen years is guilty of misdemeanor and is liable to imprisonment for two years, with or without caning. If the girl is under the age of thirteen years, he is guilty of a felony and is liable to imprisonment for three years, with or without caning.

Sections 216 and 222 of the Criminal Code Act are discriminatory against female children in Nigeria. The provisions insufficiently define acts of abuse against which female children should be protected.

ACCESS TO EDUCATION

The percentage of female children attending school in Nigeria compared with male children is very low. This is particularly the situation in the Northern part of Nigeria, where the highest rate of illiteracy (70%) was registered, and while female children attending schools are very few[31]. This is as a result of early child marriage.

CONCLUSION AND RECOMMENDATIONS

Nigeria ratified the Convention on the Rights of the Child (CRC) in 1991 and other international instruments that affects the rights of the children such as the Convention on the Elimination of all Forms of Discrimination against Women (CEDAW), the Convention against Torture and Other Cruel Inhuman or Degrading Treatment or Punishment and the Convention on the Elimination of All Forms of Racial Discrimination. It is also part of the International Convention on Civil and Political Rights and to the International Convention on Economic, Social and Cultural Rights. Further, it signed but did not ratify the Optional Protocol on children in armed conflict and the Optional Protocol on the sale of Children, child prostitution and child pornography and the African Charter on the Rights and Welfare of the Child. But the legislation to implement them, the Child Rights Act (CRA) was first drafted in 1993 and adopted in 2003. The CRA was enacted in only 10 states out of the 36 states of the federation.

Section 14(2) (b) of the Constitution of Nigeria States that "the security and welfare of the people shall be the primary purpose of a government...". It is obligatory on the government to fundamentally pursue the security and welfare of the children at all times. In order to protect the rights of the female children in Nigeria, based on the following recommendations:

(a) The CRC and other international conventions as enshrined in the Child Rights Act must be adopted and implemented in all the states of the federation.

(b) The government must ensure full compliance with the United Nation Convention on the Rights of the Child and the Child Rights Act 2003, which set the marriage age at 18 year.

(c) The government must enact law on Female Genital Mutilation and also carry out a nation wide campaign on the dangers of FGM.

(d) The government should implement policies to eradicate all forms of gender discrimination against female children, including a policy of integration in formal schools.

(e) The government should collaborate with CRC and other specialized international institutions as well as NGOs in establishing, monitoring and implementing a comprehensive programms that would promote the interest of the children.

(f) It is most obvious that the government alone cannot create awareness on the rights of the female children in Nigeria. The burden of creating awareness lies on human rights conscious individuals in various capacities be it academic, press, or organizations such as NGOs and the UN agencies.

(g) Finally, the world's attention should be on the modality for the protection of the rights of the children to help meet their basic needs, and to expand their opportunities to reach their full potentials. Therefore children need to know their rights, so that they can become human rights conscious. Parents needs to know the right of the children in order to control child violation. Government agencies need to know the rights of the children so as to enable them differentiate child rights from child privileges and charity. Legislators too need to know these rights in order to have a reorientation on the rights of the children.

NOTES

1. Constitution of the Federal Republic of Nigeria (Promulgation) Decree 1999 No. 24.
2. The general framework within which human rights are protected in Nigeria are enshrined in the Constitution of the Federal Republic of Nigeria, 1999. Chapter IV contains an elaborated Bill of Rights. The rights guaranteed include the right to life (Section 33); the right to personal liberty (Section 35); the right to fair hearing (Section 36) and the right to freedom of movement (Section 41) Section 42 prohibit unjustifiable discrimination on basis of "ethnic group, place of origin, sex, religion or political opinion". As for penal infractions, codes, Nigeria has two seperate one applying to Southern Nigeria (Criminal Code) and one applying to Northern Nigeria (Penal Code). These provide for offences against persons, including homicide, assaults and different kinds of sexual and gender-specific violations such as rape.
3. In some areas, the off-springs of such a union are still ascribed to the late husband and not the biological father, a practice which is in itself repugnant to natural justice, equity and good conscience.
4. For further reading see Ezeilo J. Women and Children's Rights in Nigeria Women's Aid Collective, Enugu, 2001 pp.25-26, Omonubi–Mc Donnell, M. Gender Inequality in Nigeria, Spectrum Books Ltd, Ibadan, 2003 p. 8.

5. It is on this score that traditional herbal practitioners have held sway in these communities with the veneration of age-long dogmas and beliefs on reproductive and health matters.
6. This is often assumed to be predicated on religious injunction as contained in the Holly Koran.
7. Some of these are social and mental problems.
8. Cap. 218 Chapter 218 Volume XI, Laws of the Federation of Nigeria, 1990.
9. Cap. 220, Vol. 8 Laws of the Federation of Nigeria, 1990.
10. Section 3(1) (e) of the Matrimonial cause Act.
11. No. 26 of 2003. This followed on the heels of the UN Convention on the Rights of the Child, 1989.
12. This would be the ordinary assumption since the constitution regards age as crucial to the exercise of the civic responsibility of participating in the political process.
13. According to a NDHS Survey, 19% of girls cited marriage as a reason for leaving school. NDHS, quoted in: Oxfam: Women and Poverty in Nigeria, CRC/C15/Add.61, 30/10/96. Also available under *htt://www.unchr.ch/tbs/doc.nsf/* (Symbol)/CRC.c.15. Add.61. En? Open Document.
14. UNICEF, quoted in Integrated Regional Information Network (IRIN), Nigeria: Focus on the challenge of enforcing children's rights, November, 2002. Available under *htt://www.irinnews.org/print.asp?. Report ID=30878.*
15. Oxfam: Women and Poverty in Nigeria, *ibid.* p.58. Available *http://www.irinnews.org/print.asp?. Report ID= 30878.*
16. The psychological trauma generated by this condition can better be imagined than seen as this could degenerate to psychiatric problems and other socially unacceptable conditions.
17. This is because the process is in no way comparable to the circumcision of the male organ, where simple circular cut is made to remove the well-defined foreskin alone. However, the various states laws and even some academic writers still refer to it as circumcision, see for example the Cross River State's Girl-Child Marriages and Female Circumcision Law, 2000, Female Circumcision and Genital Mutilations (Prohibition) Law of Edo Sate, 1999 and Rivers State Abolition of Female Genital Mutilations (Prohibition) Laws of Edo State, 1999 and Rivers State Abolition of Female Circumcision Law, No. 2 of 2001.
18. Thomas, I. M. "Female Genital Mutilation as a contradiction of Moral, Medical and Ethical Values being a keynote Address delivered at the National Symposium on Female Genital Mutilation organs by Women's Centre for Peace and Development, (WOPED) at Ikeja, Lagos on 25th May, 2000 extract in WOPED News. Vol. 2, Nos. 1 & 2, July, 2000, p. 24.
19. The World Health Organization (WHO) is an International Organization that cater for the health and welfare of the children.
20. This is an harmful traditional beliefs.
21. For further reading, see Obiora, L.A. Bridges and Barricades: Rethinking Polemics and Intransigence in Campaign Against Female Circumcision (1975) 47 Case Western Reserve Law Review, p. 275.

22. This reason appears to be common in most of the communities and countries where the practice is vague, see Slack, A. T. "Female Circumcision: A Critical Appraisal "*Human Rights Quarterly Review,* Vol. 12, No. 4 (1988), p. 437 at 445.
23. Indeed, some of these other factors can have profound influence on the productivity of females promiscuity; for instance, a girl from a broken home without proper parental care and guidance is more likely to be swayed to promiscuous conduct as she may treasure more, the companion outsiders.
24. Mainly to the men, Nahid Toubia describes such beliefs and practices as part of the global subordination of women, see Toubia, N. "Female Genital Mutilation" in Women Rights Human Rights: International Feminist Perspectives, Peter J.O. Wolper, A (eds) Routledge, Inc. 1995, p. 224 at 236.
25. For further reading see Thomas, I.M *op. cit.* p. 25.
26. For further reading see Akumadu, T.U. Repudiating Repugnant Customs: The Call to Ban Female Genital Mutilation in Nigeria, Women's Centre For Peace and Development WOPED, 2000 p. 11.
27. For further reading see Akumadu, T.U. Beast of Burden: A study of Women's Legal Status and Reproductive Health Rights in Nigeria, Civil Liberties Organization 1998 p. 39.
28. Edo State of Nigeria took a commendable lead in enacting law against female genital mutilation which is one of the dehumanizing practices in Nigeria, known as Female Circumcision and Genital Mutilations (Prohibition) Law, 1999. Section 4 (a) (b) of the law provides the categories of offenders. These include "any person who offers herself for circumcision or genital mutilation" and "any person who coerces, entices, or induces any person to undergo female circumcision or genital mutilation".
29. River State of Nigeria also enacted the Abolition of Female Circumcision law No. 2 of 2001. Section 2 (2) (a) of the Law makes it an offence for any person to deny any female her right or privilege simply because she refused to be circumcised.
30. Cap. 77 Chapter 77 Laws of the Federation of Nigeria, 1990.
31. Info taken from UNICEF, quoted in Integrated Regional Information Networks (IRIN), Nigeria: Focus on the challenge of enforcing children's rights, November, 2002.

ECONOMIC EFFICIENCY VERSUS EQUITY IN GENDER AND DEVELOPMENT APPROACH

R. R. PRASAD*

INTRODUCTION

This paper begins with a visit to the domain of economic thoughts in which the neo-classicals and neo-liberals give priority to economic efficiency over equality. It moves into the arena of Gender and Development (GAD) and highlights essential features of the Gender and Development (GAD) approach, and compares it with the Women in Development (WID). This section of the paper argues that the efficiency approach neglects distributional issues with serious implications for gender equity. It then moves to examine the neo-liberal view of gender relations in households, markets, and other economic institutions in the light of available literature based on the empirical data. With the available data this section argues that in the marketplace and other economic institution, in which efficiency gets priority, a large degree of gender inequality is accepted. The efficiency approach has generated many different forms of social inequalities, but gender is present in some form in all of them. Understanding how Gender and Development (GAD) approach challenges these concerns is the subject of the concluding part of this paper.

DEVELOPMENT: CONCEPT AND MEANING

Defining Development

Development is an extremely complex concept and an even more complex process. Differences in viewpoint naturally exist because the people who express them are really talking about different things. They express a wide range of optimism and pessimism about the future, but all are worried about it and feel that something must be done and soon. Let us look more closely at the reasons for these different interpretations of the nature of development.

According to Marshall Wolfe, quoted by Higgins (1992:26), 'development consists of systematically inter-related growth and change process in human

* *Professor & Head (CESD), National Institute of Rural Development (NIRD), Hyderabad.*

societies, delimited by the boundaries of national state, and highly independent on a world scale. He explains it further by saying that ,'development expresses an aspiration towards a better society. However, quite a different view of development is taken by Wolfgang Sachs (1992)who says that, 'development' has become a shapeless amoebae-like word. It cannot express anything because its outlines are blurred. But it remains ineradicable because its diffusion appears benign. He who pronounces the word denotes nothing, but claims the best of intentions. Development thus has no content, but it does possess a function: it allows and intervention to be sanctified in the name of a higher, evolutionary goal'. It is clear from the above definitions that development is perceived differently. However, a very simple definition of development has been given by Benjamin Higgins (1992:27) who says, '*development is a process of economic, social, and technological change by which human welfare is improved. Anything that raises the level of human welfare contributes to development; anything that reduces the welfare is anti-developmental, a subtraction from development*'.

Philosophically speaking, there are two opposing views of development. One is a *consumerist* view, and other is the *liberal* view. The consumerist view regards the human being primarily as a consumer of goods and services. Basically, 'development' is seen in this view as an expansion of the flow of consumption. For a time, development was identified with aggregate economic growth to bring about a progressively higher flow of aggregate of consumption irrespective of its distribution. Gradually, the interpersonal distribution question was raised, in terms of who *benefits* from such development *as consumers* (the 'liberal' view). The debate continues to this date; but the basic consumerist view prevails.

The neo-liberals are primarily concerned with the processes that enable *efficient* (i.e. least cost) utilisation of scarce productive resources and with the optimal growth of these resources over time, so as to produce an ever-expanding range of goods and services. They hold the view that an economy grows because it accumulates factors of production, like physical and human capital, because its labour effort grows, or because it improves the *efficiency* with which it uses the factors of production. *An efficient economy maximizes the rate of development*; that is, it maximizes the rate at which gaps between the norms of welfare accepted in a particular society and the *status quo* are reduced. The dominant development discourses also associate efficiency with the conversion of labour into capital, with the formalization of economic activities, with the indiscriminate absorption of the newest technologies and, of course, with the maximisation of growth rates. It is, thus, clear that the term '*efficiency*' has become a buzzword in development discourse. Hence, it is important to understand the meaning of the term '*efficiency*'?

Efficiency: Concept and Meaning

Efficiency of an industry or firm or of a government department, means maximizing its contribution to development , or to the increase in welfare, in the same sense. It involves minimizing opportunity costs and getting the maximum amount of physical output of the product-mix of any enterprise or any economy from a given bundle of resources. The dominant development discourses also associate efficiency with the conversion of labour into capital, with the formalization of economic activities, with the indiscriminate absorption of the newest technologies and, of course, with the maximisation of growth rates.

The crux of neoclassical concept of efficiency is that, "*an economy is efficient if its market functions in such a way that a Pareto optimum can be achieved.* There is an element of circular reasoning in this proposition: efficiency is defined in terms of the functioning of the market (Pareto optimum, marginal cost equals price, average cost minimized), and *an economy is considered efficient if its market functions in this way.* Any departure from this pattern is inefficient, and any policy that causes such a departure is a bad policy" (Higgins, 1992:36) . The trouble is that if the market is to continue to function "efficiently" on neoclassical criteria, any redistribution of income undertaken on grounds of *equity* must leave the allocation of resources unchanged, and that may turn out to be impossible (*ibid.*, p.34).

Ingrid Palmer (1992: 71) has discussed about the concept of economic efficiency in the context of the structural adjustment programme. She says that structural adjustment is about improving the *efficiency* of resource allocation in the present economy through freeing markets from restraints, while long-term adjustment (or economic transformation) is about developing new comparative advantages through an economically *efficient* distribution of investments in higher factor productivities. It would, therefore, be useful when examining the meaning of economic efficiency to bear in mind women's particular problems of access to resources and income, and of free deployment of their labour. Economic efficiency has been described in terms of (i) *static efficiency* and (ii) *dynamic efficiency*. While static efficiency is used in the context of structural adjustment programme of the government, the dynamic efficiency relates to the structural transformation programme. There are two basic assumptions of the static efficiency concept:

- that resources are free to move between different users and between different employers; and
- that every producer is faced with the same set of prices which are determined by competitive market forces.

Dynamic efficiency is defined as the most economically efficient distribution of investment in the means of higher productivity. But where should this investment lie? Short-term supply and demand would lead to different prices from a longer-term supply and demand. Therefore *static allocative efficiency* need not resemble *long-term allocative efficiency*. (*ibid.*,p.73).

The concept of efficiency has been attacked on various grounds that have long since become familiar: imperfect knowledge and foresight, incomplete information, misleading advertisements, externalities, inapplicability to public goods, etc. The concept of efficiency must include some standard for improvement, growth , and development , as well as standards for resource allocation at a point in time. It must include some standards regarding distribution of income among nations, regions, social groups, and individuals. And it must include targets or norms for public goods such as health, education, nutrition, and the like (Higgins, 1992:36).

DEVELOPMENT, GENDER AND EFFICIENCY

Development processes based on efficiency principles have generated many different kinds of social inequalities, but gender is present in some form in all of them. Understanding whether the *Gender And Development Approach (GAD)* challenges efficiency principles in development is the main purpose of this section. However, it will be necessary to discuss first about the Gender and Development (GAD) approach.

Gender and Development (GAD) Approach

The term 'gender' is generally understood to mean the social construction of sexual identity (Kapadia, 1997; 33290). This is a sufficient working definition for the purpose of our discussion. Gender and Development (GAD), and Women in Development (WID) are often used interchangeably and in many areas there is considerable overlap between the two. It is perhaps necessary to first discuss in brief the WID before examining the GAD approach.

Initiated by the ground-breaking work of Esther Boserup, the women in Development (WID) school provided a powerful critique from a liberal feminist perspective of development theories which concentrated on men as producers and household heads, and completely ignored women as simply recipients of welfare. WID units were established within agencies, seeking to bring women into development, mainly by including women's component in wider development projects and programmes. The assumption was that if women were 'made visible' and included in the development process, and there was a change of policy from welfare provision to equality, women would no longer be marginalised, and everyone would benefit. As neo-liberal approaches to economic development became popular, the integration of women into development was also seen as an 'efficiency' approach that utilised women's productive potential (Rowlands, 1997:5) This approach, however, did not question the existing social structures or the causes of women's subordination, focusing instead on women's role in production. It was (and continues to be) an approach which 'instrumentalises' women, using them as a resource for meeting other development goals such as population control, sustainable development , and so on. (*Ibid.*).

The only approach to women-in-development that looks at all aspects of women's lives and all the work that women do-productive and reproductive, private and public-and rejects any attempt to under-value family and household maintenance work, has come to be known as ';empowerment approach', or more generally, the Gender and Development (GAD) approach to women-in-development (Mosse,1993:161). The Gender and Development (GAD) approach questions the commonly accepted theories of what good development entails, arguing that there is more to development than economic growth and the efficient use of money, and challenges the idea that women want to be 'integrated' into the mainstream of Western designed development, in which they have little chance of determining the kind of society they want. The GAD approach seeks to base interventions on the analysis of men's and women's roles and needs in an effort to empower women to improve their position relative to men in ways in which will benefit and transform society as a whole. GAD is thus driven by a powerful motivation-to work for equity and respect for human rights for all people.(Williams, 1994:7).

One of the key assumptions underlying gender and development analysis is that women and men, because they have different gender roles and power, also have different gender interests. If those who plan projects and programmes were better able to understand women's gender interests, so the argument goes, they would be in a much better position to ensure that their gender needs were met. It is more useful to talk about 'gender interests' than about 'woman's interests' because this recognizes the fact that an individual women's interest may be determined as much by her social position or ethnic identity as by the fact that she is a woman; the interests that women share by virtue of the fact that they are women are therefore 'gender interests'.

The concept of GAD stems from the realization that targeting women in development programmes is not sufficient to ensure that they benefit from such programmes, A GAD seeks to:

- understand the different opportunities and constraints operating on men and women arising from different gender roles and gender inequalities.
- understand how and why these gender differences and inequalities affect programme outcomes including inequalities within development agencies and how these affect programme design and implementation.
- works towards more equitable gender relations through programmes which not only include women but enable them to change inequalities preventing them from achieving their aspirations and enable them to widen the range of choices open to them.

At the same time a GAD approach recognizes that:

- gender roles and inequalities are variable between cultures and contexts and also interact with other inequalities like class, age, gender and ethnicity to create differences between women within cultures and contexts.

- gender policies are not only about women but must also take into account men's needs and aspirations. (Mayoux, 1995:47).

GAD APPROACH VERSUS EFFICIENCY APPROACH

Social institutions such as the firm or the family may enhance efficiency, but they may also serve the interests of particular groups. Obstacles to social change are not only manifestations of lagged adjustments, they often reflect resistance on the part of powerful groups, who may be willing to pay a price, in *lower efficiency,* for continued control over a disproportionate share of output (Folbre, 1995:130). It is hardly surprising that policymakers and employers, who are predominantly male, seldom promote gender equality in the labour market beyond measures that have obvious, powerful efficiency effect, such as investing in women's education. (*ibid.,*142). The advocates and administrators of the efficiency measures see no need for a gender-aware approach and have measured their success and failures in monetary terms such as GNP. An immediate effect of the approaches to measuring the GNP is that a major section of the working women of the world disappear into a 'black hole' in economic theory. A significant proportion of women's activities, produced as part of their familiar obligations ('housework'), does not enter the marketplace, does not earn an income, and is therefore excluded from GNP estimates. It has no value as far as planners are concerned. On the other hands, since these dimensions of women's labour are either unremunerated, or else ensure their confinement to the casual and low-paid sectors of gender-segregated labour markets, the 'effectiveness' of their demand is also curtailed. They do not command the purchasing power that would allow them to meet their needs through the marketplace and must rely instead on the benevolence and efficacy of non-market forms of provision: households, states or community organizations. Thus, within a market-led framework of development planning, certain categories of 'demand' and 'supply' are given secondary status in the allocation of development resources. (Kabeer, 1994:77).

Quite a good number of studies have documented the fact that the failure to include women in development process reduces their likelihood of success which has increased the effectiveness of the claim that women are less productive. Efficiency has displaced equality as the rationale for claiming new resources. Huttington's (1975) point is that the equality argument should not be abandoned just because the efficiency argument is currently easier to make. The pursuit of women's claims based on equality and efficiency has revealed quite starkly the inadequacies of a strategy that fails to take women's reproductive labour into account.

The areas in which the efficiency approach has directly or indirectly constrained women's equal participation in their development have been examined at length by Naila Kaber and John Humphrey, Diane Elson, Ingrid Palmer, Frances Stewart, and others. The GAD approach, which questions the commonly accepted theories of what good development entails, arguing that there is more to development than economic growth and the efficient use of money,. has successfully challenged the neo-classical and neo-liberal paradigms based on the efficiency principles. The areas in which the efficiency approach has constrained gender and development, highlighted by the GAD activists and feminist scholars. are discussed below.

Efficiency Concerns in Non-traded Family Production

The silence of the dominant neo-liberal theorists on gender signifies their belief that, despite its acknowledge inadequacies, the market represent the key to resolving the problems of gender and development (Kabeer and Humphrey, 1991: 80). The neo-liberal assumptions that, if price incentives are right, women will respond to market opportunities in economically rational ways implicitly assumes a substitutability of family labour between the production of material resources and the reproduction of human resources, which does not in fact correspond to empirical reality. These are not equivalent activities, governed by the same set of decision rules, despite the fact that women's time may go into both. While some aspects of reproductive work may be transferred to the market, it is in general far less responsive to economic signals than productive work(*ibid*). This point has been clearly made in Elson's (1989) critique of structural adjustment programmes, which take for granted that women's unpaid labour will continue regardless of how development resources are reallocated, and will be enough to make up for cutbacks in social services aimed at family welfare.

Family Failures and Human Capital Formation

There is ample evidence on gender-differentials in literacy, enrollment rates, and educational qualifications(UNDP 1990) to show the widespread nature of this form of family failure. It places a large question mark over both the equity and efficiency of decisions taken within the family and the ability of market forces to override the consequences of family failures(Kabeer and Humphrey, 1994:90). If the health and well-being of women is to be a part of the development agenda, even if is solely in their capacities as reproducers and nurturers of the future labour force, such household outcomes cannot be regarded as allocationally efficient let alone allocationally equitable (*ibid.*,91).

Gender in the Labour Market

Job segregation and sex-typing shows little sign of declining, and in many areas of work, jobs continue to be strongly segregated along sex lines. Access to specific segments of labour markets is highly restricted for men and women, and the opportunities open to women are characterized by relatively low wages and limited opportunities for advancement. If such patterns persist, women's incorporation into the market will not reduce their disadvantage in work and employment or undermine their disadvantage in the household (Kabeer and Humphrey, 1994:92).

Women's Labour Participation in the Formal Sector

Women's labour participation in the formal sector is inhibited by child care responsibilities. Therefore labour is not absorbed by the formal sector efficiently.

Structural Adjustment Programmes

The neo-liberal policies favour reductions in State expenditures of health, education, and social services, and it looks to private provision to compensate for cuts. However, in certain contexts, particularly among the poor in the Third World, access to market provision of these services is either non-existent or extremely limited, so that it is women's unpaid labour which generally offsets reductions in state expenditures. As Elson notes, in the context of adjustment programmes, 'Women's unpaid labour is implicitly regarded as elastic–able to stretch so as to make up any shortfall in other resources available for reproduction and maintenance of human resources'. (1989:4).

The second major contradiction of the neo-liberal concerns the need for conditions for women's equality in the market. Women are being encouraged to enter the market at the same time as cutbacks in state employment restrict one of the few areas of work, where women have a chance of securing higher-wage jobs, and the shift to export agriculture and cash crops places an emphasis on forms of production which have been dominated by men (Elson 1989:18-20). In these circumstances, women's access to the market will be more difficult, not less. They will be forced into low-income and insecure work and their disadvantage in the labour market will be reinforced, not overcome.

Palmer (1994:74) says that there are two main sources of gender-based distortions in markets:

- unequal terms of women's and men's participation in markets;
- the reproduction tax on women.

Palmer (*ibid.*, p. 75) says that the causes of discrimination against women in markets are legendary. They have social and cultural origins. Some specifically arise from women's immobility due to domestic responsibilities, although this in itself is related to social and cultural factors. She says that gender discrimination occurs in human resource development and in access to fixed and variable factors of production as well as to credit.

The labour market suffers several sources of gender bias. There is the derived effect of discrimination in human resources development. there are cultural attitudes to what are appropriate jobs for women and men, respectively, and to the value of women's jobs relative to men's (Palmer, 1992:75).

But there are also markets within the household economy. Much of the gender biases in early human resource development arises from intra-household markets. Boys are usually favoured by parents' expenditure on education, nutrition and medicine, perpetuating the disadvantages of women. The long-term scarcity of quality female labour that intra-household markets generate is impervious to wider market influences(Palmer, 1992:77). Even where there is only one joint household enterprise family labour is often deployed in a way that does not resemble the distribution of the returns to labour. Whenever culture bonds women's (and children's) labour to the household production unit, this labour is not free to move to more efficient uses outside the household economy and it invariably used outside the household economy and it is invariably used beyond the point which marks its most efficient deployment in the wider economy (Palmer, 1992:75).

Palmer (1992: 79) has also discussed about the ways in which the women's reproduction activities distort the 'productive' labour market. How does this inefficiency operate? Any labour market entrant who is tied for periods of her/his working life to other responsibilities is unable to compete equally and for an equal length of time on the basis of intrinsic merit. A distortion in primary determining market, such as the labour market, has a knock-on effect in other *factor markets*; and distortions in factor markets create distortions in *product markets*. In this way the reproduction tax on women sends ripples of inefficiencies throughout the economy (*ibid.*, p. 79).

CONCLUSION

The problem with the efficiency approach is that it does not appreciate the nature of the resistance that the promotion of women in the development process is likely to encounter- in the household, in the market-place, and within the state apparatus. Planning for gender equity on the basis for social justice, rather than of formal equality, requires recognition of the full weight and implications of the gender division, priorities and possibilities that it gives rise to. Gender equity requires that welfare is seen as complementarily, rather than in opposition, to efficiency (Kabeer, 1994: 86). The GAD approach has very successfully challenged the distortions caused by efficiency approach in various arenas impinging on gender relations.

REFERENCES

Elson, D. (1989), ' The Impact of Structural Adjustment on Women: The Concepts and Issues', in B. Onimode (ed.), *The IMF, The World Bank and the African Debt,* (London: Zed books).

Folbre, Nancy (1995), 'Engendering Economics: New Perspectives on Women, Work, and Demographic Change', in in Michael Bruno and Boris Pleskovic (eds.) ' *Annual World Bnak Conference of Development Economics,* 1995, (Washington D.C., The World Bank.

Higgins, B. (1992), 'Equity and Efficiency in Development: Basic Concepts', in Donald J. Savoie and Irving Brecher ed. Book '*Equity And Efficiency in Economic Development* (London: Intermediate Technology Publications), p. 37-8.

Huttington, S. (1975), 'Issues in Women's Roles in Economic Development: Critique and Alternatives', *Journal of Marriage and the Family*, Vol. 37, No. 4, pp. 1001-12.

Kapadia, Karan (1997), 'Mediating the Meaning of Market Opportunities: Gender, Caste and Class in Rural South India, *Economic and Political Weekly*, December 27.

Naila Kabeer (1994), *Reversed Realities*, (London: Verso).

Kabeer, N. and Humphrey, J. (1993), Neo-liberalism. Gender, and the Limits of the Market, in Colough, L and Manor, J. (Eds.) *'Markets, Neo-Liberalism and the Development Policy Debate*, (Oxford: OUP).

Janes S. Jaquette (1990), Gender and Justice in Economic Development, in Irne Tinker,1990. *Persistent Inequalities (ed.)* (New York :Oxford University Press) pp. 54-69.

Naila Kabeer (1994), *Reversed Realities*, (London: Verso).

Rowlands, Jo (1997), *'Questioning Empowerment: Working with Women in Honduras'* (Oxfoed: Oxfam), p. 5.

Mosse, J. V. (1993), *An Introduction to Gender and Development*, (Oxford: Oxfam), p. 161.

UNDP (1990), *Human Development Report*, 1990 (Oxford: Oxford University Press).

Williams, S., *et al* (1994), *'Oxfam Gender Training Manual*, (Oxford:Oxfam), p. 7.

Palmer, Ingrid (1992), 'Gender Equity and Economic Efficiency in Adjustment Programmes' in Halesh Afsar and Carolyne Dennis (eds.), *Women and Adjustment in the Third World*. (London: Macmillan), p. 75.

Sachs, Wolfgang (1992), 'Poor not Different', in Paul Ekins and Manfred Max-Neef (ed). *Real-Life Economics: Understanding Wealth Creation* (London: Routledge) p. 165.

GENDER GAP IN EDUCATION: A CASE STUDY IN KARNATAKA

M. H. Hullur*

INTRODUCTION

Social and economic development of country depends on the development and growth of education. Education plays an important role in every society and country. It is the major unit of social and economic development. It is important to note that a nation's progress is based on quality of population rather than on quantity. In the new millennium, the prosperity, and quality of all nations will be determined by today's school going population and their ability to solve the problems that face them, their families, their communities and their country. However, with regard to the development of literacy and education, India's achievement is far from satisfactory.

After 55 years of Independence, the adult literacy for India has reached only about 60 per cent, which is as Amartya Sen (1995) pointed out is worse than even the average of the poorest countries in the world. India has been left a way behind in the field of basic education even by countries which have not done better than India in many other developmental achievements such as Ghana, Indonesia, Kenya, Burma, Philippines. Zimbabwe and Zambia. The problem of educational development in this country is even worse when we analyze this problem from regional perspective. Several diversities could be seen in the development of education. For instance, adult female literacy for the states like Rajastan, Bihar and Uttar Pradesh are 20%, 23% and 25% respectively, whereas it is 90% in Kerala, 60% in Tamil Nadu. Most of the northern states have remained socially, economically and educationally backward than southern states. Even within the states, the spread of education and institutions for learning have been uneven. Most of the states in India are facing these regional diversities. In this context G. P. Misra (1985) has remarked that the existence and persistence of spatial variations in the level of development is one of the basic structural characteristics of a developing country like India. If the adequate measures are not taken for the spread of education, the education chasm of economic disabilities, regional imbalance

* *Research Scholar, Department of Sociology, Karnatak University, Dharwad, K.R.C.P.G. Center, Belgaum, Karnataka.*

and social injustice will widen further, resulting in building up of disintegrative tendencies (Ministry of Education, G.O. I. 1985).

The Forth Education Commission (1964-66) remarks. "For the full development of human resources, for the improvement of our homes and for moulding the character of children during the most impressionable years of infancy, the education of women is of even greater importance than that of men." The proper development of children largely depends upon the education of women. Mother is the foundation on which child's socialization process depends to a considerable period of time. Educated women can very easily share in decision making about children's schooling, about family planning, about finance and over all perspectives of a family (Goswami, 1991).

DISPARITIES IN WOMEN'S EDUCATION

Even though education has been considered as important for women by various scholars, women even today encountering various hurdles and discrimination. They are not given equal opportunities to reap benefits of education and literacy. Educational structures were inadequate and insensitive to women's needs and irrelevant to their daily lives (UNESCO: 2001).

Our society is male dominated. The freedom and liberty of social life mostly enjoyed by men. There is unequal treatment between boys and girls, sons are preferred by every body. Girls and daughters are discouraged to pursue education. Girls have much lower access to education than boys do. The reasons for this is many. The over all picture of girls and women's education is one of limited opportunity. It is a reflection of their position in society, their subordinate status and their lack of control are even the simplest aspects of their own lives (*Ibid.*, 1). education of girls has been treated as a wasteful expenditure. She will be at her parental house till marriage, after the marriage, she will become the member of her husband's family. Therefore investing on daughters is uneconomic. This is the general feeling even today in some part of the country. As a result most of the Indian women are facing the problem of basic literacy.

The gap in literacy between men and women has increased from 1971-1991. However, from 1991-2001 it has been decreased. It is important to note that the gap in literacy was highest in Belgaum division than in Gulbarga division in 1971 and 1981. But in 1991 and 2001 Gulbarga division attained first position in literacy gap. This show in Belgaum division efforts have been made to improve the literacy among women. But H. K. region, instead of improving lag behind considerably.

DISPARITIES IN THE DEVELOPMENT OF WOMEN'S EDUCATION IN KARNATAKA

It is heartening to note that Karnataka has been a pioneering state in the development of education of all levels. It is known for its professional and

Table 1
Division wise Male and Female Literacy, Gender Gap in Literacy 1971, 1981, 1991 and 2001

	Items	*Gulbarga*	*Belgaum*	*Bangalore*	*Mysore*	*Karnataka*
1971	Female Literacy	10.11	20.76	25.00	23.74	20.95
	Male Literacy	31.13	45.45	44.73	40.93	41.62
	Gap between male and female	-21.02	-24.69	-19.73	-17.19	-20.65
1981	Female literacy	14.89	26.11	33.11	31.13	27.71
	Male literacy	37.77	50.54	53.10	48.81	48.81
	Gap between male and female	-22.28	-24.43	-20.00	17.68	-21.00
1991	Female literacy	26.52	43.10	50.82	49.15	44.34
	Male literacy	54.01	69.99	71.48	67.79	67.26
	Gap between male and female	-27.49	26.89	-20.66	-18.64	-22.92
2001	Female literacy	42.43	54.81	62.27	60.62	57.45
	Male literacy	67.31	76.91	77.54	78.03	76.29
	Gap between male and female	-24.88	-22.1	-17.41	-15.27	-18.84

Sources: 1. Census of India 1971, General population Tables, Mysore
2. Census of India 1981, General population Tables, Karnataka
3. Census of India 1991, General population Tables.
4. Census of India 2001, (Provisional Population Tables) Karnataka.

technical institutions. In recent years' it has achieved a great success in the field of computers and information technology. I.T graduates from Karnataka have a great demand in the international market. But, it is disheartening to note that these institutions of higher learning are not uniformly distributed through out the state. Most of these institutions have been either concentrated in urban areas or in few developed districts of the state.

Information technology revolution is taking place only in Bangalore and some other developed cities like Mangalore and Mysore. From the level of basic literacy to higher education, acute regional disparities exist in the state. 'Our educational system is basically urban oriented in the matter of location of facilities, allocation of finance and even the content curricula' (Jayaram, 1990). Most institutions of higher learning are concentrated in the developed districts of Karnataka. For instance, most of medical and engineering colleges in the state are found in Bangalore and Managalore districts. The awareness of their existing and utility is also greater these. Consequently, admission to these institutions find to be almost biased in favour of students from that districts only. The backward districts, in particular most of the districts of North Karnataka are the worse suffers of these disparities. From basic literacy to higher educational level, most of the districts of North Karnataka have remained back ward. Even in North Karnataka, the districts belonging to Hyderabad Karnataka region (Bidar, Bellary, Raichur, Gulbarga) have remained severely backward than the districts of Bombay-Karnataka. (Belgaum, Dharwad, Uttar Kannada, Bijapur).

The present study focuses its attention on the disparities in the growth and development of women's education in Karnataka. It seeks to observe the nature and extent of disparities that exist in the process and development of women's education and factors associated these disparities.

More specifically, the present study has been undertaken with the following objectives.

1. To record the historical causes for disparities in the women's education in Karnataka.
2. To examine the disparities and gap in the growth of women's literacy in the state.
3. To find out variations and gap in primary education of women.
4. To find out in balance in the growth of professional and higher education of women.
5. To analyse the implications of these disparities.

METHODOLOGY

The Field and Universe

The present study examines the gender gap in the growth of education in the state of Karnataka. To find out these disparities, the state has broadly be divided in to two (1) North Karnataka (N.K.) (2) south Karnataka (S.K.) North Karnataka and South Karnataka have been further classified into divisions. They are : Belgaum division and Gulbarga division in North Karnataka and Mysore and Bangalore division in south Karnataka. Educationally North Karnataka has remained backward and the disparities are acute in nature. Hence, study laid a special emphasis on the backwardness of North Karnataka.

The present study has two limitations.

1. This study is based on secondary sources only.
2. An in-depth analysis of the regional disparities is not possible to the constraints of time.

Tools and Techniques

Detailed information about gap in women education has been collected from the secondary sources. Some of these sources are census reports, Human Development Reports, Government Reports, Books and Journals. Information gathered from these sources have been interpreted and analyzed carefully for their accuracy and completeness.

The government of India, to reduce the disparities has taken many steps since independence. Balanced regional development has been one of the major objectives of Indian planning. Since the First Five Year plan attention has been laid on balanced regional development. But even after several plan period regional disparities in development process has remained. It is important to note that wide disparities in the development process would not only hurdle the progress the regions but also have adverse effect upon the progress of the state level. 'Because an unchecked and uncontrolled process of growth is leading to regional disparities result in numerous economic, social and cultural problems' (Rao, 1984) against this background, the present study examines the imbalanced growth that exists of Karnataka. Disparities in the growth of education are one such instance. It has been argued that disparities are more pronounced in North Karnataka. However, there are hardly any studies to know whether these disparities have been increased or decreased over a period of time. In this context, a trend study is highly essential.

CONCLUSION

The present study has been conducted to find out the gender gap in the growth and development education in Kamataka. In India, poor and the people of geographically backward region and women do not equally fit to reap the benefits of development. In this context the Hyderabad- Karnataka region has been prominently selected to examine problem of educational backwardness-primary to higher education.

For the present study Karnataka has been divided into two halves North and South Karnataka. Disparities exist between two halves in the case of educational progress and development. However, whole of North Karnataka has not remained backward. It is important to note that in North Karnataka, among two divisions, Gulbarga division has remained backward in all the spheres of socio-economic fields.

GAP BETWEEN MEN AND WOMEN LITERACY

No doubt women literacy level is far below than the men in Kamataka. However, problem of literacy among the women is varies in the districts of Karnataka. Whereas male literacy has crossed 75% however, women literacy has not gone upto 60%. Only in four districts (Bangalore, Dakshina Kannada, Udupi and Kodagu) female literacy is above ie., 70%. All these districts are there in South Karnataka. In 11 districts female literacy is above the state average (57.45%). But out of the .11, eight are in South Karnataka and only three in North Karnataka. No one districts of Gulbarga division have the literacy higher than average. Whereas only in 11 districts female literacy is higher than state average, but in the case of male literacy 13 districts have higher literacy than state's average.

In our state a wide space in literacy remained between men and women even today. According to 2001 census it is 18.84 percentage points between men and women. In both the divisions of North Karnataka, literacy gap between men and women is higher than the state average. But it is highest in Gulbarga division (24.88%) than Belgaum division (22.1%).

As we pointed out earlier the problem of illiteracy is looks obvious when we see the total number of literate and illiterate population. In this respect women's case is worst of all. Say for example, according to 200 I census Karnataka had 2,25,529 49 women population (excluding 0-6 age group) out of which 95,95,640 women are illiterates. Here also Gulbarga division possesses less women literates and Bangalore "has more women literates. Gulbarga division in 2001 had 39,32,671 women population. Out of which, only 16,48,572 knew how to read and write but rest of the women (22,84,099) do not know reading and writing. This show the misery of illiteracy in that region.

The problem of illiteracy is apparent when we look at the share of population and its share in literacy and illiteracy. In all the divisions (except Mysore) the share in women's population is less than that of men. But in all the divisions, their share in illiteracy in higher than literacy.

Women's literacy in rural areas is still a critical problem. It is below 50 per cent in most of the districts of the state.

PRIMARY EDUCATION DISPARITIES

Teachers are the primary agents of school system. The role of women teachers is even more important than male teachers. From 1977-78 to 1993-94 the Gulbarga division possessed less number of teacher than any other division. Besides this, women teachers constitute 40.88% to male teachers in Karnataka. However, the number of women teacher has gone up in all the divisions. But this has not increased uniformly in all the divisions. Rate of increase in women teachers is comparatively less in Gulbarga division (28.47%) and more in Bangalore division (47.83%) in 1993-94.

In Gulbarga division, large number of children (who are in the age group of 6-14) remained outside the school. It is least in Bangalore division. In 1996-97, 31. 880/0 of children in Gulbarga division have not gone to school. The problem of children remaining outside school is further aggravates when we look at the number of boys-girls. No doubt in all the divisions, girls out of number of boys. But severity of this problem we find in Gulbarga division. Nearly 40 per cent of girl-children have remained outside. This number is further increased above 50% in Raichur district. In 6-14 years age group Raichur district possessed a share of 28.95% in the state, but in children's enrollment in school its share is less than 19%.

Even some of children who take admission in schools do not continue their education. They discontinue in the middle of their school career. In our state, among the dropouts, the top three districts (Bidar, Gulbarga and Raichur) are in Gulbarga division. In Bidar district the dropout rate was 67.23%. In all the districts of Kamataka, dropout rate is high among girls than boys. There is a considerable gap between boys and girls in the dropout rate. This gap is highest in Raichur district (20.8%)

GAP IN HIGHER EDUCATION

Disparities in higher education are not uniformly distributed in the state. Girls are worst affected by these disparities. From the data we can see that as the girls move higher in their education their number is coming down severely. A wide gap exists between boys and girls in higher education. This gap is highest in Gulbarga division.

From the foregoing findings we can reiterate that a wide gap exists in the growth and development women's education in Karnataka. From the primary level to higher education severe disparities exist between the districts and divisions of the state. However, in all the aspects of women's education, Gulbarga division remained backward from other three divisions. To detain these disparities, to bring up the Gulbarga division on part with the other divisions similar and special efforts should be taken. A special package of education should be formulated to uplift the Gulbarga division in educational matters. We are living in stratified society. It is an andocentric society and has a hegemonic culture, and in such a society, fruits of development will not be available equally to all the groups and communities and to weaker sections especially to women. Uniform approach for the development of education will not be accepted and available to all. To develop the educational status of women and SC/ST in particular and exclusively meant for the HK region should be implemented. Instead of aggregated approach, diseagregated approach should be given utmost importance. Efforts should be made to see that all the facilities pertaining to the education must be made available for the poor, ignorant, women and low castes literacy. It is important to note that in basis literacy. HK region remained severely backward. Measures to improve the literacy level must get top priority. The number children in the age-group of 6-14 remained outside the school is highest in Gulbarga division, where once again the girls number is more than boys. This should be curbed on priority basis.

Planners must plan the programme of action to improve the women educational conditions of North Kamataka in general and Gulbarga division in pal1icular in North Karnataka and in Gulbarga itself but, not at capital city. Participatory development approach should be adopted to develop the HK region. Thus it can be finally said that educationally women in North Karnataka has remained backward. In North Karnataka women of Gulbarga division remained extremely backward. But in Gulbarga division women of Raichur district remained absolutely backward.

REFERENCES

Aziz, Abdul (1996), "*Development Strategy for H.K. Region A Critical Review*", in Abdul Aziz and Sudhir Krishna (eds.) Regional Development and Policy Measures, Concept, New Delhi.

Banks Olive (1968), "*Sociology of Education,*" B.T. Batsford, London.

Basu, Alka Malwasi (1992), "*Culture, the Status of Women and Demographic Behaviour,*" OUP, Oxford.

Basu Dilip K. (eds.) *et. al* (1998), "*Social and Economic Development,*" Sage, New Delhi.

Basu, Koushik *et. al* (2000), "*Isolated and Proximate Illiteracy,*" *Economic and Political Weekly* (*EPW*), Vol. 35, No. 1 and 2, pp. 35-39.

Census of India (1971), "*Karnataka a Population Tables,*" Director of Census Operations, Karnataka.

Dreze, Jean and Sen, Amartya (1995), "*India: Economic Development and Social Opportunity,*" OUP, New Delhi.

Hammadi, Ali (1984), "*University Administration in Developing Countries,*" Indian Bibliographers Bureau, Delhi.

Haq, Mahabub Ul (1996), "*Reflections on Human Development,*" Oxford.

BOTTLE NECKS TO GENDER JUSTICE
A STUDY WITH SPECIAL REFERENCE TO INDIA

R. N. Sharma*

HISTORICAL BACKGROUND

Woman is equal to man but during the course of civilization woman has lost her equal status. In India in early Vedic period woman enjoyed equal status with man but in the later period there was degeneration of her status[1]. Factors which are responsible for this are many viz patriarchal society, institution of slavery, evolution of the property, authoritarianism of state and law, theological attitude towards woman needs and necessities of society to utilize the labour potentials of woman etc which contributed to the lowering down of the status of women in spite of all the hypocritical respect, romantic adoration and theoretical regard which continued to be given to womanhood. Due to the age of renaissance and that of rationalism, rise of democracy and welfarism of state, recognition of human rights and fundamental freedoms etc, the nations and governments now have awakened to the need of implementing gender justice by the process of law and by the course of educating public for generation of corresponding social practice according to the established norms of justice. The celebration of the year 1975 by UNO as 'Woman's Year' seems to highlight the need for redemption and salvation of woman through out the world.

The disappointing feature of the Indian society is that motherhood and womanhood is not respected in due sense, rather it is ignored. They are some times subjected to cruelty and inhuman behavior. To ameliorate the position of woman in the society the Indian Parliament and State legislatures have enacted much women specific and women-oriented legislation to protect women against social discrimination and social evils in fulfillment of international guidelines/conventions in this direction. The question, however, is Have the women been able to reap the benefits provided to them by the State? The answer, unfortunately is not encouraging one. Still there is a long way to achieve the goal of gender justice. In this research paper an effort has

* *Faculty of Law, J. N. Vyas University, Jodhpur.*

been made to discus the social factors which can be said to be the bottle necks or speed breakers in the way of such redemption and salvation. These are:

TRADITIONAL PREJUDICIAL IMAGE OF WOMAN IN CULTURAL ETHOS OF HUMANITY

It is said that a woman's character is so flimsy that she may kill a man and then die for himself that like animals and low castes woman is fit to be beaten and thrashed.[2] Even Shakespeare's quote is *'Frailty thy name is woman (Hamlet)* it is said that the wise men of china have offered advice to husbands to listen to the counsel of wives but should act against their counsels. In Russia the old men's view is that there is only one good woman among ten women. So also Spaniards cautioned their men to save themselves from the wickedness of women who captivate men by their good looks. To Italians, view like wise horses a woman need a spur and require thrashing. So also in Japan in olden times women were not allowed even to pray or take part in religious ceremonies. In Arabia there was the custom of female infanticide. The Pagan Arabian buried their daughters alive and so the birth of a daughter was considered to be a great misfortune.[3] Now the modern age re saddles woman in her status equal to that of man. The Constitution of India gives equality to woman but the constitution of Indian society still goes on to maltreat woman and considers her to be inferior and subservient to man.

SUPERIORITY COMPLEX OF MAN AND INFERIORITY COMPLEX OF WOMAN

At the initial stages of evolution of man, it has been stated that at first like other organisms human being was a hermaphrodite, i.e. bi-sexual, both male and female. It was only later that evolution of separate male and female species took place. Thus by evolution a human being has two counterparts-a male and female as equal to each other. But the evolution of society and the course of struggle for existence has made man rough and strong while woman soft and weak in comparison to man. Man could then domesticate woman and forced her to live a subordinate existence in home as cooker of food, of bearing and rearing children, obeying and serving husband and performing all household duties laboriously and faithfully. This subordinated human existence then became the ideal concept of a woman which got also a religious and moral sanction. Such an ideal image of woman as 'Sita' and 'Savitri' was antagonized to an extent that woman herself accepted it as her ideal image and subordinated herself to the authority of her husband. Willingly and with righteous feeling she began to see herself as 'Dasi' and her husband as lord or 'Prannath'. This has created a superiority complex in male and a corresponding inferiority complex in female. The orthodox social code considers this subordination of woman a boon for social unity and integration of family and does seek its justification in the principle of division of labour and separation of functions.

In female the complex of self imposed inferiority has become now a stumbling block for salvation and redemption of woman from the bondage of man and in progressive realization of gender justice. It is tragic to realize that the most of the women still feel quite satisfied and they do not fail to take pride in their servile existence. This has given rise to many evil customs and wrong practices like purdah system, child marriages and destitution from succession rights etc, which perpetuated the dependence of woman upon man. With the era of renaissance and the age of rationalism and the rise of modern democratic theory with its equalitarian humanism, have now brought a new awakening and enlightenment of womanhood. Women are now becoming conscious of their dignified equal status as a matter of right and justice. But still the inferiority complex is lingering in their ways and doings which make them at times to react in an extreme manner to imitate wrongly masculinity of man in gambling, drinking, drug addiction and other vices. If this goes on it will vitiate the whole progress and make delivery of gender justice to woman very troublesome.

UNWORKABILITY OF MARRIAGE RELATIONSHIP

The tie or sacrament of marriage is the foundation of family in our society. All the other social institutions are therefore, oriented on man's family relationship. All the distribution of rights and duties allocation of freedom and responsibilities, distribution of powers and privileges derive their rationale from man's family relationship like that of father and son, mother and child, husband and wife, brothers and sisters etc. The fold of marriage which is the bond of family in time to come began to resemble more like a sale of woman as wife like a chattel, to be owned and disposed like other property. The course of law reform and social progress has brought about some changes in the institution of marriage. At first marriage was the expression of individual choice and free will of parties. Later it degenerated in child marriages, dowry system, and other modes and encumbrances. Marriage many times results in dowry death, cruelty, domestic violence and other exploitations. Woman's marriage still works as bondage and denial of her freedom. It causes diminution of her personality and individuality. The marriage bed endangers woman's health and happiness by repeated and unregulated pregnancies and child births. All this makes the life of a house wife more miserable and full of many plights and ordeals.

The modern yoke of marriage in spite of modern social reforms and legislations is still unworkable and proves to be a failure in a large number of cases. The fact is that the real success of marriage essentially depends upon mutual understanding, mutual faith, co-operation, adjustment and participation. Marriage basically is a mode of harmonious living in togetherness for two people for mutual fulfillment.

The people in the world today have begun to prefer now companion ship of man and woman instead of the formal mode of marriage. As a matter of fact marriage relationship need be more and more rationalized and liberalized to suit the present conditions of social living of this new age.

DOMINANCE OF MEDIEVAL FEUDAL CONCEPT OF MASTER AND SERVANT IN HUMAN RELATIONSHIP OF MAN AND WOMAN

The medieval feudal hierarchical society divided human society from the view of authority. From that view point the relationship between man and man or man and woman is not that of equality but that of superiority to and inferiority which is illustrated by the relationship of master and servant. Master is one who has right to command and servant is one who has the duty to obey the command. In the medieval feudal society the relation of land lord and tenant or serf, God and man the ruler and the ruled, father and son, husband and wife etc is the prototype of the relation of master and servant. With the concurrence of the institution of slavery this relationship was concretized as that of master and slave in which the master had the power of disposal over the life and limb of his servant or slave. Viewed from this perspective the status of woman as mother or wife or maid or son's wife was turned into the inferior status just like that of a slave. Therefore, she was treated like a slave. Reality of this fact can not be contradicted by the poetic praise and appreciation, romantic love and adoration, sympathy and kindness or favour expressed by man towards woman, for it only shows man's biological selfishness to appropriate or own woman. In truth it is only man's condescending and patronizing superiority complex of male for a female. This medievalism and feudalism of male's valuation of female still lingers in his mind and heart which imprints man's dealing with woman. This results in incidental cruelty, cosmetic violence, discrimination, mal treatment and whole sale exploitation of woman in various ways, and modes with all the good pretexts like integrity of character, unity of family, tranquility and peace of society etc.

In modern age the democratic equalitarianism, constitutional guarantees, declaration of the solemn rights and progressive responses of judiciary are making the impact on the social psychosis of man gradually. The goal to Gender Justice will be only achieved by woman's own empowerment through knowledge, education and of realization of human rights. But it is surprising that the feudal authority of man over woman and meek submission of woman to man is still accepted as a great moral and social value and the ideal of womanhood and her aspiration for rights as arrogance.

SERVICE AND DOMESTIC LABOUR OR WORK POTENTIAL OF WOMAN

Every family is just like a workshop or factory which subsists on house hold work and labour. Without the work, labour and service domestic life can not be continued. A woman in family is generally over burdened with work. This especially is the case of a house wife in a joint family. At times such work becomes too painful and troublesome to bear with. Women are also used as paid servants or maids to relieve men. As a matter of fact women suffer more than men in society. The subjugation of woman to man is also the legacy of the institution of slavery. As slaves they have no rights and opportunities. Women like slaves before were purposely kept illiterate so that they may remain subservient and may not revolt and aspire for freedom and equality. In spite of this by the end of medieval age, and beginning of modern age and even with the abolition of slavery a woman as house wife is still exploited like a slave in family life. So much so that woman's servility, his humanity and obedience is considered as virtue by woman herself. As such she is attuned to slave mentality. Woman's exploitation then becomes the moral norm and value of a good family life. The Sati Savitri image of woman is given high credence in social ethics. The voluntary acceptance of her servile status becomes a part of social morality which makes woman to forget or loose most of her economic and social rights and give license to men to exploit women who are often subjected to maltreatment, domestic violence, and other deprivations. All these wrongs directly or indirectly can be traced to the institution of slavery including marriage of which the woman perhaps is the first victim in social anthropology and the history of human civilization.

SEXUALIZATION OF WOMAN AS A GREAT SEX SYMBOL IN HUMAN SOCIETY

Woman is considered as the fair sex. Infatuation for woman is most general in man. Nature has given power to woman to captivate man. More attraction between sexes is necessary for procreation and continuity of human life. But our civilization has given a wrong turn to the creative urge of man. Firstly, undue regard is given to woman's sex and less to her being. So a woman is adorned beyond measure, love to woman is romanticized excessively, her beauty and grace is over emphasized. Her body is given priority over her soul. She is pursued like a game, and is used for enjoyment and satisfaction exclusively. Aspiration for more women has given rise to polygamy. Excessive indulgence in sex leads to prostitution. Sex relation at early age through marriage leads to hazards of woman's health. It gives rise in woman's mortality and increased population due to frequent child births. Woman is due to this has been debarred from normal physical development.

Woman is used as sex symbol, but a constant undervaluing of woman goes on in society through out the ages, her youth and sex potential is noticed and advertised for glamour and romance. Her chastity, modesty and purity are extolled in art and literature, over projection of sex in cinema and means of entertainment give boost to crimes against woman and corruption in society.

Man's religious faith consequently reacts strongly against the seductive power of woman. Attraction towards woman of 'Kama' is considered a great obstacle to God's realization. This again creates a prejudicial attitude towards woman. This creates hatred of woman in same religions which is quite irrational and wrongful.

Therefore a normal attitude towards woman as woman is necessary even at the cost of diminishing most of the glamour and romance of sex in life. It will make the road to gender justice clear and smooth.

DECLINE IN THE PHYSICAL POWERS AND MIGHT OF WOMAN DURING THE COURSE OF CIVILIZATION

In the hunting stage of civilization woman who was as powerful and militant as man. But in agricultural stage her physical power and strength in comparison to man was reduced considerably due to stationary domestic life and household work of cooking and that of breeding children. Her complexion became fair but her life became less adventurous and more dependent on man with less of physical struggle and fight. She accepted male's domination and control consequently began to follow his command. With the evolution of the concept of property and institution of slavery, woman in spite of all theoretical respect and regard became a merchandize to be bought and sold like a chattel. In religion woman was considered an obstacle to spiritual progress. In society the doors of knowledge learning and enlightenment were closed to her in order to keep her docile and dependants. All the so-called admiration and praise of women then amount to man's opportunism and selfishness only and nothing else.

Remedy lies in woman's empowerment through law reform, legal assistance, declaration of rights, construction of women's forums and positive social response etc. Without empowerment of woman i.e. without increasing physical power, strength and vitality of woman she can not enjoy her rights, can not resist and take action against them for protection and exercise of these rights.

We should also set up national mechanism and create and develop institutions for rendering service for gender equality. Sufficient resource allocation for such institutions, authorities and commission be made available. Programmes and policies should also be evolved in order to make strategies to amend and repeal laws, to ensure participation of people to create networks, have lobbying to have enactment and enforcement of laws, to initiate research for evolving means, methods and techniques to ensure gender justice.

For promotion of economic and social security of woman as a worker and labour there should be adequate infrastructure, the contribution of woman to nation's economy be recognized, rights of woman to hold acquire and dispose of property be made more concrete, more sensitive responses be engendered to help women in conflicting situations or when they are suffering from disasters so on and so forth.

SOCIAL BACKWARDNESS, POVERTY AND OVER POPULATION

One of the greatest obstacles in the successful delivery of gender justice and empowerment of woman is apathy or indifference towards the very notion of gender justice in the mind of its prospective recipients which is due to social stagnation or backwardness, that creates in the mind of a human being strong faith in fatalism and the absence of the will to change. In this state of things all the wrongs, hardships, cruelties and sufferings are considered as misfortunes and mishaps of life which ensue from some higher source called as irreversible fate or destiny. According to this fatalistic attitude all the so called social injustice is the just allotment of ones share due to one's fate. Man's social backwardness is generally associated with deficiency of resources, insufficient satisfaction of wants, absence of comfort and leisure, acute struggle for existence, feeling of helplessness and despondency of temperament, which creates impassivity against change, improvement and reform. One harbours in himself fear of change and feels safe to follow the trodden path. In such a state of things bad customs, superstitions, irrational practices like child marriages, destitution of females from Inheritance, and restraints like prohibition of widow re-marriage, prohibition of woman's education, etc prevail. Even when due to political independence, social reform or declaration of constitutional rights woman gets equal rights, she does not want to avail them due to her old settled beliefs and expectations, and due to her unwillingness to hold and enjoy her rights and liberties. She goes on tolerating and suffering wrongs and injustices without resistance, struggle and protestation.

Over population and poverty further deaden woman's will to change. In such a state of affairs, degradation, devaluation and social exploitation of woman is a natural and necessary out come. One may say that prevailing social exploitation of woman and their subjection to unregulated pregnancies resulting in unwanted child births became the social routine and a part of accepted social morality. Only due to poverty and over population woman is considered backward in the society.

In India only the elite and educated people seem to give more academic importance to Human Rights of woman. The message of Human Rights and fundamental freedoms fail to reach the heart of rural India due to poverty, over population, and primitive social modes of living. In spite of all the constitutional guarantees, social reforms legislative enactments, social support and publicity of woman's rights, we find that oppression, discrimination and social injustice in case of women goes on unabated.

Women are forced to accept unjust conditions of life in order to meet their bare necessities of existence. They lack will and determination to rise against their own victimization to which they become gradually habituated, and remain primitive and regressive in out look. They have no time to think of waging war for attainment and enforcement of women's right when they are sinking in poverty and flooded with over population, gender justice is left by them to be sought by sophisticated women folk only. Therefore, population control, poverty alleviation is at least cognate if not prior to delivery of gender justice to a greater portion of women in India. We can not reap the rich harvest of woman's welfare with out their removal. Further we can accelerate the process of delivery of gender justice by enhancing participation of women in politics and by inculcating the leadership capabilities in them.

INEFFICACY OF LAW REFORM AND INSUFFICIENCY OF JUDICIAL RESPONSE

Our rules of law and legislative enactments can exercise only an indirect and external influence over the actions and behavior of our people. All the civil and penal sanctions of law with various other dictates and directions falter and fail due to the inbuilt procedural limitations, dilatory judicial process, and mercantile professionalism of lawyers. All the assertions and pronouncements to administer gender justice are liable to become nugatory and trifling due to passive indifference and cool complaisance of women themselves. Most of the domestic violence, marital cruelties and incidents of denial of rights go unreported and unnoticed due to poverty, ignorance, back of initiative and publicity, and due to far off forums of justice.

To woman in general and to rustic woman in particular the knowledge and awareness of human rights and constitutional guarantee and all the avenues for knocking the door of justice in case of violation of their rights seem some what irrelevant and of no use to them, only sophisticated, forward and progressive looking ladies, who can seldom cope with hard realities of social life with its incidental burns and Pains, should resort to them for relief.

The revolutionary consciousness of human rights and liberties and generation of super sensitive against their violations can only be engendered by pervasive women's education and enlightenment, legal aid and insurance, social investigation and prompt action, publicity and public censure etc. Not only this we have to explicate the connections between the law and social, political, and economic system to achieve the goal. Further we have to explore sociologically the conditions under which law can become a principled component of social life.

WOMAN VERSUS WOMAN HOSTILITY

One special impediment of gender justice which we encounter in the hearths and homes of our people is the cankerous malice of woman against another woman. Most of the instances of such malice we see in the relationship of wife and mother in Law, wife and sister in law, where woman herself becomes a party to the violence against another woman. Most of the cases of dowry deaths and domestic cruelties reveal this fact. Further we see that oppressed wife in later age becomes oppressive mother in law to her own son's wife, so also militant and potent wives exploit their mother in laws in reverse when their turn comes. Only sympathetic understanding and concord between them are always missing. Much is to be done in order to ease the tension and mitigate hostilities, between them.

The gist of the aforesaid discussion of gender justice brings to us a tragic feeling of the life of woman who has become disabled and helpless to get respite. In my submission I remember what our one of the greatest modern poet has told the very story of her life as.........

O' woman your tale, is told as simply this-

अबला जीवन तेरी यही कहानी,

you have milk for humanities but tears for yourself,

आँचल में दूध और आखों में पानी,

I want to address woman and tell to her to change this story and remember the story of Jhansi Ki Rani about whom it is sung ....,

खूब लड़ी मर्दानी वह तो झांसी वाली रानी थी,

We the people of India should give a clarion call to woman–

Hail woman, awake arise and not be fallen,

Be potent to hold your rights,

Fight and resist every invasion of your rights,

Be brave and victorious,

Attain solace bliss and happiness of human life.

Lastly it is submitted that while performing the holy task of empowering our woman with their rights, we must remember that all the so-called rights are in their ultimate analysis real services either to individual or to society or to both. We must then be aware that in the name of enforcing rights we are in fact making our womanhood more potent to defend her due rights, thereby we are making her more responsible and more amiable but not more arrogant, aggressive and irresponsible beyond all the expectations.

We should not forget:

That there is always a woman behind the success of every man.

That the public activities undertaken by men are only possible because the woman is inhibited in private sphere.

That a man can perform all his duties because he lives with a wife.

NOTES

1. Protection to Women in Matrimonial Home,Vijay Sharma, p. 13, Deep and Deep Publication, Delhi.
2. त्रिया चरित्र जाने न कोय, पुरुष मारकर सती होय, शुद्र पशु और नारी है ताड़न के अधिकारी, औरत पांव की जूती की तरह है उसे सिर पर चढ़ाने की जरूरत नहीं।
3. Woman Law and Social Change, Shamsuddin Shams Preface, (1991), p. (IX), Ashish Publication House, New Delhi.

GLOBALIZATION AND ITS IMPACT ON INDIAN WORKING WOMEN

P. SRINIVAS SUBBARAO*

Capitalism's expansion across the globe has depended on a massive influx of tens of millions of women into the workforce who had traditionally been dependent on husbands and male relatives. Globalization has brought great freedom to women, especially those living in traditionally conservative countries like Indonesia, Ireland and Thailand, where women are able for the first time to be economically independent of men and to have at least some choice in their personal lives. Ultimately, by bringing women into the workforce, globalization has given women a power they lacked in the past—the power to end the system that breeds poverty, exploitation and oppression.

Globalization has opened up broader communication lines and brought more companies as well as different worldwide organizations into India. This provides opportunities for not only workingmen, but also women, who are becoming a larger part of the workforce. With new jobs for women, there are opportunities for higher pay, which raises self-confidence and brings about independence. This, in turn, can promote equality between the sexes, something that Indian women have been struggling with their entire lives. Globalization has the power to uproot the traditional views towards women so they can take an equal carriage in society.

Globalization is a double edged process as far as women are concerned. On the one hand, majority of women in India find themselves uncovered off the benefit of social security, government subsidy protection of labour rights and than safety nets. On the other hand there are possibilities of better education facilities and opportunities at the transnational sense which are very attractive to the privileged few. It is however necessary to understand that effective development requires full integration of women in the development process as agents of change as well as beneficiaries because Indian women can be utilized as development resources in many ways. This paper explains the positive and negative effects of globalization. The following are some of the benefits of globalization for women.

* *Head of the Department, MBA & MHRM, M.R.P.G. College, Vizianagaram-535001. A.P., Email: ss_pasumarti@yahoo.co.in*

WOMEN IN INDIAN WORKFORCE

The share of women in the country's workforce has increased during the last three decades, but it still stood at a poor 25.68 per cent in 2001 even as there are more women workers in rural areas than in the urban centers. The proportion of women in the total workforce in 1981 was 19.67 per cent and it rose to 22.73 per cent in 1991, further rising to 25.68 per cent in 2001, according to the statistics of the Registrar General in India.

The work participation rate for women in rural areas was 30.98 per cent as compared to 11.55 per cent in the urban areas. In rural areas, women are mainly involved as cultivators and agricultural laborers, while in the urban areas, almost 80 per cent of the women workforce was working in unorganized sectors like household industry, petty trades and services and construction activity.

In the organized sector, women workers constituted 18.4 per cent of the workforce in 2003 as compared to 18.1 per cent in the previous years. As on March 31, 2003, there were about 49.68 lakh women workers employed in the organized sector. However, despite improvement, the work participation rate for women continues to be substantially low in comparison to that of men. In 2001, the work participation rate for men was 51.93 per cent, which was more than double that of their women counterparts.

POSITIVE IMPACTS OF GLOBALIZATION FOR WOMEN

Opportunities to Grow Through NGOs

Different non-profit organizations have been brought to India from around the globe. These organizations have given women the skills they need to advance, such as literacy and vocational skills. One *http://global_india1.tripod.com/main page.htmhttp://global_india1.tripod.com/*main page.htmorganization, Indiacorps, has brought in a range of programs to help women help themselves. One program in Ahmedabad, India has taught poor women how to create different crafts to generate income. With this program, women are able to earn their own personal money and enable the children to attend school instead of having to work to make more money. The women also gain business skills that inform them about career opportunities.

The Self-Employed Women's Association (SEWA) in India is a union of women laborers willing to work hard and seize any work opportunities they might get. Globalization has aided their opportunities in various ways. SEWA has established a Women's Cooperative Bank with 125,000 members, and through the aid of globalization, they have even reached the women in the rural areas of India. Markets in different areas can now be reached by Indian women who have a part in businesses, or by craft-making women who have licenses to export their goods. As per AKF-ISP News with more freedoms and opportunities, these women are raising their standard of living by generating more income.

Using of Modern Technology: Because of globalization and liberalization policies today the low cost and high quality technology products are available to the consumers at affordable prices. Technology that may seem out-dated to the United States is viewed as modern technology to India. With the aid of satellites and computers, SEWA has been able to reach more women to share self-help knowledge. Even the telephone is an advancement to many women in their business ventures. After one of the SEWA women took out a loan of four dollars to buy a telephone, her income was increased because she could reach more people (AKF-ISP News).

Development of Media and Communication system: After globalization there is vast development in Information and communication technology (ICT). Media can be viewed as a positive aspect of globalization. Media has the opportunity to reach people, and convey a message to people all over the world. A magazine called Femina is the top women's magazine for Indian women. It was started in 1959 and since it showcased its website in 1996, it has received much feedback from Indians all over the world. Femina shows the accomplishments of different Indian women from all over and provides inspiration to the women who read it.

Exposure to International Markets/organizations: Post globalization provides opportunities to expose several international markets for Indian products. One of the SEWA women, Mauna Dave, has made tremendous advancements and is sharing her knowledge of the global world and economy with other Indian women so they can establish a better life for themselves. Dave attributes the skills she has obtained to SEWA since she had the opportunity to speak and listen to other women in this organization. This UNIFEM Social Responsibility Award recipient is the director of Kutchcraft, which is an association of 110 craftswomen's groups with over 6,000 employees. She helped organize the craftswomen into an empowered group that have obtained bargaining power to compete in the international market. Dave said that some of the most difficult challenges are to keep current on the global economy and the fast-paced changes in India itself. Globalization has helped her and other Indian women share ideas and network in the international markets (UNIFEM).

PROBLEMS OF MODERN WOMEN WORKERS IN POST GLOBALIZATION

Globalization has had such negative consequences for women and children that some commentators argue that 'globalization is a man'. They point to the way women suffer disproportionately from IMF and World Bank policies as public services are cut and they are forced to care for sick, disabled and older relatives, as well as earn a living.

Globalization has had negative implications for Indian women. Their plights are similar to those of women in other developing regions such as Africa and Asia. Globalization has made many international corporations richer by the billions. However, what most people are not aware of is that women in these developing countries are suffering enormously due to this expansion of corporate empires. According to estimates from World Development Indicators, "Women work two-thirds of the world's working hours, produce half of the world's food, but earn only ten per cent of the world's income, and own less than one per cent of the world's property (Tomlinson)". According to Vandana Shivea, and Indian ecofeminist and scholar, globalization along with the support of organizations such as the World Bank and the International Monetary Fund, have created slave wages. These wages are not necessarily the result of "unjust" societies, but of the fact that global trade devalues the worth of people's lives and work (Aujla). While globalization has brought jobs to rural, developing areas such as India where there was previously no employment, these jobs seem to be wolves in sheep's clothing. The work available to women is almost always poorly paid, mentally and physically unhealthy, demeaning, or insecure.

Women are suffering two fold. As women in developing countries move into the work force, their domestic responsibilities are not alleviated. Women work two full time jobs. One in a factory, where they are paid next to nothing, the second is in the home where they are paid nothing (Moghadam). According to Merlin A. Taber and Sushma Batra, editors of the book Social Strains of Globalization in India, development for poor women has meant the migration of men to cities, higher prices for commodities, poorer job opportunities. "The mixture of corporate capitalism and Western culture models is dissolving family and community social controls as witnessed by higher rates of family violence, rape, divorce, and family breakdown."

One example of women's labor being exploited would be the Noida Export Processing Zone, which is 24 km from New Delhi. These "zones" prefer to hire women because they are "more obedient and more productive in men." In short, they are easier to control and less likely to retaliate against less than ideal working conditions, which are exactly what thousands of women encounter 12 hours a day. The zone is dangerous, hot, and unsanitary. Unnecessary body searches are routine. There are no maternity benefits and minimum wage is never enforced. Women who become pregnant or marry are immediately fired. Overtime is compulsory but women are paid lower rates than men. In order to avoid being fired, women turn to unsafe abortions performed by unqualified "doctors." In the zone, "respiratory problems, pelvic inflammatory disease, and sever cases of dehydration and anemia are common." (Rajalakshmi).

Globalization has affected both the quantity and the quality of work available to the majority of women in India. Some of the reasons are:

Loss of traditional works: The traditional role of women in agriculture, livestock and animal husbandry, Khadi and village industries including handicrafts, handlooms fisheries, etc, is being undermined because mechanization and automation is becoming prevalent in the market based economy which will adversely affect the village based traditional economy.

Privatization: Privatization and reduction of public services will reduce regular employment opportunities for women. Trade liberalization will allow MNCS to enter into food processing and other feminized industries which will lead to reduction in low skilled women labour. Globalization has increased the number of low paid, part-time and exploitative jobs.

State provisions: Curtailment of state provisions in child care, community care and social security, will increase the dual burden of employment and family responsibilities for women in general. Occupational sex segregation will be a stark reality in the open economy. This will tend to result in worse working condition, lower pay and inferior career opportunities.

Effects of Migration: With male migration on the increase from the rural to urban sectors, the women have to bear the triple burden of caring, farming and paid employment in the rural sector. Migration of women especially for economic reasons often gives rise to exploitation and trafficking in women at the local, regional and global levels.

Multiple Responsibilities: In the neo liberal work practices, contract work, unsocial hours of work,, cooperative practices, payment by result make it very difficult for women to cope with their multiple responsibilities.

No skills training to women students: Women are not taught specific skills and are themselves diffident to take up skill training. The government's existing ITI network has a low number of women students. There is a need for improvement of courses and optimal use of space and teachers.

Problems in Special Economic Zones: Implementation of Export oriented model and competition for foreign investment has led to the opening of more and more Special Economic Zones (also Free Trade Zones and Export Processing Zones etc.). In these zones labour laws are generally not applicable. Women are being used as 'cheap labour' force. They work under harsh working conditions. There is the abuse of labour and human rights and several instances of sexual harassment at workplace. Governments have had tendency to turn a blind eye to the abuse by capitalists to keep foreign investment.

Night Work for Women particuerly in BPO industry: Gliobalisation gives opportunity to develop Business process outsourcing has resulted into thousands of call centres employing young, computer savvy, and English knowing women for night work. Women's Movement is divided over this issue. One point of view supports night duty if, the safety of women is ensured by safe transport facility, group of women doing night duty together and absence of sexual harassment at workplace. Majority of women abhor night duty as they find it difficult as their family members oppose, at times it unsafe and injurious to their children's interests. In Mumbai, bar girls campaigned to work at night, as their work is possible only during that time and also more remunerative. According to ILO, 'night signifies a time period of 'at least 11 consecutive hours, including an interval between 10 p.m. and 7 a.m. But many women workers face a lot of problems due to work at night including sexual harassment, molestation and rape. It is unfair to put a blanket prohibition on night work is discrimination against women to prevent access to jobs and contravening the principle of equality. The questions regarding sexual harassment and assault on them needs to be addressed.

RECOMMENDATIONS FOR BETTER EMPLOYMENT FOR WOMEN

Need of Women employment policy: A policy for women's employment has to include strategies for challenging the sexual division of labour and gender ideology inside as well as outside the workplace.

Policies for access- include access to employment, education, training, credit etc.

1. Policies to improve the quality of employment, including her position in the household.
2. Policies to preserve employment and to protect material and human resources and assets.

Proper Implementation of Existing Laws and Schemes

The existing labour legislation, i.e. the Industrial Disputes Act, the Factories Act, the E.S.I.S. Act and the Minimum Wages Act, should not be withdrawn but strengthened to cover all workers. Some mechanism is required to evaluate the value of work under ERA. Minimum wages need to be strictly implemented with ward level committees of workers.

Employment Guarantee Scheme: The central and state government has to ensure macro policies that will absorb workers in labour intensive units and occupations. The Employment Guarantee Scheme needs to be expanded and improved for urban workers. The focus of such employment schemes can be on building infrastructure, slum development and housing. The National Renewal Fund should be extended to cover the unorganised sector and a substantial part should go into the retraining of workers.

Maternity Benefit: For all working Mothers irrespective of the number of employees or as per the Factories Act Crèches should be provided for children of all workers and not merely women workers irrespective of the number of employees. There could be a common fund for each industry and it should be financially supported by the concerned state Governments.

Family Leave: The minimum paid maternity leave period to be applicable to all working mothers irrespective of the necessary length of continuous service or the number of employees, irrespective whether married or un married and whether the child is natural born or adopted. Birth or adoptive fathers of a new child entitled to paid paternity leave on the birth or adoption of a child

Employees to have a right to take time off to care for children, disabled or sick dependants. The options available include: unpaid leave with automatic re-entry to an equivalent post in terms of grade, type of work etc., Part time working, Temporary re-arrangement of working pattern, Flexi-time Request Right available to working parents with young children (below 5 years of age or employees who have to care for disabled or sick dependants. The request can cover: the employee will have a right to return to work following availing of any of the above leave. The staff member must undertake in writing to return to work. No employee will suffer a detriment, be unfairly dismissed or be discriminated against for a reason connected, with pregnancy, childbirth, maternity, paternity, adoption, dependant care leave or the right to request flexible working, or time off to take care for a dependant. There shall be no loss of seniority, sick leave entitlements and incremental progression. [16]

Legal Protection for Informal Sector

Legal protection has to be given to the informal sector worker in the form of regular employment, notice period, compensatory pay or some form of unemployment insurance. It has been a long-standing demand of the representatives of the informal sector workers, trade unions and NGOs (Non Governmental Organisations) that workers should be registered as daily or piece rated workers with an identity card. This single act would provide information on the number of irregular workers and access to them for welfare measures. Social welfare for the informal sector workers can be implemented by levying a cess on employers in industrial estates. Social services can be dispensed to the workers through existing government infrastructure and tripartite boards. [17]

*Emphasis on Education and Skills:*A clear emphasis needs to be given to education, type of education of poor and especially of women. Women's access to employment is limited (amongst other reasons) because of lack of education and skills. The central and state government has a free education policy for girls but there is no follow up on the number of dropouts. Girls usually drop out from the high school. Special attention and incentives should be given to girls and parents for them to return to school.

*Capacity Building and Training:*Extra allocations of funds will be necessary for tying up the training institutions with job placement organisations or industries. Trainings for jobs have to be combined with additional inputs around building other life-skills towards critical awareness about women's status, improvement in negotiating skills and programs around building and maintaining women's assets including savings.

CONCLUSION

Even today in the modern, developed world, surveys show that parents still prefer to have a boy rather than a girl. One longstanding reason why boys have been seen as a greater blessing has been that they are expected to become better economic providers for their parents' old age. Yet it is time for parents to think again. Girls may now be a better investment. Women are now a permanent part of the global workforce. In the aftermath of the Asian financial crisis of the late 1990s women lost their jobs and resumed employment at much the same rate as men. Women workers suffer the worst working conditions, poorest pay *and* have to care for children and other dependants. Globalization can be a major force for prosperity only if it is backed by adequate national policies and conducive social and economic environment.

REFERENCES

Horgan G. (2001), 'Changing Women's Lives in Ireland', *International Socialism* 91 (Summer).

Ibid., p. 221.

Kim, S. (1992), *Anthropology and the Global Factory*, New York.

M. Wong and M. Wong (2001), 'Breaking Barriers, Building Alliances: Asia-Latin America Women's Exchange Workshop', in *Asia Labour Update*, No. 38.

Oaff B.(2001), 'New Economy, Same Old Story for Women', in *The Guardian*, 12 May.

Rajput, Pam, ed. (1994), Globalisation and Women. New Delhi; Ashish Publications. Goswami, P. R. Literacy, Information, and Governance in the Digital Era: An Indian Scenario, *Libr. Rev. 34; 2002; 255-70.*

Raynolds L. T. (2001), 'New Plantations, New Workers: Gender and Production Politics in the Dominican Republic', in *Gender and Society*, Vol. 15, No. 1, p. 17.

Siwal, B. R. (1998), Structural Adjustment Macro Perspective, *Social Welfare*, 45, 1, 6-8 & 48.

Sood, A. D. (2001), How to Wire Rural India: Problems and Possibilities of Digital Development, *Economic and Political Weekly*, 27, 4134-41.

Social Security for the Informal Sector. Edited by Wouter Van Ginneken, Asian Women Workers, *Newsletter*, Vol. 23, No. 1, January, 2004.

Wichterich, C. (2000), *The Globalized Woman: Reports from a Future of Inequality*, London, p. 47.

World Bank (1995), *Priorities and Strategies for Education: A World Bank Review*, Washington DC.

GENDER INEQUALITY IN DAIRY SECTOR IN AGRA DISTRICT OF UTTAR PRADESH

JYOTI GOGIA*

"There is no chance for the welfare of the world unless the condition of women is empowered. It is not possible for a bird to fly on one wing."

–Swami Vivekanand

INTRODUCTION

Indian economy is predominantly an agricultural in nature. About 45 per cent of the geographical area is under cultivation. Indian agriculture is a symbiosis of crop and animal production. India is endowed with the largest livestock population in the world. It accounts for 57 per cent of the world's buffalo population and 16 per cent of the cattle population. The country had about 218 millions cattle and 94 millions buffaloes at the beginning of the New Millennium, respectively (Shastry, 2003)[1] as compared to 155 millions and 43 millions in 1951. India stands the first place in its share of dairy production in the international scenario. This ever-expanding industry provides gainful employment to a vast majority of the rural households. It employs about 8.47 million people on yearly basis out of which 71% are women. (India Business Directory).

Milk production in India is generally practiced on majority of farms as a supplementary or complementary enterprise. About 73 per cent of the rural households own one or other kind of livestock. About 67% of the landless, small and marginal rural workforce is engaged in agriculture either as cultivator or farm labour. In a normal year, crop production can generate employment for this workforce for only 90 to 120 days. For the remaining period, they are virtually unemployed. In this situation, dairying sets right this imbalance in employment. The dairy sector today provides triple benefits to 80 million farm families-Nutritive food, Supplementary income, and productive employment for family labour, and mainly for women. In India, women accounted for 93 per cent of total employment in dairy production and indoor jobs like feeding and cleaning live stocks are done by women in 90 per cent families (APHCA-2004).[2]

* *Lecturer, Dei (Deemed University) Dayalbagh, Agra (UP), E-mail: Jgogia07@Yahoo.co.in*

Management, of livestock is one of the important allied agricultural activities in which Indian women contribute a lot i.e. entire management of dairy animals, starting from cutting, collection and chaffing of fodder to feeding, milking, preparation of milk products, cleaning of cattle shed and cattle, collection of dung and dung cakes etc. Women have also evolved several practices in caring for sick animals. Despite their considerable involvement and contribution, women's role in livestock production has often been underestimated or, worse, ignored. Gender-blindness is partly the result of a paternalistic bias, but also of the attitudes of women themselves, who may have been conditioned by their culture and society to undervalue the worth of the work they do.

METHODOLOGY

The data were collected from both primary as well as secondary sources. All the primary information were collected from selected households through survey with the help need based self designed schedules and questionnaire. Secondary data used were obtained from the office of Provincial Co-operative Dairy Federation, concerned block offices, journals, reports and other published sources.

The sampling process for primary data consists of three stages viz. selection of blocks, selection of villages and selection of sample cases. At the first stage of sampling, out of 15 blocks of Agra district, two blocks viz. Jaitpur Kalan and Bah were selected purposely since these blocks were supplying maximum quantity of milk to P.C.D.F (Provincial Dairy Co-operative Federation).At the second stage of sampling, five villages from each block were selected randomly. Thus ten villages were selected for present study. At the final stage a list of all the households keeping milch animals was prepared and a sample of 150 cases was drawn from the list randomly.

RESULTS AND DISCUSSION

Educational Status of the Respondents: Literacy is a very significant and common attribute of the social as well as economic status. Its connection with awareness of the respondents is not difficult to understand. Hence, education is considered an influential determinant of the progressive nature of the family members, as it is supposed to affect their level of adoption of the modern concepts, use of new technology and their attitude towards the women. The family leader decides about farm plans and arranges inputs for the production, which is largely based on farmer's experience and awareness, which to an extent associated with his level of education. The education level of the respondents (male and female) is given in Table 1.

The Table 1 reveals that overall maximum respondents, both men and women, were illiterate or less educated and per cent of illiterate women (26) is more as compared to men (12.7). The table also indicates that women get less chance to attain education as compared to men because as the status of education increases, the per cent of women is decreases in comparison to men which shows that in family, preference to get education is given to a boy than a girl.

Table 1

Educational Status of the Respondents

(Per cent)

Educational Status	*Female*	*Male*	*Total*
Illiterate	26.0	12.7	38.7
Primary	18.0	21.3	39.3
High-school	04.0	10.0	14.0
Inter-mediate	02.0	04.7	06.7
Graduate	00.0	01.3	01.3
Total	50.0	50.0	100.0

Contribution of Women in Dairy Income: Rearing one or two animals for milk is an important source of livelihood for women. Possession of dairy animals means more increased income for them; it means financial security, status, self-confidence and an opportunity to have some control over their lives. Preferring this alternative to exhausting agricultural labour, the women are self-employed, with flexible working hours and maintain better health as a result. Women play an important role and performing almost all work as labour, therefore to know the contribution of women in dairying, the best way to estimate their contribution in the income earned through dairy.

Table 2

Contribution of Women in Per Household Income from Dairy

Work hours per year				*Contribution (Rs)*	
Male	*Female*	*Total*	*Net Income (Rs.)*	*Male*	*Female*
153.45	291.85	445.30	75057.50	25864.75 (34.46)	49192.75 (65.54)

(Figures in parentheses indicate percentages).

The Table 2 indicates that out of total per household hour's contribution, women and men contributed 291.85 and 153.45 respectively. Further it can also be easily concluded that women's contribution to per household net income from dairying is 65.54 per cent where as men contributed only 34.46 per cent. Thus, it can be generalized that women contributed more in the family income from dairying as compared to men.

Extent of Decision Making Regarding Dairying Activities: Women have traditionally been centre of participate in home, farm and dairy activities in the rural areas. They share abundant responsibilities and perform a wide spectrum of duties. Besides being home makers, they have been time-honored partners to men in rearing livestock. To know the extent up to which a woman participate in decision making with respect to various activities of dairying is broadly categorized in to three categories viz. *Nil*-when women do not participate up to any extent in the decision about a particular activity, *Consulted*-before and after taking decision women are consulted for their advice but the decision is mainly taken by the male members of the family and *Dominated*-activities for which female take major decision individually.

Table 3
Extent of Participation of Women in Decision Making

(Per cent)

Activities	*Nil*	*Consulted*	*Dominated*
Disposal of milk	19	50	31
Sale of animal	57	32	11
Sale of animal	57	32	11
Breeding	75	17	8
Vaccination	78	14	8
Type of feed	-	64	36
Type of fodder	-	64	36
Investment of income	59	30	11

A close perusal of the table reveals that most of the women didn't participate in the decisions regarding sale and purchase of animals, breeding, vaccination and investment of income. Overall majority of family women were consulted in the activities like disposal of milk, type of feed and type of fodder. Decision on investment of income is very important one and there were only 11 per cent women who were dominant regarding decision making. Thus, from the above discussion it may be concluded that for most of the activities the women were only consulted for making decisions, sometimes their participation is nil. The major role regarding decision making is playing by male members of the family.

Level of Liberty and Women's Participation in Social Front: Rural women play a significant role in domestic and socio-economic life of the society and therefore this is an important and substantial segment of our society. Mr. Atal Bihari Vajpayee had observed that political empowerment of women alone would not do, along with it there should come social and economic empowerment. Women's role in farm management and other decision-making processes varied partly in relation to their status in the household and partly in the farm enterprise. To evaluate the status of the women in the family as well as in the society, the level of liberty they enjoyed and their participation in the social front is necessary to evaluate.

The Table 4 reveals that overall in majority of cases women have very low level of liberty regarding thoughts; the same levels were observed in case of liberty of expression. As the liberty of belief is concerned the majority of the women have moderate level. Further it can also be observed from the table that most of the women enjoy very high level of liberty of faith and worship. It can be concluded that women are not enjoying high level of liberty; they are not free to express their views and ideas.

Table 4
Opinion of the Respondents Regarding Different Levels of Liberty

(Per cent)

	Levels of Liberty		
Items	*Very high*	*Moderate*	*Very low*
Thought	2	45	53
Expression	3	47	50
Belief	28	59	13
Faith	62	35	3
Worship	91	9	-

The Table 5 gives a clear picture of the women's participation in the social front. Majority of women are treated as wife, mother and daughter in their family. As the liberty to take decision in the family matters by the women is concerned most of the women have partial liberty to take decisions which mean that they were not free to take independent decision. Mostly women are not aware about the equality and their development. 95 per cent women never struggle for social justice and 77 per cent are even not aware of the social rights and power given to them. 33 per cent women never went outside for dairy activities while they are contributing a lot in production process.

Table 5
Extent of Women's Participation in the Social Front

Activities	*Response*	*(Per cent)*
Liberty to take family decision	Yes	10
	No	27
	Partially	63
Awareness about the equality, development of women	Yes	2
	No	72
	Partially	26
Struggle for social justice in the family and society	Yes	5
	No	95
Moving out for dairy activities	Never	32
	Sometimes	22
	Often	46
Viewed as a wife , mother or daughter in the family	Yes	86
	No	-
	Sometimes	14
Awareness of the social rights and power	Yes	-
	No	77
	Cant' Say	23

CONCLUSION AND SUGGESTIONS

The empowerment of women involves not just an improvement in their physical and social conditions but also an increased involvement in decision-making and control over resources. The male head of a family, however, takes important decisions relating to dairy farming. It is always a male who participates in the activity where cash economy is involved. For instance, a male member will collect the money the sale of milk fetches. It is also the male member who will take decision to sell or purchase a dairy animal. Loans under various government agencies are sanctioned mostly to the male members. Only a male member of a family participates in a dairy farming-related training occasionally organised by concerned government institutions under a 'development project'.

It indicates the invisibility of the majority of women, who act as unpaid workers on the family farm. Care of livestock is a female domain but as dairy work is becoming modernized, women are losing control of both management and economic returns. Training of women in animal husbandry is found to be totally neglected. The level of improved household technology, too, is very unsatisfactory, more especially in backward regions where the majority of women are still working with age-old tools. Over half the respondents had no leisure time.

While the literature on women speaks of empowerment and while we believed that empowerment is important to sustain long term change in the role of women, we have not been entirely clear on what empowerment means much less how to encourage it. We could see that in a world where the male is dominant women's roles change only when they possess the confidence, the courage, the commitment and the perseverance to promote and even force change. We now believe we have some clues as to what in fact empowerment is, as well as how to encourage it. We can see empowerment in decision-making. Who participates in a decision, and who actually decides are measures of empowerment. A further dimension is the nature of the decision. Who takes the decision to buy a new cow or buffalo, or how to feed the animal while she is pregnant, whether to artificially inseminate or naturally service a cow on who to vote for as a managing committee member? These are the decisions of importance. Who takes the decision is an indicator of empowerment. These are also illustrative of the areas where women have generally had a limited, if any, role in decision-making.

Women must not only be empowered to take decisions, they must be reinforced by results, which means learning to take good decisions and to assess, in advance and after the consequences of those decisions. It is, we believe, important to educate men as well as women, if we are to promote changes in the quality we seek. Rural men can and must be transformed into allies instead of opponents to change. We intend to begin this effort at home by helping our male officers of the NDDB to become sensitive to gender issues.

We have also learned-perhaps the hard way that financial inducements are often a poor way to encourage societal change. We no longer offer a package of funds to unions that are willing to undertake activities such as the Women's Dairy Co-operative Leadership Programme. We will support such programmes with training, with consultancy, with our personnel but with money only when it is crucial to the outcome.

In all of these areas if we want the benefits of our work to reach and affect the lives of dairy farmers, particularly in developing countries, then we must think how we can reach out in particular to women with our messages, what we can do to empower women to participate in crucial decisions, how we can support women to adopt new methods and practices and how we can help them to ensure that they too benefit from their labours so that future generations of women are educated, healthy, and standing tall shoulder to shoulder with their men, share equally the responsibility of making a better life for us all.

NOTES

1. Shastry, NSR (2003), Buffalo Management Scenario in small farmer holdings of India: Observation and suggestion. Proceedings of the 4th Asian Buffalo congress. Feb. 25-28, New Delhi (India).
2. Animal Production and Health Commission for Asia and the Pacific, Twenty-eighth Session's Report (2004).

REFERENCES

Amrita Patel (1998), "Women and the White Revolution", (*Source*: *Co-op. Dialogue,* Vol. 8, No. 1, Jan.-June, pp. 20-25.

Azad, D. S. and Sinha, R. S. (1985), "The Participation of Women in Agriculture and Allied Enterprises". A Case Study of Biduhna Block of District Etawa in U.P. Ph.D. *Thesis Submitted to Agra University, Agra.*

Barger M. (1985), "The Monetary Value of a Housewife–A Replacement Cost Approach", *American Journal of Economics & Sociology,* Vol. 33.

Bhuvaneswari and Khanna, K. (1998), "Women in Agriculture and Rural Development", *Indian Journal of Agricultural Economics, 54(3): 102-105.*

Janelid, I. (1975), The Role of Women in Nigerian Agriculture, Rome: FAO.

Jyothi, K. S., Gracy C. P. and Prakash, S. (1999), "Environment and Decision-making by Rural Women–An Economic Study in Karnataka", *Indian Journal of Agricultural Economics, Mumbai,* Vol. 54, No. 3:308.

Kaur, Manjit and Punia, R. (1988), "Participation of Women in Home, Dairy and Farm Activities", *Indian Journal of Dairy Science,* 25 (2): 168.

Ponghal, S., Kumar, A, and Singh, S. I. (1986), "Comparative Working Efficiency of Men and Women Labour in Different Operation in Haryana", A Case Study of Rohtak Distt, *Indian Journal of Agriculture Research,* 48(2): 32-35.

Saikia, A. (1995), "Role of Farm Women in Agriculture and their Involvement in Decision Making", *Indian Journal of Agricultural Economics,* 28(2): 113-118.

Singh, B., Kumar, N. and Dhaliwal, S. K. (1999), "Contribution of Farm Women in Decision Making with Respect to Investment and Farm and Non-Farm Activities in Punjab", *Indian Journal of Agricultural Economics, Mumbai,* Vol. No., 54, No. 3, 303-304.

GROWING INTERSECTORAL IMBALANCES AND GENDER INEQUALITIES IN WAGES AND INCOMES IN INDIA

GEETANJALI SHARMA*

INTRODUCTION

Economic development has historically been associated with structural changes in the national economies. It has, in fact, most often, been defined as a process combining economic growth with changing share of different sectors in the national product and labour force. The most common structural changes that have been observed historically have followed a sequence of shift from agriculture to industry and then to services. Thus, an underdeveloped economy is characterised by a predominant share of agriculture; with development, the share of industry increases and that of agriculture declines, and subsequently after reaching a reasonably high level of development, the services sector increases in importance, becoming a major component of the economy. This pattern has not only been observed historically, but it also holds across the countries with different levels of development. Structural shifts and changing sectoral shares are found to hold both for the national product and the workforce.

Structural changes do not only characterise economic development, they are also necessary for sustaining economic growth. The neoclassical view that sectoral composition is a relatively unimportant by-product of growth has been convincingly questioned by structural economists like Kuznets, who have empirically demonstrated that growth is brought about by changes in sectoral composition. This is so both for the reasons of demand and supply. Though the emphasis laid on different factors by different economists has varied, the broad line of reasoning advanced by pioneers like Fisher and dark and followed with some elaborations and modifications by later analysts has been as follows: income elasticity of demand for agricultural products is low; that for industrial, particularly manufacturing goods, is high; and, for services, it is still higher. As a result, with rising levels of income, the demand for agricultural products

* *Lecturer in Economics, Malviya National Institute of Technology, Jaipur, India, E-mail: geetanjali20@rediffmail.com*

relatively declines and that for industrial goods increases and, after reaching a reasonably high level of income, demand for services increases sharply. Accordingly, the shares of different sectors in the national product get determined by the changes in the pattern of demand. On the supply side, agriculture being mainly dependent on a fixed factor of production, namely land, faces a limit on its growth and is subject to early operation of the law of diminishing returns. Industry, specially manufacturing, on the other hand, offers large scope for use of capital and technology, which could be augmented almost without limit with human effort. Labour supply could constrain expansion of industry, but it is possible to overcome it by introducing labour-saving technological changes. The same applies to services, where application of technologies seems to offer much larger scope, as shown by the experience over the past few decades'.

The paper highlights the multi-dimensional context of gender inequalities prevalent in Indian labour markets stemming from the socially derived structures, division of labour, sex segregation and labour market segmentation that provide the basis for propagation and perpetuation of wage and income inequalities, while examining the economic aspects to assess the credibility of oft-repeated justifications offered in lieu of these imbalances in wage earnings across men and women.

Does educational attainment and human capital attributes differentiating labour supplies explain differential returns to workers, or are such variations an offshoot of super-imposition of social status and valuation of work on to economic, labour market spheres? Have there been any major changes visible in the trends of female employment and what are the implications for their levels of vulnerability? Are the compulsions of poverty induced, survival oriented livelihood still operational? If so, can economic growth and women's increasing labour market participation propel wages upwards?

Wages and incomes in India have been rising over time; however, the gender inequalities have not been bridged. Changes in women's workforce participation have influenced the remuneration and returns due to them; however the wage imbalances across men and women remain. An examination of the trends in the economy reflects the stubborn persistence of the structure of inequalities in the sphere of occupational concentration, where women continue to be concentrated at lower end jobs, thereby receiving lower wages. The discrimination and biases against women witnessed in social spheres gets mirrored on to economic spaces not only through direct, legitimate routes but also via the resilience in perceptions and mindsets among the agents of the labour markets that reconfigure to retain elements of gender imbalances. This paper highlights the weak potential of economic growth and increasing women's economic participation towards eliminating these inequalities, unless supported by concerted efforts at altering attitudes towards women's roles and contribution that are harboured by different agents within the labour markets.

REGIONAL IMBALANCES

Regional equity is a subject whose importance goes beyond the national level because it is a major international problem. In India there is a long standing and persistent problem that is similar in kind, though not in degree ; it is a problem of regions that have more and regions that have less. These gaps in income are a source of tension and discontent as elsewhere in the world. The regions of India have been studied under alternative classification schemes by economists, geographers and sociologists. The economist's attention tends to focus naturally on the relative performance of India's regions from the standpoint of the economic welfare of their inhabitants.

No national or international economy can be thoroughly understood without analyzing its regional structure, the nature and functioning of the various regional economies comprising it, their interaction among themselves, and their relationship to the national and world economies. It is a well recognized fact that material wellbeing of a society depends not only on absolute wealth and purchasing power/but also on their distribution among individuals and families. There is no universally accepted criterion for judging regional disparities but a wide variety of facts suggest that individual wellbeing does differ from one region to another. One cannot really speak of "regional development" and "increasing the efficiency of the national economy," as if these were two quite distinct things, between which any society with scarce resources must make marginal choices. Rather regional development is a key component of any policy for raising the efficiency of national economy.[1]

REGIONAL DISPARITIES AND HUMAN CAPITAL

Regional disparities within countries are quite common. Taking the three census years 1981,1991 and 2001 as benchmarks, the disparity ratio is approximately 1:3 between the most and the least developed states, Punjab and Bihar may be easily matched elsewhere. But in India, these disparities refer to basic economic conditions rather than to different levels of productivity and income as in developed countries. Moreover, such disparities seem to be increasing in India whereas the trend is towards convergence in developed countries.

The last few years have seen a renewed interest in growth issues and the concept of convergence. Two recent studies have shown that regions in India are converging. Few studies have established the evidence of absolute convergence of regions in India, since much of earlier literature on regional disparity has shown a tendency of increase in the disparities, these recent results for India are rather surprising.

People are the real wealth of a nation. The basic objective of development is to create an enabling environment for people to enjoy long, healthy and creative lives. Economists have long been aware of the importance of human resource development. Adam Smith stressed the importance of education at various points in "The wealth of Nations" and he specifically included "the acquired and useful abilities of all the inhabitants or members of society" in his concept of fixed capital.' Similarly Alfred Marshall emphasised the importance of education "as a national investment" and in his view, "the most valuable of all capital is that invested in human beings". But not until the late fifties did economists and other social scientists paid much attention to the role of investment in human beings as an important determinant of economic development. It is important to point out that T.W. Schultz highlighted the idea of human resource development. According to him there are five ways of developing human resources: (i) health facilities and services, broadly conceived to include all expenditure that affect the life expectancy, strength and stamina and the vigour and vitality of the people; (ii) on the job training; (iii) formally organised education the elementary, secondary and higher levels; (iv) study programmes for adults that are not organised by firms and (v) migration of individuals and families to adjust to changing job opportunities. Similarly according to S. Kuznets "The major capital stock of an industrially advanced nation is not its physical equipment; it is body of knowledge amassed from tested findings and discoveries of empirical science and the capacity and training of its population to use this knowledge effectively".[2]

As a result, the concept of human capital formation came to limelight. Human capital can be defined as the body of knowledge possessed by the population and the capacity of the people to use this knowledge effectively. Human development is a process of enlarging people's choices. In principle these choices can be infinite. But at all levels of development, the three essential ones are for people to lead a long and healthy life, to acquire knowledge and to have access to resources needed for a decent standard of living. Human development, thus, has two sides. One is the formation of human capabilities such as improved health, knowledge and skills. The other is the use people make of their acquired capabilities for productive purposes, for leisure or for being active in cultural, social and political affairs. Human resource development treats human beings primarily as an input in the production process a means rather than an end.[3] By 1980's the concept of human development reinforced. the belief that people should participate in the development process and benefit from it. Recent experience with attempts to accumulate physical capital at a rapid rate in poor countries bears out the necessity of due attention to human capital. It has become evident that the effective use of physical capital itself is dependent upon human capital. Economists like Harbison, Schultz, Denison, Meier observed that one of the important factors responsible for the rapid growth of the American economy is their increasing allocation of outlays on education resulting significant improvement in the level of human capital formation. In a similar vein, a recent World Bank Study across countries has established that increasing the average level of schooling by three years was associated with a 27% increase in the countries rate of economic growth. Increasing education by six years lifted economic growth rates by 39%. While the case for investment in human resources is gaining wider acceptance, the means of attaining an increase in this type of investment have still received only superficial consideration.[4]

GENDER INEQUALITIES IN INCOME AND WAGES IN INDIA

Income Inequalities in India

Growth of State Domestic Product is the single most important indicator of development for a State. Ideally, the SDP series of each State should be fully consistent with the national accounts estimates of GDP. However, this is not the case. Information on SDP compiled by the State Governments is collected by the Central Statistical Organisation and is used as one of the inputs of national accounts estimation. In this process, the CSO takes notes of the differences in methods of estimating the SDP in different States, but it does not refine the series to make them statistically comparable with each other and with the national accounts. Accordingly, we restrict the use of the data to comparison of the trends in growth rate only in order to reduce the error margin inherent in the data and avoid direct inter-State comparison of data as far as possible. We look at the trend rates of growth for State domestic product from 1960s to 1990s of major States only, as comparable data are not available for smaller States and new States created during this period. With the exception of Assam, Haryana, Himachal Pradesh and Punjab, the State income data from 1960-61 is available for all of the other major States. For Assam, Haryana and Punjab, data for 1960-61 and from 1965-66 onwards is available. For Himachal Pradesh the data set begins from 1967-68. Base years taken for arriving at the trend real rates of decadal growth are 1960-61, 1970-71, 1980-81 and 1993-94 for the four decades respectively. Although the first data series continues through 1984-85, we have taken 1960-61 to 1979-80 to be the first period. This is because with effect from 1980-81 a second data series came into existence, incorporating improvements in method and extension of coverage. The 1980-81 series was in use till 1997-98. A third series with 1993-94 as the base year was introduced in 1999, with changes in the coverage of economic activities. In our analysis of the growth experience of individual States; we will thus be making use of these three distinct data series. The source of the data is the Central Statistical Organisation.

In the nineteen sixties, the highest growth rates were recorded by the erstwhile unified Punjab and adjoining areas (now Himachal Pradesh, Punjab and Haryana). In this decade, Bihar was the slowest growing State economy recording less than 1 per cent growth, which implied a decline in per capita income. Uttar Pradesh, Rajasthan, Madhya Pradesh and Andhra Pradesh-recorded less than 2 per cent growth. In the seventies, the pattern of rates of growth remained largely unchanged. Along with Punjab, Haryana, Jammu &

Kashmir, the western States of Maharashtra and Gujarat, and the southern States of Karnataka and Tamil Nadu began to register higher rates of growth. Madhya Pradesh and Kerala were at the bottom with negative real per capita income growth in this period. The national average of economic growth picked up from the 3.6 per cent of the previous decade to 5.6 per cent in the eighties. Individual States showed the greatest consistency in their growth record during this decade[5] as reflected in the decrease of measure of inter-State disparity from 2.20 to 1.39. The difference between the highest and the lowest values for the rates of growth across States was 4.0 percentage points. Haryana, Rajasthan, Punjab, Maharashtra, Karnataka and Tamil Nadu recorded the highest growth. Jammu and Kashmir and Assam slipped to the lower end of the growth. The new series of GSDP data was released by the CSO in August 2000 and subsequently updated in November, 2001. Table 1 gives the trends of growth in GSDP from 1993-94 onwards for the decade of nineties (with base year 1993-94) based on the new series.

Table 1

Trends in Rates of Growth in Gross State Domestic Product Current Prices-Decades of Eighties and Nineties*

	Gross States Domestic Product		*Gross States Domestic Productper capita*	
States	*1980-81to 1990-91*	*1993-94 to 1998-99*	*1980-81 to 1990-91*	*1993-94 to 1998-99*
Karnataka	5.4	8.2	3.3	6.4
Gujarat	5.1	8.0	3.0	6.2
Tamil Nadu	5.	6.8	3.9	5.8
Maharashtra	6.0	7.1	3.6	5.4
Rajasthan	5.9	7.7	3.8	5.3
West Bengal	4.8	6.8	2.6	5.0
All India	5.6	6.8	3.3	4.8
Goa	5.5	8.3	3.9	4.5
Kerala	3.2	5.5	1.7	4.2
Himachal Pradesh	5.0	6.7	3.1	3.9
Haryana	6.2	5.8	3.9	3.6
Andhra Pradesh	5.4	5.0	3.5	3.0
Orissa	5.0	4.3	3.1	2.9
Bihar	4.7	4.2	2.5	2.6
Madhya Pradesh	4.0	4.4	2.1	2.3
Uttar Pradesh	4.9	4.5	2.5	2.3
Jammu & Kashmir	2.2	.7	- 0.4	1.6
Delhi	7.6	6.7	3.2	1.6
Assam	3.6	2.7	1.4	1.0

* Govt. of India, Planning Commission (2001) Tenth Five Year Plan, Vol. III, p. 36.

The overall disparity in inter-State growth of NSDP and per capita NSDP of States has increased considerably during the nineties as compared to the eighties and the seventies In recent decades, the decade office eighties seems to be a period in which horizontal inequity across States was a minimum compared to other periods. In the nineties the magnitude of disparities was the maximum. A comparison of the trends in rates of economic growth for all the States in the Nineties is given in Table No.1. It may be seen that less developed regions including the north eastern States, Orissa and the heartland States of Bihar, Uttar Pradesh & Madhya Pradesh have generally recorded growth rates below the All India average during the most recent period of 1993-94 to 1998-1999. This trend suggests a widening of the gap between the more and the less developed States. The growth experience of the nineties has two alternative interpretations. One, that the faster growth experienced in some States is at the expense of others and is an outcome of a lessening of the equalising role of Centralised Planning. Alternatively, it could be argued that the reformed economic climate allowed some individual States to harness more of their true economic potential; this was not at the expense of other States. The national average growth stepped up by 1 percentage point in the nineties and most States experienced improved growth in this decade.[6]

STRUCTURAL CHANGES IN INCOME AND WAGES

The economy of the States have been experiencing major structural changes as would be expected in the structure of a developing economy. There has been a shift from the primary sector to secondary and tertiary sectors. Figures for all the 19 States taken together suggest major structural changes away from the predominantly agriculture-based economy that the country has traditionally had. Comparable data regarding net State domestic product at current Prices available for 19 States indicate that in the last three plan periods, the percentage share of the primary sector marginally increased between 1987-88 and 1993-94 and declined to a low of 30.83 per cent in 1999-2000. The trend for the secondary sector is exactly the opposite, as it should be, and it stood at 14.02 per cent in 1999-2000. However, the share of tertiary sector has been steadily increasing from 49.14 per cent in 1987-88 to an all time high of 55.14 per cent in 1999-2001. Against the normal pattern of development, exceptions are, West Bengal, where there were significant falls in the share of the "witnessed a decrease in the growth of employment secondary sector in income in the case of Arunachal in the agriculture sector in spite of a sharp increase in the growth of the sectoral income; and Delhi, which experienced an increase in the growth of employment share of agriculture in spite of a sharp decrease in the growth of income from the sector.[7]

Of the 1.3 billion of the world poor, 70% are women and 570 million rural women in developing countries i.e. 60% of women rural population live below the poverty line. Now for only 09 countries Gender Empowerment Index values are above 0.6 and 24 countries are below 0.6 whereas 45 countries have a Gender Development Index value below 0.5 and only 32 countries have a Gender Development Index value above 0.8. Many studies show that much of women's work remains unrecognised and undervalued. At present, 16 billion dollar of global output is invisible out of which 11 billion dollar is produced by women. A review of 131 countries revealed that (a) Women work longer time than men of the total burden of work, women carry 53% in developing countries and 51% in industrial countries (b) of men's total work, two third is spent on paid SNA and one-third is unpaid non-SNA activities in industrial countries. These shares became reversed for women. In developing countries, more than three fourth of men's work is in paid SNA activities and one fourth is in unpaid non-SNA-activities. On the other hand, these shares became reversed for women. Thus, women's work remains unpaid, unrecognised and undervalued.[8]

In 1991 the UNDP evolved the Human Development Index that takes into account a country's achievements in terms of three aspects of human development (i) the opportunity that it offers its citizens to lead a long and healthy life, (ii) to acquire knowledge and (iii) to have access to the resources needed to acquire a decent standard of living.. To capture gender inequalities, the UNDP in 1995 introduced two more indices; (i) the Gender Development Index and (ii) the Gender Empowerment Index. The Gender Related Development Index is calculated to reflect inequalities between men and women in the three dimensions used in calculating. The three indices, namely, life expectancy index, education index and GDP index are calculated separately for men and women, and an equally distributed index is calculated for each dimension. The Gender Empowerment Index focuses on women's opportunities and captures gender inequality in three areas: (1) Political participation and decision-making power: measured by women's and men's percentage shares of parliamentary seats. (2) Economic participation and decision-making power: measured by two indicators: (a) Women's and men's percentage share of positions as legislators, senior officials and managers, and (b) Women's and men's percentage shares of professional and technical positions; and (3) Power over economic resources: measured by women's and men's estimated earned income. As we move forward with the implementation of the Millennium Development Goals, it is important that we are fully committed to investing in policies and programmes that empower women and promote gender equality.[9]

Women both in the traditional and modern social structure have always been the victims of the greatest exploitation. Especially for poor women in Third World Countries, who are at the bottom of every hierarchy, oppressions are further magnified as they toil under the double burden of gender and economic deprivation. The Gender Equality Doctrine is an outstanding contribution of twentieth century social thought as a practical objective for the welfare of human race. The UN Declaration of Women's Rights, 1967, postulated the Equalitarian Doctrine of achieving equal rights for women as that of men and advocated its universal recognition in law by all countries as an unavoidable necessity. Maximum participation of women as well as men in all fields of human activity is essential for the full and complete development of country, the welfare of the world and the cause of world peace. Any discrimination against equal rights of women or their subordination amounts to injustice to half of humanity. Prevention of the participation of women on equal basis with men in political, social, economic and cultural life of their country is a great obstacle to the full development of the potential of women in the service of their country and of humanity. The UN General Assembly reaffirmed its faith in the fundamental human rights and in the equal rights of men and women. The Equalitanan Doctrine is a revolutionary theory. Gender discrimination of inequality from womb to tomb is a patent fact in the traditional cultures of the developing countries.[10]

There has been a long drawn debate throughout the world as to how gender equity be achieved so that women may be empowered to come as an equal partner in power sharing of economic, social or political activities. There is no denial of the fact that the women, throughout the world, have been the victim of exploitation of all shorts, may be because of the biological reason or inherent subjunctive nature in them. Even though in earlier days or even today, by sheer individual efforts or initiative they have far excelled than their male partner in almost every area of human achievements. However, it comes to practice the women are exploited in one or the other way. It has been calculated that at every moment of time the women become the victim of rape, domestic violence and subjugation in one or the other part of the globe. Then the question arises, is all that have been said good for the women are rhetoric or it has something to do with reality?[11]

Women constitute about 48 per cent of the total population of the country as per the 2001 census of India, they suffer many disadvantages as compared to men in terms of literacy rates, labour participation rates and earnings. In order to address issues relating to social and economic advancement of women, the Department of Women and Child Development under the Ministry of Human Resource Development has been implementing various schemes.

REDUCTION OF GENDER INEQUALITIES DURING FIVE YEAR PLANS IN INDIA

Development of women remained focal point in different plan periods. The first plan (1951-56) treated it as welfare subjects, in second plan (1956-79) reflected the welfare approach Besides giving priority to women education and launching measures to improve maternal and child health service. The shift and approach from welfare to development of women could take place only in the 6th plan (1980-85) which adopted a multi-disciplinary approach with special thrust on health, education and employment in the seventh plan!(1985-90), the development programs continued with the major objective of raising their economic and social status. The eighth plan (1997-2002) made two significant changes in conceptual strategy of planning for women. First

Empowerment of women became one of the nine primary objectives of the plan period. It directed both the centre and states to adopt a special strategy of 'Women's Component Plan' (WCP) through which not less 30% of Funds flow to women from all development sectors. The 10th plan (2002-07) adopted a sector-specific 3-fold strategy for empowerment for women, based on the transcription of national policy for Empowerment of women which included :

Social Development

To create an enabling environment through various affirmative development policies and program for the development of women besides providing them easy and equal access to all the basic minimum services so as to enable them to realise their fill potential.

Economic Empowerment

To ensure provision of training, employment and income generation activities with both backward and forward linkage with unlimited objectives of making all potential women economically independent and self-reliant.

Gender Justice

To eliminate all forms of gender discrimination and thus allow woman to enjoy not only demure but also the de-facto rights and fundamental freedom on par with men in all sphere of life. So the gender justice is the main parameter for the real social justice and empowerment of women, particularly academic empowerment which becomes the root cause of empowerment. The Eleventh Five Year Plan emphasises about "Appropriate Provisions" for "Gender Balancing".

During Ninth Plan 'National Policy for Empowerment of Women' was adopted to eliminate all types of discrimination against women and to ensure Gender Justice besides empowering women both socially and economically. 'Year 2001' was celebrated as 'Women's Empowerment Year' to create awareness generation, remove negative thinking, besides building up confidence in women through the process of conscientization so that they can take their rightful place in the mainstream of the nation's social, political and economic life.

We do believe that equitable representation of women in the highest decision-making bodies of our country is also urgently required. Therefore, serious efforts have to be built broad-based consensus on the issue of reserving 33 per cent seats in Parliament and State Legislatures for women. Our experience with such reservation at the Panchayat level has been very encouraging, even if not uniformly successful across the country. The time his come for us to scale this experiment upto the national level and the very centre of our legislative process that is represented by our Parliament. India's quest for freedom and dignity or a life of dignity and self respect for all our citizens can never become a living reality unless our women are equal partners in all processes of development and governance.

Employment of women in productive activities has been recognized as the 'critical entry point for women's freedom and her integration in the mainstream development. The poor and deteriorating status of rural women has been attributed to their declining economic participation and other factors like the modernization of the agricultural sector. These days, need for giving a better deal to the rural women is being widely recognized. It is now accepted that the participation of women themselves in development activities is the most effective tool for the promotion of the access of women to the benefits of development. At the same time. a study shows that women among the poor families are even more powerless. In the economic sphere, women have fewer opportunities than men, they earn about half of men's income, and they have particularly no ownership of resources. They face segmented labour markets and unequal earnings structures. The problem is mainly the limited mobility of women which does not allow them access to improved opportunities in skill development or economic betterment. It is also revealed that in most sectors of the economy, women tend to be employed in the low paid, most menial tasks, using the least technology. In agriculture, for example, women engage in labour intensive tasks such as transplantation and weeding. The study points out that a systematic gender bias in industrial and agricultural sectors of employment invariably surfaces at micro level Operations like ploughing that fetch higher wages are male preserves, whereas transplanting, which commands lower wages, is a females preserve. Study illustrates, women's development and social conflicts, apart from the differentials in wages for the same jobs, discrimination against women is strengthened by having lower rates for the job traditionally done by women, viz., sewing, weeding, transplanting, winnowing, threshing and harvesting, as against ploughing-normally done be men only.

INDIA'S GLOBAL POSITION IN GENDER DEVELOPMENT

India's Global Position in Gender Development has been shown in Table 2.

Women in Development and Gender and Development are sometimes used interchangeably but there are some basic differences. The WID approach was developed in the 1970s, with the objective of designing actions and policies to integrate women fully into development. Margaret Snyder and Mary Tadesse, in their book, 'African Women and Development A History,' defined women and development as follows:

"Women and Development"[12] is an inclusive term which is used to signify a concept and a movement whose long-range goal is the well being of society- the community of men, women and children.

Balanced Regional Development is not to be pursued through a process of levelling down by preventing states from reaching their full growth potential. What is needed is that well-managed states must be encouraged to reach their

Table 2
India Global Position in Gender Development*

	Human Development Index	*Gender Development Index*	*Maternal Mortality Ratio (per one lakh live births)*	*Adult Female Literacy Rate*	*Female Economic Activity Rate (FEAR)*
Norway	0.963	0.960	16	-	60.3
Austalia	0.954	0.954	8	-	56.7
United States	0.944	0.942	17	-	59.6
China	0.755	0.754	56	86.5	72.4
Sri Lanka	0.751	0.747	92	88.6	43.5
India	*0.602*	*0.586*	*540*	*47.8*	42.5
Pakistan	0.527	0.508	500	35.2	36.7
Nepal	0.526	0.511	740	34.9	56.9
Bangladesh	0.520	0.514	380	31.4	66.5
Mozambique	0.379	0.365	1000	31.4	82.6
Ethiopia	0.367	0.355	850	33.8	57.2
Niger	0.281	0.271	1600	9.4	69.3

*UNDP. Human Development Report, 2005, p. 33.

full growth potential and their superior performance could then serve as a model for others to emulate. This process is bound to generate some differences in growth performance across states but such differences can have a healthy demonstration effect. The priority tasks to equalise development across regions would be:

(i) The investment in agriculture needs to be stepped up especially in the lagging region. The backward and forward linkages of agriculture in poorer regions need to be emphasised more. Investment in water harvesting, soil conservation, rural roads warehouses, processing activities and promotion of high value crops should be emphasised. Since agricultural growth is found to be more disparate, steps to equalise it will certainly reduce the regional imbalances.

(ii) Service sector has been found to be the new driver of the growth process. Especially the banking and insurance sector and infrastructure have contributed to acceleration of many states. There is a need to promote these sectors, on priority, in backward regions.

(iii) Improvement in basic infrastructural facilities like power, transport, telecommunication and irrigation in backward states is a precondition to improve the quality of life of people and to usher in sustainable development in them. Availability of assured power supply, developed transport system and modern telecommunication facilities are important factors to attract private investments into these states.

(iv) The governments of backward states are fiscally weak and lack resources. Liberalisation process and various reforms have further weakened their financial position. It is hoped that resource flows to the states via Finance Commission awards and Planning Commission dispensation will continue and are likely to remain positively discriminating in favour of backward states. In fact, these transfers are found to be progressive in reducing regional disparities. However, direct public sector investment by the central government in the states are likely to dry up gradually due to severe budget constraint of the Centre, Under the above circumstances an important factor that influences the speed of economic progress of a state is the quality of governance. A better administered state is more efficient in raising revenues and putting them to better use. There are few states which will attract more private investment both from domestic and foreign sources. Such states are also in a position to prepare viable projects and successfully bid central assistance or external funding. Hence. governance needs to be given immediate attention, especially in the backward states.

Thus, the solution lies not merely in increasing resource flows to backward regions but in creating an enabling environment to attract more resources, using them properly and assuring a fair deal to the investors. The overall investment climate and governance need to be upgraded.[13]

NOTES AND REFERENCES

1. Shrinivasa Gowda, M. V. (1995), Regional Development in India, Deep and Deep Publications, New Delhi, p. 23.
2. Gautam, V. (2002), Human Resource Development, Vikas Publishing House, New Delhi, p. 39.
3. Singh, B. (1995), Current Trends in Human Resource Development, Deep and Deep Publications, New Delhi, p. 16.
4. World Bank (2003), Economic Development in India: Achievements and Challanges, The World Bank, Washington, p. 33.
5. Srinivasa Gowda, M. V. (1995), *Ibid*, p. 55.
6. Govt. of India, (Planning Commission) (2001), *Tenth Five Year Plan*, Vol. III, p. 37.
7. Govt. of India (Planning Commission) (2001), *Ibid*, p. 39.
8. UNDΓ (2005), Human Development Report, 2005, Oxford University Press, pp. 88-97.
9. UNDP (2005), *Ibid*, p. 103.
10. Banerjee, N. (2004), Women, Work and Ideology in Third World, Asia Publishing House, New Delhi, p. 11.
11. Banerjee, N. (2005), *Ibid*, p. 23.
12. Rhoda, R. (2000), "Why Gender? Why Development? Oxford University Press, New Delhi, p. 17.
13 Govt. of India, Ministry of Information and Broadcasting (2006), *Yojna*, October, 2006, p. 7.

SEXUAL HARASSMENT OF WORKING WOMEN– A CRITICAL ANALYSIS

GURPREET PANNU*

INTRODUCTION

With the beginning of modern industrial era and industrial revolution, there was change in the nature of work of women. Women have to go out of the four walls of their houses in order to augment their family income. Women become victims in many spheres i.e. social, economic, political and employment. Physical and mental torture, humiliation, sexual abuse and harassment of working women is as old as history of family life. Historically, sexual harassment is seen as being perpetrated by men in possession of physical, political and economic power against women.[1] It is also seen as an outcome of male dominated society. Women are sexually harassed as sex is a primary tool of oppression and men show their power through harassment.

Now women workers constitute an important component of Indian labour force. An increasing number of women are today compelled to leave the security of their homes and venture out in search of work depending upon the socio-economic status. With the change in the outlook, attitudes and approach towards living, it has now become necessary by and large for the families to supplement their requirements through additional earnings. For this reason, women have recorded impressive gains in employment from 1991 onward as it is clear from economic surveys.[2] As per survey, total number of women employees in 1990 was 36.44 lakhs and it increased to 49.49 lakhs in 2001; there was an increase of 35.81%.[3] Now globalization has accelerated the way for women to enter the field of employment. But other side of picture is that it has led to many evils e.g. gender discrimination, physical and mental harassment and more specifically sexual harassment at work place. According to report of ILO, one-third of women in industrial society are sexually harassed at workplace. Now, it has became a global issue.[4]

According to a survey, 68% of women suffer mental harassment out of which 26% suffer physical harassment.[5] In India, according to the statistics

* *Reader, Department of Law, Punjabi University, Patiala.*

recorded by National Crime Records Bureau, the number of cases recorded on sexual harassment in the year 2001 was 9746, it increased to 10155 in 2002 and again increased to 12325 in 2003. In the year 2004 number of recorded cases on sexual harassment were 10001 and in 2005 it was 9984. There was 0.2% decrease in number of cases in 2005 over 2004.[6]

MEANING OF SEXUAL HARASSMENT

Sexual Harassment is a violation of one's freedom and personal integrity. Sexual harassment refers to a conduct of sexual nature.[7] It occurs in employment establishments. Comprehensive illustrations of sexual harassment are also given by National Commission of Women in India. It states that unwelcome sexual conduct includes eve teasing, unsavoury remarks, jokes that causes or are likely to cause awkwardness or embarrassment, innuendos and taunts, gender-based insults or sexist remarks, unwelcome sexual tone, obnoxious telephone calls, displaying pornographic or other offensive or derogatory pictures, cartoons or pamphlets, touching or brusing against any part of another's body and the like.

In American Employment Law, it is any unwelcome sexual advance or conduct on the job, having the effect of making the workplace intimidating, hostile or offensive. Sexual harassment is considered as a form of illegal discrimination.[8]

According to Lin Farley, sexual harassment is best described as "unsolicited non-reciprocal male behaviour that asserts a woman's sex role over her function as a worker".[9]

According to Somers and Clementson Mohr "sexual harassment may include verbal abuse, sexist remarks regarding women's clothing, of body patting, pinching or brushing up against a woman's body, leering or ogling, demand for sexual favours in return for hiring, promotion or tenure, physical assault, rape."[10]

Catharine MacKinnon defines sexual harassment as "unwanted imposition of sexual requirements in the context of relationship of unequal powers".[11]

Kathleen Gallivan defines sexual harassment as "any type of unwanted sexual or gender-oriented behaviour that has adverse job-related effects"[12]

According to Malaysian Code "sexual harassment includes any unwanted conduct of sexual nature having the effect of verbal, non-verbal, visual, psychological or physical harassment."[13]

Sexual harassment is a sort of sex discrimination that occurs in the workplace. Unwelcome conduct of sexual nature that effects the work environment or leads to adverse job related consequences for victim of harassment.[14]

Our Apex Court has defined sexual harassment to include "such unwelcome sexually determined behaviour (whether directly or by implication) as:

(a) physical contact advances;
(b) demand or request for sexual favours;
(c) sexually-coloured remarks;
(d) showing pornography;
(e) any other unwelcome physical, verbal, non-verbal contact of sexual nature.

Where any of these acts is committed in circumstances whereunder the victim of such conduct has a reasonable apprehension that in relation to the victim's employment or work, whether she is drawing salary or honorarium or voluntary, whether in Government, public or private enterprise, such conduct can be humiliating and may constitute a health and safety problem. Indeed, it is discriminatory, for instance, when the woman has reasonable grounds to believe that her objection would disadvantage her in connection with her employment or work including recruiting or promotion or when it creates a hostile work environment. Adverse consequences might be visited if the victim does not consent to the conduct in question or raises any objection thereto."[15]

The proposed Sexual Harassment of Women at the Workplace (Prevention and Redressal) Bill, 2004 defines sexual harassment to mean "any unwelcome sexually determined conduct whether physical, verbal or non-verbal, including but not limited to sexual advances, demands or requests for sexual favour, molestation, sexually nuances gestures, comments, remarks or jokes either verbal, textual, graphic or electronic."[16]

From the analysis of all definitions it is quite clear that no specific meaning can be assigned to the term sexual harassment because it is a multitude problem having different facets. It is a form of sex discrimination against working person who suffers from it and the society in which she lives. An analysis of all these definitions shows that it is a form of sex discrimination which working women are forced to face due to their feminine character and hence the definition of the phrase sexual harassment can be broad and controversial depending on each individual's opinion of what harassment is.[17] It must be remembered that emphasis of law is on protecting women.

INTERNATIONAL INITIATIVES ON SEXUAL HARASSMENT

The Commission on the Status of Women, a functional Commission of Economic and Social Council, was established in 1946. This Commission meets once in two years in Vienna to examine women's progress towards equality throughout the world. Its function is primarily to prepare recommendations and to make reports to the Economic and Social Council of United Nations. In 1949, the Commission initiated work on the Convention on the Political Rights of Women. The Convention, the first legal instrument dealing exclusively with women's rights was adopted by General Assembly in 1952. Commission has focused on many topics relating to women such as role of women in development, family planning, education and economic rights of women.

The Universal Declaration of Human Rights, adopted on 10 December 1948 set out the general ban on discrimination of any kind, including on the basis of sex. It was followed by two international covenants i.e. Covenant on Civil and Political Rights and Covenant on Economic, Social and Cultural Rights adopted on 16 December 1966 likewise prohibiting discrimination on that basis in general terms.

But the most important step that the General Assembly of UN took was the adoption of Convention on the Elimination of All Forms of Discrimination against Women (CEDAW) on December 18, 1979, laying down the broad definition of discrimination specifically against women that gained worldwide acceptance. Art. 11 of the Convention require states "to take appropriate measures to eliminate discrimination against women in the filed of employment" followed by Art. 22 which states, "equality in employment can be seriously impaired when working women are subjected to gender specific violence such as sexual harassment at the workplace and Art. 24 further requires that "states should include in their reports, information about sexual harassment and on measures to protect women from sexual harassment and other forms of violence or coercion in the workplace." It was followed by General Recommendation No. 19 on violence against women which was adopted by the committee on the Elimination of Discrimination against women in January 1992. Although this Recommendation is not binding on ratifying states but it is important because it further clarifies the term sexual harassment given by CEDAW and to be used by the national courts dealing with claims relating to sexual harassment where the domestic law might be silent or not clear.[18]

International Labour Organization, one of the specialized agencies of the UN has always been in the forefront to highlight the issue of sexual harassment through the adoption of the Discrimination (Employment and Occupation) Convention, 1958 (No. 111). The Committee of Experts on the Application of Conventions and Recommendations lists a number of examples of sexual harassment in employment. The ILO is the only international body to have adopted an instrument containing protection against sexual harassment.

The ILO's concern is also manifested in a number of non-binding instruments; the 1985 International Labour Conference resolution on equal opportunity and equal treatment for men and women in employment, the conclusion of the 1989 ILO Meeting of Experts on Special Protective Measures for Women and Equality of Opportunity and Treatment. The conclusions of the 1992 Tripartite Symposium on Equality of Opportunity and Treatment for Men and Women in Employment in Industrialized Countries referring specifically to sexual harassment as well as the 1991 International Labour Conference resolution concerning ILO action for women workers, requesting the International Labour Office to develop guidelines, training and information materials on issues of specific and major importance to women workers, such as sexual harassment in the workplace.

All these Conventions, Recommendations and Resolutions adopted by the UN and the ILO from time to time make it amply clear that they have been fully conscious of the growing problem of sexual harassment. In fact, through these Conventions and Recommendations, they have laid down the guidelines to be followed by the member-states to tackle the issue of sexual harassment.[19]

INDIAN LAWS

Constitutional Provisions

The Constitution of India, the law of the land and which is considered one of the most progressive Constitutions in the world ensures gender equality by making it a fundamental right. Fundamental Rights are enshrined in Part III of the Constitution of India. It must be borne in mind that when fundamental rights are infringed, the natural basic human rights, inherent in human being are violated. The relevant Articles conferring constitutional rights upon women are:

- *Article 14* equality before law and equal protection of law to every person. It not only prohibits discrimination but also makes various provisions for the protection of women.
- *Article 15(1)* provides that the state shall not discriminate against any citizen on ground only of religion, race, caste, sex, place of birth or any of them.
- *Article 15(3)* empowers the state to make special provision for women namely, "nothing in Article 15 shall prevent the state from making any special provision for women and children."
- *Article 16* guarantees equality of opportunity for all citizens in matters relating to employment or opportunity to any office under the state and forbids discrimination on the grounds only of *inter alia* sex.
- *Article 19* ensures two basic freedoms i.e. freedom of speech and expression [Article 19(1)(a)] and freedom to practice any profession or to carry out any occupation, trade or business [Article 19(1) (g)].
- *Article 21* says, "no person shall be deprived of his life or personal liberty except according to procedure established by law." Women workers have a right to lead a dignified and honourable life with liberty.
- *Article 23* guarantees the right against exploitation. It prohibits traffic in human beings and other similar forms of forced labour and makes contravention of this provision to be an offence punishable under law.
- *Article 32* the right to more to Supreme Court by appropriate proceedings for the enforcement of these rights. Art. 32 is a

fundamental right and provides that Supreme Court shall have power to issue directions or orders, writs for the enforcement of any of the rights conferred by Part III of Constitution.

In addition to these fundamental rights, Part IV of the Constitution which incorporates Directive Principles of State Policy, also ensure dignified life to working women. The important provisions are:

- *Article 39(a)* ensures that the citizens, men and women equally have the right to adequate means of livelihood.
- *Article 39(d)* states that there will be equal pay for equal work for both men and women.
- *Article 39(e)* states that the health and strength of workers, men and women... are not abused.
- *Article 42* ensures that the state shall make provision for securing just and humane condition of work and for maternity relief.
- *Article 51 A(e)* makes it a fundamental duty of every citizen to renounce practices derogatory to the dignity of women.

The effect of Article 51,73, and 253 is to impose international obligation on the state to enact legislation to curb the evil of sexual harassment to uphold fundamental right of gender equality of women.

These are the guidelines to be followed by all the three organs of the state: legislature, executive and judiciary that are committed to make, enforce and interpret law and to combat sexual harassment to women.

Indian Penal Code, 1860[20]

There is no direct legislation dealing with sexual harassment as a crime in India. However, Indian Penal Code contains provisions relating to obscenity and acts that are considered as violating the modesty of a woman, which can be invoked against a person committing sexual harassment.[21] Section 294 makes obscene acts in any public place punihsable.[22] Penal Code prescribes punishment for the offence of assault or use of force on women with intent to insult the modesty of a woman.[23] Eve teasing or sexual teasing of woman is also punishable. It consists of making verbal remarks relating to sex. Under the Delhi Prohibition of Eve Teasing Act, 1988 eve teasing is a non-bailable offence.

Labour Legislations

There are many labour legislations, which protect the right of women workers to ensure equality in employment and to lead a dignified life. Industrial Disputes Act, 1947 provides that it is an unfair labour practice to discharge a person by way of victimization.[24] Thus who is an employee and is unfairly dismissed or denied employment benefits by her employer as a consequence of rejection of sexual advances, the employee can take up matter against the employer. This provision is confined *quid pro quo* sexual harassment. Otherwise sexual harassment does not form part of labour legislations as it is done in some of the developed countries of the world.[25] After Vishaka's case, The Industrial Employment (standing orders) Act, 1946 was amended and sexual harassment has been made misconduct.[26]

JUDICIAL RESPONSE

Law relating to sexual harassment in India was laid down by Supreme Court. In this background, the role of judiciary assumes great importance in dealing with cases of sexual harassment. In the absence of enacted law to provide for effective enforcement of the basic human right of gender equality and guarantee against sexual harassment and abuse, more particularly against sexual harassment at workplace.

In *Vishaka* v. *State of Rajasthan and others*[27] there was a social workers who was brutally gang raped for her crusade against child marriage. Public interest litigation was field and Supreme Court laid down guidelines and norms that should be observed at all workplaces until a law is enacted. While formulating guidelines and norms, the judges had due regard to the international conventions and norms to achieve the object of protection of women workers from sexual harassment and to make their fundamental right meaningful. They clearly perceived the nexus: "In the absence of domestic law occupying the field to formulate effective measures to check the event of sexual harassment of working woman at all workplaces, the contents of international conventions or norms are significant for the purpose of interpretation of the guarantee of gender equality, right to work with human dignity in Arts. 14, 15, 19(1)(g) and 21 of the Constitution and the safeguards against sexual harassment implicit therein. Any international convention not inconsistent with the fundamental rights and in harmony with its spirit must be read into these provisions to enlarge the meaning and content thereof to promote the object of the constitutional guarantee. This is implicit from Article 51(c) and the enabling power of Parliament to enact laws for implementing the international conventions and norms by virtue of Article 253 read with entry 14 of the Union list in Seventh Schedule of the Constitution Article 73 is also relevant.[28]

It was further stated that, "gender equality includes protection from sexual harassment and right to work with dignity, which is a universally recognized basic human right. The common minimum requirements of this right has received global acceptance."

The Apex Court has emphasized that the following guidelines and norms be treated as the law under Article 141 of the Constitution:

Duty of the Employer

It shall be the duty of the employer and other responsible persons in workplaces and other institutions to prevent or deter the commission of acts of sexual harassment and to provide the procedures for the resolution, settlement or prosecution of acts of sexual harassment by taking all steps required.

Appropriate Peventive Steps

All employers or persons in charge of workplace whether in the public or private sector should take appropriate steps to prevent sexual harassment, without generality of this obligation they should take following steps:

(a) Express prohibition of sexual harassment punishment and circulate in appropriate ways.

(b) The Rules/Regulations of Government and Public sector bodies relating to conduct and discipline should include rule/regulations prohibiting sexual harassment and provide for appropriate penalties.

(c) As regards private employees, steps should be taken to include the aforesaid prohibition in the standing order.

Appropriate Work Conditions

Appropriate work conditions should be provided in respect of work and women workers should be ensured that there is no hostile environment towards them at work places and no woman employee should have reasonable grounds to believe that she is disadvantaged in connection with her employment.

Criminal Proceedings

Where such conduct amounts to a specific offence under the Indian Penal Code or under any other law, the employer shall initiate appropriate action in accordance with law by making complaint with the appropriate authority. In particular, it should ensure that victims or witnesses are not victimized or discriminated against while dealing with complaints of sexual harassment. The victims of sexual harassment should have the option to seek transfer of the perpetrator or their own transfer.

Disciplinary action by Employer

When such conduct amounts to misconduct in employment as defined by the relevant service rules, appropriate disciplinary action should be initiated by the employer in accordance with those rules.

Complaint Mechanism in Employer's Organization

Whether or not such conduct constitutes an offence under law or a breach of the service rules, an appropriate complaint mechanism should be created in the employer's organization for redress of the complaint made by the victim. Such complaint mechanism should ensure time-bound treatment of complaints.

Complaints Committee

- The complaint mechanism should be adequate to provide, where necessary, a Complaints Committee, a special counselor or other support services, including the maintenance of confidentiality.
- The Complaints Committee should be headed by a woman and not less than half of its members should be women. Further, to prevent the possibility of any pressure or influence from senior levels, such complaints committee should involve a third party, either NGO or another body who is familiar with the issue of sexual harassment.
- The complaint committee must make an annual report to the government department concerned of the complaints and actions taken by them.

Workers Initiative

Employees should be allowed to raise issue of sexual harassment at worker's meeting and in other appropriate forum and it should be affirmatively discussed in Employer-employee meetings.

To Create Awareness

Awareness of the rights of female employees in this regard should be created in particular by prominently notifying the guidelines (and appropriate legislation when enacted on the subject) in a suitable manner.

Harassment by Third Party

Where sexual harassment occurs as a result of an act or omission by any third party or outsider, the employer and person in-charge will take all steps necessary and reasonable to assist the affected person in terms of support and preventive action.

The Central/State Governments are requested to consider adopting suitable measures including legislation to ensure that the guidelines laid down by this order are also observed by the employers in private sector.

These guidelines will no prejudice any rights available under the Protection of Human Rights Act, 1993. Supreme Court took into account the provisions of the conventions and treaties when interpreting the provisions of constitution and the Beijing Statement of Principles the Independence of the Judiciary, 1995 and the CEDAW to lay down the law of sexual harassment and to achieve gender equality and gender justice within the framework of the constitution. The thrust of decision was that at woman had the right to gender equality, to dignity and honour, to work in an environment free from sexual harassment and abuse.

In *Apparel Export Promotion Council* v. *A.K. Chopra,*[29] sexual harassment was committed by a superior ranking employee against a lower ranking employee. The High Court found that respondent's dismissal was unjustified on the ground that he was only trying to molest the employee and had not actually established physical contact with her. On appeal to Supreme Court, Anand, C. J. held that:

"Any action or gesture, whether directly or by implication, aims at or has the tendency to outrage the modesty of female employee, must fall under the general concept of the definition of sexual harassment the respondent's behaviour did not cease to be outrageous for want of physical contact and the observation made by the high court to the effect that the respondent did not actually molest the victim because he did not establish such contact which are unacceptable. The courts should examine all evidence to determine the genuineness of the complaint and should rely on the evidence of a credible victim. The respondent's conduct offended against morality, decency and victim's modesty. The punishment imposed on respondent was commensurate with the gravity of his objectionable behaviour. Any reduction in punishment is bound to have a demoralizing effect on women employees and is a retrograde step."

In *Shennaz Mudbhatkal* v. *Saudi Arabian Airlines*[30], a high court in India was for the first time contronted with a sexual harassment case. The victim Shehnaz Mudbhatkal was an employee of Saudi Arabian Airlines and the harasser was Station Manager, Abdul Allah Bahrani. The sexual advances started with offers of lunch and dinner and soon the station manager began to ask her intimate questions. She objected to such sexual advances made by him and made a complaint. She was forced to give an apology for her complaint and when she took the matter to higher authorities, her services were terminated. The court decided case in the favour of victim.

Rupan Deol Bajaj v. *K.P.S. Gill and another*[31] involved sexual harassment. The victim was slapped on the bottom by Gill, D.G.P. of Punjab. She complained of indecent behaviour. Mr. Gill was convicted and was fined Rs. 2,50,000/- in lieu of three months rigorous imprisonment.

Another important issue to be considered here is whether monetary compensation could be awarded to victim of sexual harassment. In the case of Vishaka, the court did not specifically rule on this question, yet it seems clear from the decision that compensation could be provided to a victim of sexual harassment. The Supreme Court, High Courts and other Courts in India have power to award damages. The Supreme Court in *Chairman, Railway Board and Other* v. *Mrs. Chandrima Dass and Others,*[32] the employer was vicariously held liable to compensate the victim of a gang rape who was a foreign national, committed by its employees within its premises. In this case compensation of 10 lacs was awarded. Thus, if a woman employee or a stranger is subjected to acts of sexual harassment of grave nature wherein the offender is another employee, the liability of employer can be fixed.

In *K.S. Triveni* v. *Union of India,*[33] the Andhra Pradesh High Court struck down section 66(1) (b) of Factories Act, 1948 as unconstitutional which prohibits the employment of women in night shifts, the issue of sexual harassment assumes all the more importance. Contention of women's forum that women should be allowed to work in nightshifts was upheld. The court issued elaborate guidelines in furtherance to the Vishaka's case.

In this background, the union cabinet decided to lift the ban on women working in night shifts between 7 p.m. to 6 a.m. at factories by ratifying the Protocol of 1990 to ILO Night Work (Women) Convention and amending the Factories Act, 1948. This amendment allowed women to work between 10 p.m. to 6 a.m. can benefit those working in special economics zones, textiles and IT sector (call centers etc.)

Thus higher judiciary of our country has played dynamic role in upholding the dignity and human rights of women as enshrined in the Constitution of India and declared by many international conventions and instruments.

CONCLUSION AND SUGGESTION

The proceeding discussion makes it clear the nature and magnitude of the problem of sexual harassment. Till the day there is no codified law to curb this social menace. There is urgent need to legislate on the topic of sexual harassment. Undoubtly, the Supreme Court's decision in *Vishaka* is an excellent example of judicial law making to fill the lacuna that existed in the law. There is proposed Sexual Harassment of Women at their Workplace, 2005, but that is still in the pipeline. There is need to enforce legislation to curb this evil. The following suggestions are offered:

- The Supreme Court's decision in *Vishaka* was designed to protect only women against sexual harassment. But, actually both men and women are victims of sexual harassment. The law should apply not only to women but also to men. The guidelines issued in *Vishaka* and proposed Bill deals with sexual harassment at workplace only and not anywhere else, but sexual harassment is all-pervasive; it exists in educational institutions, hospitals, courts etc. So new law should not only cover sexual harassment at workplaces but at other related places also.
- Sexual harassment should be declared as a civil wrong and courts should be empowered to award exemplary damages. It can have deterrent effect.
- Usually the victims of sexual harassment are women or girls, so women judges should be included in panel of judges handling the cases of sexual harassment.
- N.G.Os. should come forward to create awareness among working women regarding their rights.
- Physical training should be given to working women to tackel with such situation.
- Human Rights Commission should be authorised to handle such cases.

NOTES AND REFERENCES

1. N.C. Jefferson (1999), *Power and Gender: Issues in Sexual Dominance and Harassment,* McFarland and Co., p. 460.
2. Aruna Goel (edited), 'Violence against Women-issues and Perspectives'–*Sexual Harassment of Working Women: The Legal Approach,* by Ranbir Kaur, p. 171-184 at p. 172.
3. Economic Survey, 2003-04, Ministry of Finance, Govt. of India, p. 55.
4. S.C. Srivastava (2004), *Sexual Harassment of Women at Workplaces: Law and Policy",* *IJIR,* Vol. 39 No. III Jan., p. 364.
5. D. K. Srivastava (1999), *Recognizing Sexual Harassment as a Tort,* Hong-Kong Lawyer (September), p. 38-33.
6. *Crime in India 2005,* National Crime Records Bureau, Ministry of Home Affairs, New Delhi, 2008.
7. D. K. Srivastava and Charu Sharma (2000), Corporate Liability for Sexual Harassment in the Workplaces, *Journal of Corporate Law,* pp. 170-91.
8. *http:/en Wikipedia org./wiki/sexual harassment.*
9. Lin Farley (1978), *Sexual Shake-Dow: The Sexual Harassment on Women on the Job,* New York, McGraw Hill, pp. 14-15.
10. A Somers Patricia and Judith Clemenstton-Mohr: *Sexual Extornition in the Workplace, the Personal Administrator,* (April 1970), p. 23.
11. Catharine MacKinnon (1979), *Sexual Harassment of Working Women,* New Haven, Yale University, Press, p. 32.
12. Kathleen Gallivan, *Sexual Harassment of after Janzon V. Play: The Transformation Possibilities,* Hall, Toronto Fac. L. Rev., p. 27, 29.
13. Article 4 of Malysian Code Practice on the Prevention and Eradication of Sexual Harassment in the Workplace, 1999.
14. Lina Gonsalves (2001), Women and Human Rights, A.P.H. Publishing Corporation, p. 73.
15. *Vishaka* v. *State of Rajasthan,* AIR 1997, SC 3011 at p. 3016.
16. Section 2 (o).
17. *Supra note* 8.
18. *Supra note* 2, p. 175.
19. *Ibid.*
20. Act no. 45 of 1860.
21. C. Raj Kumar and K. Chockalingam (Edited), "Human Rights, Justice and Constitutional Empowerment": *Sexual Harassment and Violence against Women in India: Constitutional and Legal Perspectives* by D.K. Srivastava, Oxford University Press, 2007, p. 486-513 at p. 493.
22. Section 294, Whoever, to the annoyance of others–(a) does any obscene act in a public place, or (b) sings, recites or utters any obscene songs, ballad or words, in or near any public place, shall be punished with imprisonment of either description for a term which may extend to three months, or with fine, or with both.

23. Section 354, Whoever assaults or uses criminal force to any woman intending to outrage or knowing it to be likely that he will thereby outrage her modesty shall be punished with imprisonment of either description for a term which may extend to two years, or with fine, or with both.

    Section 509, Whoever, intending to insult the modesty of a woman, utters any word, makes any sound or gesture, or exhibits any object, intending that such word or sound shall be heard, or that such gesture of object shall be seen by such woman, or intrudes upon the privacy of such woman, shall be punished with simple imprisonment for a term which may extend to one year, or with the fine for with both.

24. Schedule 5 Rule 5 (a) of Industrial Disputes Act, 1948.

25. In Canada, France, New Zealand, Spain, Belgium etc. labour laws explicitly prohibit sexual harassment.

26. Rue 17 (1), Industrial Employment: (S.O.) Central Rules, 1946 framed under the IE (SO) Act provides that disciplinary action may be taken *inter alia* in cases of sexual harassment which includes such unwelcome sexual determined behaviour as (i) physical contact and advances or (ii) a demand or request for sexual favour; or (iii) sexually coloured remarks (iv) showing pornography or (v) any other unwelcome physical, verbal or non-verbal conduct of sexual nature.

27. AIR 1997 SC 3011.

28. *Ibid.*, para 7, p. 3013-14.

29. AIR 1999 SC 625.

30. *http://www. indianetpress.com/ie/daily/19881126/33050884p.html.*

31. (1995) 6 SCC 194.

32. AIR 2000 SC 988.

33. 2002 Lab CAP 1714.

SARVA SHIKSHA ABHIYAN AND GENDER EQUALITY IN EDUCATION: REACHING THE UNREACHED

M. SUGIRTHA* & K. MADESWARAN**

INTRODUCTION

Education can be viewed as a process of expanding human capacities to contribute to the making of a just and compassionate society. Education is the first step towards empowerment and the most crucial factor in overall development of the individual and an effective instrument for social and economic development and national integration. It also helps one free from ignorance, exploitation and poverty.

Ever since civilization came into existence, women have been deprived of their right to equality in almost every field, including education, the most vital element of overall human development. In a male dominated society, the subordination of women and discrimination on the basis of gender prevails irrespective of country, culture, society and civilization. While causes and consequences may vary from country to country, discrimination against women is widespread and deep rooted. A developing country like India can ill afford if half of the human capital remains unutilized thereby being a liability and not an asset for the nation. This paper is an effort to capture the emerging picture with respect to girls' and women's education in India and especially in Tamilnadu.

INTERNATIONAL EFFORTS ON GENDER EQUALITY IN EDUCATION

The *World Declaration on Education For All*, Jomtien 1990 was an important milestone in the march towards universal elementary education and girls' and women's access to basic education. The rights perspective on educational access and equality got a tremendous boost during the International Conference on Population and Development, Cairo 1994. *Everyone has a right to education, which*

* *Lecturer (S.S), Political Science Wing, DDE, Annamalai University, Annamalainagar, Chidambaram, Tamilnadu.*

* *Lecturer, Political Science Wing, DDE, Annamalai University, Annamalainagar, Chidambaram, Tamilnadu.*

shall be directed to the full development of human resources, and human dignity and potential, with particular attention to women and the girl child. Education should be designed to strengthen respect for human rights and fundamental freedoms, including those related to population and development[1].

The very fact that a population conference forced the international community to look into the inter-linkages between population, poverty, gender inequality and development, was a major departure from the past. Women's and girls' education was placed centre stage in the struggle for human development and social justice in the Copenhagen declaration on social development in 1995. *We affirm that, in both economic and social terms, the most productive policies and investments are those that empower people to maximise their capacities, resources and opportunities.* (Paragraph 7 of the Copenhagen declaration, 1995). The Fourth World Conference on Women, Beijing 1995, reaffirmed the commitments made by governments and called upon the international community to intensify efforts. Four important world conferences, one after another, bombarded our world with messages of equality, empowerment, human rights and universal access to the tools of knowledge– i.e. education.

NATIONAL SCENARIO

Gender equality has been a key objective of educational policy in India for over six decades. The Government of India has expressed a strong commitment towards Education for All. At the time of independence, India inherited an educational system which was not only quantitatively small but was also characterized by regional, gender, caste and structural imbalances.

At the school level, free education provided by the State and supported by incentives such as free textbooks, stationery, school uniforms and mid-day meals, has led to increased school attendance. Special schemes such as lumpsum grant to students and parents, mid-day meals, free text books, pre-matric hostels, and non-formal education (NFE) centres have helped in raising the enrolment of girl students considerably. There has been a tremendous growth in all areas of education system, be it expansion of institutions, infrastructural facilities, expenditure or quality of education.

The National Policy of Education provides that "the education of girls should receive emphasis not only on ground of social justice but also because it accelerates social transformation". In 1976, through the 42nd Constitutional amendment, education was incorporated in the Concurrent List and it became a joint responsibility of both Centre and the State[2].

Table 1 exhibits that female literacy is increasing gradually. But compared to male literacy, it is much low. Low weightage to girl students, their high dropout rate, poverty and present social system can be attributed for this.

Table 1
Litracy Rates (1951-2001 Census)

(In percentage)

Census year	*Persons*	*Males*	*Females*	*Male-Female*
1951*	18.3	27.2	8.9	18.3
1961*	28.3	40.4	15.4	25.1
1971*	34.5	46.0	22.0	24.0
1981**	43.6	56.4	29.8	26.6
1991**	52.2	64.1	39.3	24.8
2001**	64.8	75.3	53.7	21.6

Source: Census India 2001.
*- Aged 5+, **Aged 7+

FACTORS RESPONSIBLE FOR LOW LITERACY LEVEL AMONG FEMALES

Historically, a variety of factors have been found to be responsible for poor female literacy rate[3], viz.,

- Gender based inequality
- Social discrimination and economic exploitation
- Occupation of girl child in domestic chores
- Low enrolment of girls in schools

While these are certainly true, there are numerous other factors responsible for the low levels of literacy among females,

- *Inadequate School Facilities:* Many states do not have enough classrooms to accommodate all school-age children. And the classrooms that are available often lack basic necessities such as sanitary facilities and water.
- *Lack of Qualified Female Teachers:* Girls are more likely to attend schools if they have female teachers. Girls are more comfortable and more vocal with lady teachers, thus actively focusing and participating in the learning process. Also, parents-especially in rural areas-are hesitant to send their girls to schools that have only male teachers. Nearly all committees and commissions that have looked into illiteracy have recommended increased recruitment of women teachers.
- *Lack of Transport Facilities:* Particularly in rural areas, transportation is needed for girls to attend middle and secondary schools, which are often far away from their homes. Primary education is often accessible much closer, but secondary education facilities assume that children will drop out as they age, and therefore fewer schools are established to cater to older children. Necessarily, therefore, these schools tend to be inaccessibly far away from many school-age girls.

- *Lack of Hostel Facilities for Girls:* Many girls desirous of pursuing education above middle level, facilities for which are available away from their homes, cannot avail themselves of these facilities due to lack of hostel arrangements. Girls, particularly those belonging to Scheduled Castes and Scheduled Tribes would continue their education at middle and above levels if they could find free or inexpensive residential facilities nearer the educational institution.
- *Fear of Sexual Harassment:* Parents often complain about insecurity for girls attending schools. Instances of abduction, rape and molestation of girls dampen the enthusiasm of parents and girl students in pursuing education beyond a certain age; thereafter they remain bound to their homes.

These factors combine to produce unattractive environments in which girls must run the gauntlet of difficulties to remain in school, as a result of which their learning is severely compromised even if they do remain. A discriminatory attitude builds up among teachers and the greater society that witnesses girls dropping out in large numbers. In India, a survey shows that the dropout rates of girls, specially from the marginalized sections of society and the rural areas continues to be grim. 9 out of every 10 girls enrolled in school do not complete schooling, and only 1 out of every 100 girls enrolled in class 1 reaches class 12 in rural areas[4].

In order to overcome these hurdles and bring out the girls to mainstream of education, the Lok Sabha unanimously passed 93rd Constitution Amendment bill after 55 years providing right to education as a guaranteed right. The 93rd Constitutional Amendment thus, gives the legally enforceable right to free elementary education to children between 6 and 14 year of age.

SARVA SHIKSHA ABHIYAN

Apart from that, the Indian Government launched a programme called Sarva Shiksha Abhiyan(SSA) in November, 2000. Sarva Shiksha Abhiyan is an effort to universalise elementary education by community-ownership of the school system. It is a response to the demand for quality basic education all over the country. The SSA programme is also an attempt to provide an opportunity for improving human capabilities to all children, through provision of community-owned quality education in a mission mode.

The programme covers the entire country with a special focus on educational needs of girls, scheduled castes and scheduled tribes and other children in difficult circumstances. The broad aim of Sarva Shiksha Abhiyan is to provide useful and relevant elementary education to all children in the 6 to 14 age group by 2010 and to bridge social, regional and gender gaps, with the active participation of the community in the management of schools.

The following are the specific objectives of SSA[5]:

- All children in School, Education Guarantee Centre, Alternate School or 'Back-to-School' camp by 2005.
- Bridge all gender and social category gaps at primary stage by 2007 and at elementary education level by 2010.
- Universal retention by 2010.
- Focus on elementary education of satisfactory quality with emphasis on education for life.

The following are some of the norms for interventions under SSA[6]:

- One teacher for every 40 children in Primary and upper primary.
- At least two teachers in a Primary school.
- One teacher for every class in the upper primary.
- Within one Kilometre of every habitation.
- Provision for opening of new schools as per State norms or for setting up EGS like schools in unserved habitations.
- As per requirement based on the number of children completing primary education, up to a ceiling of one upper primary school/section for every two primary schools.
- A room for every teacher in Primary & upper Primary, with the provision that there would be two class rooms with verandah to every Primary school with at least two teachers.
- A room for Head-Master in upper Primary school/section.
- To all girls/SC/ST children at primary & upper primary level within an upper ceiling of Rs. 150/- per child.
- State to continue to fund free textbooks being currently provided from the State Plans.
- As per norms already approved under Education Guarantee Scheme & Alternative and Innovative Education, providing for the following kind of interventions.
- Setting up Education Guarantee Centres in unserved habitations.
- Setting up other alternative schooling models.
- Bridge Courses, remedial courses, Back-to-School Camps with a focus on mainstreaming out of school children into regular schools.

Sarva Shiksha Abhiyan takes note of the fact that provision of elementary education is largely made by the government and government aided schools. There are also private unaided schools in many parts of the country that provide elementary education. Poorer households are not able to afford the fees charged in private schools in many parts of the country. There are also private schools that charge relatively modest fees and where poorer children are also attending.

Some of these schools are marked by poor infrastructure and low paid teachers. While encouraging all efforts at equity and 'access to all' in well-endowed private unaided schools, efforts to explore areas of public-private partnership will also be made. Government, Local Body, and government aided schools would be covered under the Sarva Shiksha Abhiyan, as is the practice under the Mid Day Meal scheme. In case private sector wishes to improve the functioning of a government, local body or a private aided school, efforts to develop a partnership would be made within the broad parameters of State policy in this regard.

The financial assistance under the programme of Sarva Shiksha Abhiyan was on a 85:15 sharing arrangement during the IX Plan. During the X Plan, SSA has a funding pattern of 75:25 between the Centre and the States, During XI Plan, the funding pattern between Centre and States/UTs is 50:50. SSA was partially funded to the tune of Rs. 4700 crores from 2003-04 to 2006-07 by the World Bank, European Commission and UK.

The implementation of SSA since its inception has made significant achievements in the field of education. Special emphasis was laid to ensure inclusion of all out-of-school children in the field of education. The focus has been on improving the existing infrastructure of regular schools as well as on alternate strategies for mainstreaming children who have been left out of the schooling process due to various reasons. As a result, the number of out-of-school children declined from 320 lakh in 2001 to 95 lakh as on October 2005. Towards the objectives of improving infrastructure, 1,17,677 new schools have been opened against the approval of 1,20,661 schools. Likewise, 3,86,458 teachers have been appointed till March 31, 2005, against the sanctioned limit of 5,96,245 teachers to ensure proper pupil-teacher ratios. Two independent survey shows that 93 per cent of the children in the age group of 6-14 years are in schools. Recognizing its good performance, outlay for SSA has been increased from Rs. 7,156 crore to Rs. 10,041 crore in 2006-07[7].

TOWARDS ACHIEVING GENDER EQUALITY IN EDUCATION: SSA IN TAMILNADU

As per the Census 2001, the total Population of Tamilnadu is *6,24,05,679* comprising *3,14,00,909* male and *3,10,04,770* female members. The urban population is 2,74,83,998 and that of the rural is 3,49,21,681.

The school educational structure in Tamilnadu has four levels namely, Primary, Upper Primary, Secondary and Higher Secondary. The Primary comprises I to V classes, Upper Primary VI to VIII classes, Secondary IX and X classes and Higher Secondary XI and XII standards[8].

It is evident from Table 2 that though the literacy rate has been increasing over the years, the male-female gap in literacy rate has not decreased. In order to bridge the gender gap in education, the government of Tamilnadu is taking arduous efforts to implement the SSA programme effectively in the State.

Table 2
Literacy Rate Trend-Tamil Nadu Literacy Rate (1901 to 2001)

	Tamil Nadu Literacy (in percentage)		
Year	*Male*	*Female*	*Person*
1901	14.10	1.00	7.60
1911	17.10	1.50	9.20
1921	18.60	2.40	10.40
1931	20.00	2.90	11.30
1941	25.60	6.90	16.20
1951	31.70	10.10	20.80
1961	51.59	21.06	36.39
1971	59.54	30.92	45.40
1981	68.05	40.43	54.39
1991	73.05	51.33	62.66
2001	82.33	64.55	73.47

Source: A Report of Department of Education, Tamilnadu.

SSA PLAN FORMULATION IN TAMIL NADU[9]

In Tamilnadu, the District Elementary Education Plan (DEEP) under SSA Mission is prepared in a decentralized and participatory manner. The core planning teams at Village/school, Block, District and State levels are in place. As envisaged in the SSA framework, the 'bottom-up' approach of planning has been adopted to analyse the problems and issues and to address them appropriately.

The State Core Planning Team takes care of planning for urban areas as well. The State core planning team consists of Director of School Education, Director of Elementary Education, Director, Teacher Education, Research & Training, Joint Directors (SSA), Consultants in Finance and Planning and Academic Coordinators. The District Core Planning team comprises District Programme Co-ordinator (DPC)/Chief Educational Officer (CEO), District Educational Officers (DEO), Additional District Programme Co-ordinator/ District Elementary Educational Officer (DEEO), Assistant District Programme Co-ordinator (ADPC), Statistical Officer (SO), DIET Principal/ faculty member (Planning), two Block Resource Centre Supervisors (BRCS), two Assistant Elementary Education Officers (AEEO), two Block Resource Teacher Educators (BRTEs) and inter-departmental representatives.

The Block-level Planning Team consists of Block Resource Centre Supervisor, Block Development Officer (BDO), Block Resource Teacher Educators (BRTEs), Assistant Elementary Education Officer(s), Headmaster(s) and Teachers. The School-level Core Planning Team comprises Headmaster, President/Ward Member, Teachers, Parents and Women Self Help Group Members.

The Programme is implemented through various Project Management and Institutional Structures viz., Village Education Committees (VECs)/Parent

Teacher Associations (PTAs), Cluster Resource Centres (CRCs), Block Resource Centres (BRCs), District Project Offices (DPOs) and State Project Office (SPO).

In Tamilnadu, there are 51,777 schools, including EGS centres (all categories). They consist of 33,909 Primary schools, 8,552 Middle Schools (Upper Primary Schools), 4,436 High schools and 4,632 Higher Secondary Schools. There are 247 EGS centres functioning in all Districts[10].

During 2001-2002, 452 Primary Schools were opened and 197 Primary Schools were upgraded into Upper Primary Schools, and in 2002-2003, 304 Primary Schools were opened and 479 Primary Schools were upgraded into Upper Primary Schools. During 2003-2004, 356 Primary Schools were opened and 399 Primary Schools were upgraded into Upper Primary Schools and in 2004-2005, 1,031 Primary schools have been upgraded into Upper Primary schools. During 2005-2006, 162 Primary Schools have been opened and 684 Primary Schools have been upgraded into Upper Primary Schools. During 2006-2007, 126 Primary Schools have been opened and 234 Primary Schools have been upgraded into Upper Primary Schools.

Table 3
Tamilnadu-Teachers in Primary Schools *(Management-wise)*

Government Schools			*Private Aided*			*Private Unaided*			*Total Teachers*		
Male	*Female*	*Total*	*Male*	*Female*	*Total*	*Male*	*Female*	*Total*	*Male*	*Female*	*Total*
19198	55898	75096	5908	22851	28759	3020	30352	33372	28126	109101	137227

Source: DISE 2006.

Regarding the number of teachers, there are 1,37,227 teachers serving in Primary schools in Tamilnadu. As many as 75,096 teachers work in Government Primary Schools comprising 19,198 male and 55,898 female teachers. There are 28,759 teachers working in Private aided schools and 33,372 teachers working in Private unaided schools. Of significance is the fact that there are *more women than men among the teachers in Elementary Education. Women Teachers make up nearly three-fourths of the total number of teachers constituting 73.95%*.

Table 4
Teachers–Upper Primary Schools/Upper Primary Classes in High Schools and Higher Secondary Schools *(Management-wise)*

Government Schools			*Private Aided*			*Private Unaided*			*Total Teachers*		
Male	*Female*	*Total*	*Male*	*Female*	*Total*	*Male*	*Female*	*Total*	*Male*	*Female*	*Total*
17372	44344	61716	10407	24417	34824	2355	8967	11322	30134	77728	107862

Source: DISE 2006.

At Upper Primary Level, there are 1,07,862 teachers working either in Upper Primary Schools or in Upper Primary Classes in High School and Higher Secondary Schools. They consist of 30,134 male and 77,728 female teachers.

Around 61,716 teachers work in Government schools, comprising 17,372 male and 44,344 female teachers. There are 34,824 teachers working in Private aided schools and 11,322 teachers serving in Private unaided schools. At Upper Primary level also, *more than two-thirds of the teachers are women with their percentage as high as 67.6%*

There is a total of 1,04,45,841 elementary school-age children in the State of Tamilnadu, who are possibly comprise 66,65,309 children in the age-group of 6-11 years and 37,80,531 children in the age group of 11-14 years.

As per the Household Survey conducted in 2001, the total number of out-of-school children in 6-14 age group was 5.74 lakh, which was the target for the year 2002-2003. The target and achievement in respect of out-of-school children from 2002-2003 to 2006-2007 are presented in the Table 5 that follow.

Table 5
Out-of-School Children Target & Achievement (2002-2003 & 2007-2008)

	Target and Achievement		
Year	*Target*	*Achievement*	*Percentage*
2002-03	574069	108000	18.81
2003-04	466069	255144	54.74
2004-05	279458	201007	71.93
2005-06	169262	116918	69.08
2006-07	111989	97296	86.88
2007-08	103261	84326	81.66

Source: Monthly Review Report.

Enrolling and mainstreaming *Out-of-school children* has been a major challenge for the State. This is the typical 'last-mile' problem: all those who could be enrolled have been enrolled without much effort; the hardest to enrol are those in remote pockets and scattered habitations reaching whom is a stupendous task. However, thanks to the concerted efforts and various interventions, as many as, 1,16,918 children have been enrolled and mainstreamed against the target of 1,69,262 children during 2005-2006.

With the objective of educating girls since literacy have a direct impact on empowerment of women, special strategies have been adopted.

GIRLS EDUCATION

Objectives of Girls Education

- Educating Girls is imperative to achieve the goal of Universal Education.
- Girls Education and Literacy have a direct impact on empowerment of women.
- To achieve 100% NER (Net Enrolment Ratio) among girls and to retain the girls already enrolled in schools.

Activities under Girls Education

1. Vocational Training–for upper primary girls.
2. Remedial Coaching–for upper primary girls.
3. Life Skills Training–for upper primary girls.
4. English Communication skills Development Training–for upper primary girls.

Table 6
Girls Education–Beneficiaries 2002-03 to 2007-08

Year	*Vocation training*	*Remedial Coaching*	*Life skill training*	*English Communication skills Development Training*
2002-03	33530	0	0	0
2003-04	444743	0	0	0
2004-05	1011153	0	100	0
2005-06	750817	0	6155	0
2006-07	29000	116000	34800	0
2007-08	340077	0	35879	119951

Source: Monthly Review Reports.

During 2002–03, 33530 children were covered under vocational training and during 2003-04, 4,44,743 girls were given vocational training. During 2004-05, as many as 10,11,153 girls were given vocational training and 100 Girls were covered under Life skills training. During 2005-06, 7,50,817 girls were given vocational training and 6,155 Girls were covered under Life skills training and during (2006-07), 29,000 girls were given vocational training and 34800 Girls were covered under Life skills training. During 2007-08, 340077 girls were given vocational training and 35879 Girls were covered under Life skills training. 119951 girls were given English Communication skills Development Training.

Thus, it is evident from the above discussion that the Sarva Shiksha Abhiyan (SSA) programme has been achieving its goal by reaching the unreached in the field of education.

CONCLUSION

Access to information and literacy became part of women's attempt to redistribute power, and education got infused with or broadened its objectives to one that would:

- Enhance the self-image of women,
- Encourage women's active participation in the process of change.
- Build collective and alternative visions of their environment.
- Question injustice and inequality.
- Reduce household drudgery.

- Help women to assert themselves and
- Modernize policies.

The lamp of knowledge must be lit inside every child of India and this should be done fast. As a very popular mantra says,

> *"From illusion lead us to enlightenment From Darkness unto Light From death to immortality"*

The light, which illuminates the truth, which wipes out darkness, brings enlightenment and immortality, comes through knowledge. We owe it to ourselves to give this knowledge to our girls.

NOTES AND REFERENCES

1. *Agenda for Action*, International Conference on Population and Development, 1994, p.10.
2. D. D. Basu (1997), *Introduction to the Constitution of India*, New Delhi, Prentice-Hall of India Pvt. Ltd., p.431.
3. *A Report of Government of India*, Ministry of Information & Broadcasting, 1996, p. 79.
4. Gursharan Singh Kainth (2006), "A Mission Approach to Sarva Shiksha Abhiyan", *Economic and Political Weekly*, July, p. 3288.
5. *http://www.ssa.nic.in* accessed on 12.11.2008.
6. *Ibid.*,
7. *Ibid.*,
8. *www.tngov.nic.in* accessed on 23.10.2008.
9. *www. tnssa.nic.in* accessed on 3.10.2008.
10. *A Report of District Information Source of Education*, Tamilnadu.

THE LEGAL PROCEDURES OF MARRIAGE AND DIVORCE AMONG THE MUSLIMS BETWEEN BANGLADESH AND INDIA: A COMPARATIVE ANALYSIS

Neaz Ahmed*

INTRODUCTION

Marriage and divorce are two legal concepts, which exist in almost all societies in the world. Indeed, no country in the world is found without these two institutions, irrespective of religion, caste etc. Bangladesh and India are not exceptional though the forms of marriage and divorce and their procedures may differ from one religious community to another. Marriage is a legal relationship between a man and woman. This relationship is based on contract mostly among Muslim and Christian communities. Among Hindus, marriage is a sacramental bond, though legal aspects of marriage cannot be ignored from them. Although far more than a contract from religious, cultural, biological, psychological and philosophical perspectives, marriage is also a contract.[1] The man promises that he will be a husband, the woman that she will be a wife. Each promises that whatever changes are wrought by the winds of time they will continue to perform their respective duties in a spirit of loving, honouring and cherishing for the remainder of their lives. In reliance on these assurances, each spouse invests in this marriage, thereby sacrificing current and future love invests and other life choices.[2] Some might object to the characterization of marriage as a contract. They observe that marriage seems more like status than contract. That is, it is the state defines and specifies most of the explicit rights, duties and privileges of marriage rather than the parties.[3] From physiological point of view, marriage is a permanent form of monogamous erotic relationship.

As such, marriage represents a distinct advance ethically; it is also evolutionary in as far as, it gives the fullest opportunity for the primitive ages, which are initially purely self-regarding and self-centered, to extend themselves in action and consciousness towards altruistic object i.e. the preservation and

* *Associate professor, Department of Social Work, Shahjalal University of Science and Technology, Sylhet, Bangladesh, Email: neazahmed-2002@yahoomail.com*

welfare of other persons.[4] Sexual urges cannot be ignored from marriage. It is one of the marital rights and duties. Like marriage, divorce is a socially sanctioned arrangement whereby marriage is formally terminated and the family group dissolved.[5] It is also a universal phenomenon. Divorce is practiced in most societies but varies in the conditions that must be met, the sanctions it implies, the frequency with which it is used, procedure and ceremonies that legalize it. In legal languages, it might appear as a simple phenomenon, but in practical life, its implications are massive. Divorce represents the end of the hopes that two people had for each other; it is certificate that their relationship failed.[6] It is truly a complete turn from the way of life the couple had so far.[7] In the psychological literature through the 1950s, divorce was most often attributed to pre-existing psychological disorder.[8] The implication of this approach is that divorce happens only to rich not those who are well or who get adequate help. But the recent trend is different. Regarding the personal matters of marriage and divorce, among Muslims in Bangladesh and India, same laws are not followed although both the country posses' mostly *sunni* faith. A comparative analysis has been given in this paper considering the existing laws of marriage and divorce that exit in Bangladesh and India.

INSTITUTION OF MARRIAGE

In every known human society, some form of the institution of marriage exists, fulfilling the basic needs of society and of the individual in that society. Marriage provides the formal bases for stable heterosexual relations and for the formation of nuclear families. In addition, marriage institutions therefore aids the fulfillment of many basic individual needs (besides sex). In short, the stability and continuity of the social order and the need satisfaction and achievements of individuals depend on the marital institution.[9] Marriage is an ancient sustainable social institution. Whenever, we look at the history or the contemporary world, whether at civilized people or the most primitive, we find that social life is molded by a large social institution.[10] Institution like marriage existed from the beginning of civilized society, but within this institution, certain changes in marriage take places in terms of its forms, nature and customs.[11] In western societies, marriage is occurring later and less often, divorce has become more common as having families with only one parent (usually the mother). Sex without marriage is rampant and problems of marital life are more frequent than other countries. Through Asia, marriage behavior is also changing. Young people are waiting later to marry, couples are having fewer children and more married women are working outside the home. There are some challenges in marriage like non-interaction, incompatibilities, feminine intellectuality, repugnance and early motherhood, the problem of relatives, suspiciousness etc.[12]

Islam as the basis of society recognizes marriage. It is universal. Islam regards it (marriage) as a most sacred institution and makes it incumbent on all Muslim, unless prevented by valid physical or economic incapability to lead a married life.[13] Marriage is an important social institution both amongst Bangladesh and Indian Muslims. It is one amongst the number of powerful institutions, which cut across class distinctions, to shape rules and status of women in general. Parents usually select spouses' for their children, although men frequently exercise some influencs over the choice of their spouses. Marriage is generally made between families of similar social status although a woman might properly marry a man of somewhat higher socio-economic status. Financial and social status of groom may consider for getting prospective bride in all societies in Bangladesh.[14] There are three main features in the traditional form of marriage. They are (a) the proposal of marriage is initiated by the groom's party; (b) the marriage usually takes place in the bride's home (c) marriages are arranged by the parents, other relatives, friends or acquaintance of the party concerned.[15] It is a huge gathering in both the countries among Muslims. There are many phases of marriage festival like, engagement, marriage feast, walima etc. In fact, this social institution is a great institution cutting across the educational background, social status etc.

THE MUSLIM MARRIAGE BETWEEN BANGLADESH AND INDIA

Among *Mussalmans* conjugal relation begins with the contract of marriage, which is a sacred religious institution. The first principle on which this institution based on the free consent of man and woman who has arrived at the age of puberty is as freer as man. No marriage can take place without the presence of the witnesses.[16] Muslim marriage is known as *nikah.* It has been defined in Islam as a contract for the legalization of intercourse and the procreation of children.[17] There is a general debate about whether a Muslim marriage is a sacrament or a civil contract. Perhaps, it would be most appropriate to state that Muslim marriage is a combination of both contract and sacrament. According to Islamic law, a Muslim marriage is a contract and not a sacrament. The institution of marriage, has three aspects says Fyzee.[18] They are legal, social and religious. From the legal point of view, Muslim marriage is a contract. However, as far as social and religious aspects are concerned, it is a sacrament. It follows that it must be made between parties who are of sound mind. As in all contracts a formal proposal has to be made or on behalf of one of the parties to the marriage. It is essential to the validity of a marriage under the *Muhammadean* law that the words of proposal and acceptance must be uttered by the contracting parties or their agents in each others' presence and hearing and in the presence and hearing of two males or one male or two females witnesses who must be sound/sane and adult Muslims and who were transaction must be completed at one meeting.[19] A proposal made at one meeting and acceptance made at another meeting does not constitute a valid marriage.[20]

The laws relating to the personal matters like marriage, divorce, inheritance etc are applicable among Muslims in India are Muslim Personal Law (*Shariat*) Application Act 1937, The Dissolution of Muslim Marriage Act 1939, The Child Marriage Restraint Act 1929, etc. except the state of Jammu and Kashmir. For the people of Jammu and Kashmir "The Jammu and Kashmir Muslim Marriages Registration Act 1981" is applicable. It says, every marriage contracted between Muslims after the commencement of this act, shall be registered as hereinafter provided within thirty days after the conclusion of the *nikah* Ceremony.[21] Moreover, a Muslim is governed by his personal law of marriage and divorce, unless he has been or his marriage has been registered under the special marriage act (The Special Marriage Act 1954).[22] This personal law, which forms part of the compendium known as *Muhammadean* law is uncodified law derived from the Quran and various judicial decisions.[23] In addition, disputes related to such matters usually settled by All India Muslim Personal Law Board and their decisions are to some extent final. The board established Islamic Courts in all states of the country and mobile Islamic courts for rural areas to settle the disputes.[24]

In Bangladesh, regarding family matters, The Muslim Family Law Ordinance 1961 is applicable apart from other laws. Muslim marriage must be registered otherwise it will be a punishable offence. There is a *nikahnama* and both the parties must fill it up. However, in India, among Muslims, for the all states, there is no common *nikahnama*. Marriage is not registered at all though law says that it is a contract. This contract is not made written. A model *nikhnama*, which, some Islamic scholars and women's right activities have drafted, is meant to make every Muslim aware of these stipulations.[25] However, such initiative has not been made so far.

Neither writing nor any religious ceremony is necessary to the validity of marriage[26]. In India, after the enactment of *Kazi*'s Act, then for Madras Province, the Bengal legislature had erected the *Muhammadean* Marriages and Divorces Registration Act 1876. It was a law providing the facility of voluntary registration of Marriages and Divorce with registrars appointed by the province Government.[27] The act does not impose a legal duty upon any person to register a marriage or divorce. It provisions are wholly for the benefit of the persons concerned which they may or may not avail. The act also makes it clear that non-registration of a marriage or divorce, which is otherwise valid under Muslim law, shall not invalidate it in any sense.[28]

Age is an important aspect of marriage. No particular age has been specified in the Islamic law; in fact, with the difference of climate conditions, there would be differences as to the marriageable age in different countries. However, the Holy Quran does speak of an age of marriage which it identifies with the age of majority "And test the orphans until they (the age of) marriage (*nikah*); then if you find in them maturity of intellect, make over to them their property, and do not consume it extravagantly and hastily, anticipating their attaining to full age" (4:6). Thus, it will be seen that the age of marriage and the age of maturity of intellect are identified with full age or the age of majority. A man or a woman who has not attained to puberty is unable to decide whether he or she will like or dislike a certain woman or man as wife or husband.[29]

In Bangladesh, there is a specific age of marriage for boys and girls. These are 18 years for girls and 21 for boys. The Government of India has enacted several laws to increase the age at marriage. The first Child Marriage Restraint Act was passed in September 1929, and was introduced with effect from April 1930. It prescribed the minimum age of marriage as 14 years for girls and 18 years for boys. In March 1978, by a fresh legislation on the subject (Child Marriage Restraint Amendment Act) the Indian Government raised the minimum age at marriage for girls and boys to 18 and 21 years respectively.[30] Regarding the age at marriage, Bangladesh and India follows the same age.

A conclusion, which is arrived from the procedures of marriage in Bangladesh and India, is that there are some similarities between two countries. Marriage institution and festival of marriage are equally existed in both the countries. In India Muslim, marriage is called contract but in Bangladesh, it is regarded as a civil contract. Since Muslim marriage is a civil contract in Bangladesh, registration of marriage is mandatory but marriage is a contract in Indian Muslims, so registration is not so mandatory. No formal *nikahnama* essential in marriage contract in India but Bangladesh has formal *nikahnama* and also marriage registrars. However, other matters like acceptance and proposal, witnesses of marriage existed in both the countries. It can be said that India enjoys *shariat* and *Muhammadean* law, which, is based on entirely *Quran* and *Hadith*. However, Bangladesh may not follow directly *shariat* law but laws existed in Bangladesh among Muslims are based on Islamic laws. It has only made some good provisions like registration of marriage and divorce, which is appreciated, by many scholars and conscious persons.

INSTITUTION OF DIVORCE

Divorce is an institution, which gives us systematic institutionalized framework. It follows certain procedure to get it proper shape. Any kind of institution gives some norms, rules and regulations. Divorce is not exceptional from them. As an institution, divorce trends to reflect the predominant value of a given culture. If this is a sociological fact, it is not surprising that our own matrimonial institutions change, adapt and proliferate according to the value of a given time and place.[31] The procedure of divorce implies that it is an institution. Without institutional framework, none can obtain divorce. The family law of respective religions gives certain rules and provisions settlings the divorce cases. It is a complete institution though this institution is changing due to changing society. Indeed, divorce is the way of institution to defuse our problem and take a harmonious family life. In that sense, it is a perfect positive social institution, but its consequences are more than its advantages.

THE MUSLIM DIVORCE BETWEEN BANGLADESH AND INDIA

As marriage links together man and woman and makes them sharers in the happiness of their lives, so death and divorce (whether availed by the man or wife) cuts as under the ties and brings about a separation in their relation. In addition, Islam has provided special laws for these emergencies.[32] There are four procedures the voluntary dissolve a marriage: the legal procedures for obtaining a civilly recognized divorce, legal separation, annulment and the illegal procedure of desertion. The legal ways of voluntarily dissolving marriage can be very complex and costly. With desertion, once spouse voluntarily ends the marriage simply by leaving it. Annulment, which formally and legally declare that the marriage never existed in the first place. A legal separation which is permitted in most cases, does not really terminate the marriage but merely limits the privileges of the spouses, who are still regarded as married.[33] Marriage contract under the Muslim law, may be dissolved in any of the following forms: (i) by the husband, without the intervention of courts (*talaq*); (ii) by mutual consent, without the intervention of the court *(khula and mubara'et);* (iii) by a judicial decree, at the suit of husband or wife; (iv) by wife, provided such a stipulation is made in the marriage contract.

A Muslim husband has the unilateral right to dissolve the marriage by divorce at any time he wishes. This is the well known right of the husband called the right of *talaq*. Divorce is considered to be distasteful although its necessity in cases is considered and recognized. It is therefore accepted in Islam as unavoidable. In addition, it places the tools of this necessary evil primarily in the hands of the male. Undeniable Muslim law allows the husband wide powers to pronounce divorce and he may do so without sufficient cause and at his will or whim. In the case of *talaq,* no consent is required by the wife; and the pronouncement or declaration of *talaq* is extra-judicial, in no way subject to any external check.[34] Muslim jurisprudence confers on the husband almost absolute power to divorce but denies like freedom to the wife.[35] Consequently, the wife can obtain divorce only when the couple mutually agrees to the dissolution *(mubara'et)*; or the husband agrees to the wife's proposal for divorce and she either forgoes her dower or gives him something in return for his consent to release her from her marital bond (*khula)*.[36] The husband may also, if only he wishes to delegate his right of divorce to her (*talaq e tawfeez)*. Failing the above, after 1939, the wife may under the Dissolution of Muslim Marriage Act of 1939 go to court for contain specific reasons and pray for dissolution of marriage (*faskh)*.[37] On the other hand, Islam does not require the couple to hang on to and ill-founded marriage tie. When the husband and wife can not live together in peace and harmony, there are given the option to separate[38] but there such a separation it is recommended that there is an attempt at reconciliation, The Quran (IV:35) counsels arbitration between spouses. If ye fear a beach between them twain, appoint (two) arbiters, one from his family and the other from hers; if they wish for peach God hath full knowledge and is acquainted with all things.[39] Ali commenting on the verses, states that is clear that not only must be a good cause for divorce, but that all means to effect reconciliation must have been exhausted before resort is had to this extreme measure. The impression given is that a capricious use of *talaq* is a grave distortion of the Islamic institution of divorce.[40] It can be argued that Islam condemns the husband giving *talaq* to his wife unreasonably and encourages reconciliation between that couples before a haste decision is made by the husband.[41] This is perhaps a good provision given by Islamic laws.

In India, husband has unilateral power of divorcing his wife, which is called *talaq*. Other's forms of dissolution of marriage like *mubaraet* and *khula* exited in a limited way. These two forms of divorce depend on man's will. If the husband does not want, then wife cannot exercise. It is a great plight of Muslim women in India. In many cases, women/wives try to convince their husband for getting it. But they usually fail. Another form like *taleq-e-tawfeez* is not existed, as marriage is not registered. Women legally do not get the divorce by their husband. They can enjoy the benefit of Dissolution of Muslims Marriage Act 1939, but they hardly go to the court, as most judges are different in religions. There is no specific provision of arbitrations in Indian Muslims regarding marriage dissolution while such a provision is given in the Muslim Family Laws Ordinance 1961 applicable in Bangladesh. Anges Flavia[42] pointed out that could an Indian Muslim wife approach a civil court for a decree of divorce. This questioned is often answered in the negative.

The Muslim Family Laws Ordinance of 1961[43] that is applicable in Bangladesh lied imposed certain procedural restrictions on men's right to divorce. There is a strong provision of arbitration but husband rights of divorcing his wife at his own will without intervention of court does not omit. Thus, now divorce does not become effective by a mere triple pronouncement. However, one has to wait for three months after notifying the chairman of Arbitration Council and the wife for the divorce to take effect. It must however be mentioned here that whatever the procedural restrictions are men's one right to divorce command full respect, though husband can delegate the right of divorce him to the wife under specific conditions or without any reason. The right has to be delegated at the time of marriage and to be recorded in the *nikahnama*. If this right is granted, a woman can divorce her husband without the intervention of court. Apart from these, according to the Muslim Marriage Dissolution Act of 1939, women can apply to the court for divorce on one or more on the grounds as prescribed by the Act.

Divorce procedures among Muslims in Bangladesh are: (a) any man who wishes to divorce his wife shall, as soon as may be after the pronouncement of *talaq* in any form whatsoever give the chairman notice in writing of his having done so, and shall supply a copy thereof to the wife. (b) Whoever contravenes the provisions of sub-section (1) shall be punishable with simple imprisonment for a term which may extend to ten thousand taka or with both. (c) Save as provided in sub section (5) a *talaq* unless revoked earlier expressly or otherwise, shall not be effective until the expiration ninety days from the day on which notice under sub-section (1) is delivered to the Chairman. (d) Within thirty days of the receipt of notice under sub-section (1) The Chairman shall constitute an Arbitration Council for the purposes of bringing about reconciliation between the parties and the Arbitration Council shall take all steps necessary to bring about such reconciliation. (e) If the wife is pregnant at the time of *talaq* is pronounced, *talaq* shall not be effective until the period mentioned in sub-section (3) or the pregnancy, which ever be later ends (f) Nothing shall debar a wife whose marriage has been terminated by *talaq* effective under this section, from remarrying the same husband, without an intervening marriage with a third person, unless such termination is for the third time so effective.

Bangladeshi Muslim women are little ahead than the Indian counterpart. In many cases, wife gets right of power divorcing her husband with or without causes. In addition, wife easily can exercise that power. Ahmed[44] in his study finds that ninety seven per cent of divorced women got power of divorcing her husband at the time of marriage. However, such a provision does not existed among Muslims women in India. There is a mandatory provision of Arbitration to minimize the incidence of divorce, which is very much necessary particularly for the wives. Sometimes man pronounces divorce with an angry mode. Arbitration can bring the husband in his earlier stand, which also can correct himself and restore their conjugal life. In fact, Indian women may not even enjoy such a provision. It is worth to say that Muslim women in Bangladesh enjoy little freedom regarding divorce than the Indian women.

PROVISION OF DOWER IN MARRIAGE

The basic ingredients of a Muslim marriage are offer, acceptance and dower.[45] Under the Muslim law, marriage is a contract and dower is a necessary result of it, being a part of the consideration of her agreement to become her husband's wife by consummating.[46] This provision is must for any Muslim marriage. The amount of dower differs from one place to another place. There is no fixed rule as to the maximum; in fact, the amount of dower depends on the social position of the parties and conditions of society. There is no limit to the amount of dower-it may be to a very large amount considering the position and circumstances of the bridegroom, but is minimum is never less than ten *Dirhams*.[47] As per the provisions of S 10 of the Muslim Family Laws Ordinance 1961, where no details about the mode of payment of dower are specified in the *nikahnama* or the marriage contract. The entire amount of dower shall be presumed to the payable on demand. High dower is fixed to prevent the husband from divorcing the wife capriciously. There are two form of dower. One is prompt and another deferred.[48] The wife may refuse to live with her husband and admit him to sexual intercourse so long as the prompt dower is not paid.

The amount of dower may be fixed either before or at the time of marriage or after marriage[49] and can be increased after marriage.[50] The wife may remit the dower or any part thereof in favour of the husband or his heirs. Such a remission is valid though made without consideration.[51] But the remission must have been made with free consent. A remission made by a wife when she is in great mental distress is not one made with free consent and is not binding on her.[52] If the dower is not paid, the wife and after her death, her heirs may sue for it. The period of limitation for a suit to recover deferred dower is three years from the date when the marriage is dissolved by death or divorce where, however, prompt dower has not been fixed a demand and refusal is not a condition precedent for filing a suit for its recovery.[53] Dower is a major part of Muslim marriage. In fact, Muslim marriage cannot take place without the fixation of dower. Both Bangladesh and India follow the dower provision very strictly, though the amount of dower usually differs from one to another.

MAINTENANCE PROVISIONS FOR DIVORCED WOMEN

Under the Muslim law, a woman is entitled for maintenance only during *iddat* (waiting) period, which extends to three month. This provision is applicable in Bangladesh under the Muslim Family Laws Ordinance 1961. Under these circumstances, it will be very difficult for her if she is not having substantial amount for her livelihood. Keeping these facts into consideration, the pre-Islamic institution of dower was recognized in Islam. Ameer Ali[54] says that the custom originated in ancient times with the payments made by husbands to their wives as a means for their support and as protection against the arbitrary exercise of the power of divorce. From the women's view point it is seen that the wife who has spent her whole life and labour for her husbands household, which was not rewarded, should not just be turned out of her house without any subsistence. In Bangladesh, these problems are articulated gradually. The high court division of the Supreme Court had taken steps to provide for post divorce maintenance. In *Hefzur Rahman vs Shamsun Nahar Begum*[55] it was held that a person after divorcing his wife is bound to maintain her on a reasonable scale beyond the period of *iddat* for an indefinite period till she loss the status of a divorcee by remarriage another person. The verse in the holy *Quran* (2:241) translated by Abdulllah Yusuf Ali was relied on: For divorced women maintenance (should be provided) on a reasonable scale. This is a duty on the righteous.[56]

In India, a good provision has been made by the Act called "The Muslim Women (Protection of Rights of Divorce) Act 1986"[57] which gave maintenance provisions after the divorce. Here maintenance is not for only *iddat* period but extends further where the court came to a conclusion that if the divorced woman/wife is able to maintain herself, the husbands liability ceases with the expiration of the period of *iddat*, but if she is unable to maintain herself after the period of *iddat*, she is entitled to have recourse to section, 125 of the Code of Criminal Procedure. Under this section, the magistrate is given power to order a monthly allowance for the maintenance of a man's wife or child or father or mother including divorced woman. A Muslim divorced woman is unable to maintain her after the period of *iddat*, the magistrate is empowered to make an order for the payment of maintenance by her relatives who would be entitled to inherit her property on her death according to Muslim law in the proportions in which they would inherit her property. If any of such relatives is unable to pay his or her share on the ground of his or her not having the relatives who have sufficient means to pay the shares of these relatives also. But where a divorced woman has no relatives or such relatives or any one of them has not enough means to pay the maintenance or the other relatives who have been asked to pay the shares of the defaulting relatives also do not have the means to pay the shares of the defaulting relatives the magistrate would order the state *wakf* Board to pay the maintenance him or the shares of the relatives who are unable to pay.

Government of India has made an appropriate provision for divorced women thought it is not mandatory in Islamic law. The Government had faced huge constraint from the Muslims in India at that time. But, it is a historic law for the Muslim women. It gave minimum economic security for the divorced women. Such a provision is no way existed in Muslim Family Laws Ordinance 1961, which is applicable in Bangladesh. In comparison, it is worth to say that regarding the provision of maintenance, Indian divorced women get maintenance that are not applicable among Muslim divorced women in Bangladesh.

CONCLUSION

The comparative discussion shows that there are some similarities in the procedures of marriage and divorce laws among Muslims in Bangladesh and India. At the same time, differences are viewed by reviewing the laws existed both the countries. However, one thing is very common that the laws, which are framed by both the Government, respected the Mohammedan laws or *Quran* and *Hadith*. It was reframed by the need of hours and considering the demands of the society. Many Muslim countries of the world have already abolished Islamic laws and made new laws. Tahir Mohmood had made a survey of the state of Muslim personal law in some 20 countries.[58] He says except in a very few countries like Saudi Arabia, where it holds full sway the Islamic law is applied only in regard to family rights or personal status. Even so, it is not uniformly applied. /Turkey[59], Cyprus, Tunisia, Algeria, Iraq and Iran do not give a Muslim husband the right to divorce his wife unilaterally. A Muslim husband seeking to divorce his wife must apply to the court of law. The same provision prevails in Ccylon, Singapore and in four states of Malaysia. Turkey and Albania are the only two countries with a Muslim majority, which have abandoned the Islamic law. In Bangladesh, Islamic laws have not abandoned directly but Government enacted law like Muslim Family Laws Ordinance 1961 by respecting the Islamic law, which has given uniformed status for all Muslims living in Bangladesh. In India, though Muslims follow the *Mohammedan* and *Shariat* Law but some states have separate laws regarding marriage registration. Moreover, All India Muslim Personal Law Board dominates the matter like dower and other related issues. Women are the victim of law hence; it is because of non-existence of equal right. In a democracy, every one should have equal right but Muslim personal laws do not give equal right of Indian Muslim women. There is a need to make law considering the demand of the need of the society. In addition, divorce should be granted on certain grounds, not without any reasons at the will of one, without the intervention of court both from the husband and the wife as marriage is a sacred bond between two opposite sexes.

NOTES AND REFERENCES

1. This chapter reflects the most current statement of my thought on the subject of marriage and divorce. My earliest and somewhat more complete statement on the subject appears in Cohen (1987). See also Cohen (1998 p- 618) and Cohen (1995).
2. There has been much discussion in the legal literature of whether marriage is the best understood as a contract relation or alternatively, as a status relations. Some commentators have argued "that because the law, not the parties, defines the obligations of spouse," the relationship is truly one of status rather than contract (Babcock, 1978, p. 564).
3. Cohen, Lioyd R. (2002), Marriage: The Long-term Contract, In *The Law and Economics of Marriage and Divorce* (ed) Antony W. Dnes and Robert Rowthorn, Cambridge University Press, p. 10.
4. Velde, Van De. H. (1976), *Ideal Marriage: Its Physiology and Technique,* Allied Publishers Ltd. New Delhi,.
5. Bertrand Alvin L. (1967), *Basic Sociology,* Appleton-Century Crofts, New York.
6. Sancturay, Gerld and Others (1970), *Divorce and After,* Victor Goliancz Ltd, London.
7. Pothen S. (1986), *Divorce, its Causes and Consequences in Hindu Society,* Vikas Publishing House Pvt., Ltd., New Delhi.
8. Bachrach, L. (1975), *Marital Status and Mental Disorder: An Analytic Review,* US Government Printing Office, Washington D.C.
9. In all parts of the world, married men and women have lower death than those in the same sex and age groups who are unmarried-whether never married, divorced or widowed (US National Center for Health Statistics 1970). As yet there is no explanation for this phenomenon
10. Johnson Hary (1970), *Sociology: A Systematic Introduction,* Allied Publishers Private Ltd. Bombay, India.
11. Campling (ed) *Family, State and Social Policy,* Macmillan Press Ltd, London, UK, 1996.
12. Kapoor J.D. (2002), *Laws and Flaws in Marriage,* Konark Publishers Pvt. Ltd, Delhi, India.

13. M. M. Siddidqui, *Women in Islam*, p. 40.

14. Islam Sirajul (ed.) (2002), *Banglapedia: National Encyclopedia of Bangladesh*, Asiatic Society of Bangladesh ,Vol. 7, pp. 424-426.

15. Aziz Ashraful, K.M. (1979), *Kinship in Bangladesh*. International Diarrheal Disease Research, Dhaka, Bangladesh.

16. Sultan Jahan Begum (1980), Nawas H.H. Muslim Married Couple, Award Publishing House, New Delhi.

17. A.A.A. Fyzee, *Outlines of Muhammadan Law*, p. 90.

18. A.A.A Fyzee *op.cit*, p. 90.

19. *Aklemennessa vs. Md. Halem* 1LD 31 cal 849:8 Cal WN 705 at p. – 710 *Sahabi bibi Vs Kamaruddin* 1S Cal WN. 91. *Kazi Siddique Vs. Salima Khatoon* 61. Cal WN 187.

20. Mulla on *Muhammadan Law*, 17th ed. p. 256 and 252.

21. Act No XXIII of 1981. 3

22. Conditions relating to solemerization special marriages namely, neither party has a spouse living; neither party is incapable of giving a valid consent to it in consequence of unsoundness of mind, has been subject to recurrent attacks of insanity or epilepsy the male as completed the age of 21 years and the female the age of 18 years, the parties are not within the degrees of prohibited relationship.

23. Engineer Asghar Ali (1992), *The Rights of Women in Islam*. Sterling Publishers Pvt. Ltd, New Delhi, pp. 172-175.

24. Dharatiya V. P. (1996), *Muslim Law*, Eastern Book Company, Lucknow.

25. Anges, Flavia (2004), '*Muslim Wives and Marriage Dissolutions*, The Asian Age, (6) August 24.

26. Roland Wilson on *Anglo-Muhammadan Law* 26th ed. p. 700, S. 24

27. *Bengal Muhammadan Marriages and Divorces Registration Act 1876*, Sec. 3.

28. Id Section 26 (a)

29. Muhammad Ali; Maulana (1950), '*The Religion of Islam*, The Ahmadiyyah Anjuman Ishaat Islam, Lahore, Pakistan, pp. 618-619.

30. Sureender S. (1992), Age at Marriage, *Social Welfare* No. 4-5, July–August.

31. Silverman, S.P. (1976), *Divorce: Its causes and Consequences American*, Book Company, New York.

32. *Ibid.*, At 1980.

33. Saxton, L. Lloyd (1977), *The Individual, Marriage and the Family*, Wadsworth Publishing Company, Inc California, pp. 354-365.

34. Peare, David (1987), *A Textbook on Muslim Personal Law*, 2nd Edition, Croom Helm, London, p. 100.

35. Huda, Shahnaz (1994), Untying the Knot–Muslim Women's Right of Divorce and other Incidental Rights in Bangladesh in the *Dhaka University Studies*, Part F. Vol V. No. 1, pp. 133-157.

36. Fyzee A. A. (1964), *Outlines of Mohammedan Law*, Oxford University Press, London, at p. 162.

37. Feroze, Muhammad Roshid (1962), *Reform in Family Laws in the Muslim World in Islamic Studies*, Vol. I, No. 1, pp. 0102-130, at 108.

38. Ahmed, *Supra note,* 11 at 4.
39. Ysuf Ali, *Supra note* 6. at 6.
40. Maulana Muhammad Ali (1982), The Religion of Islam 627 (Lahore 1936) Tahir Mahmood, A Unreported Judgment on the Islamic Law of Divorce, In *Islamic and Comparative Law,* Quarterly, 47-48.
41. Ahmed Ali, *Supra note,* 1 at 432.
42. See *Smt. Nasre Begum Vs. Rigurn Ali* AIR 1980. All 118.
43. *The Muslim Family Laws Ordinance enacted 1961* When Bangladesh was part of Pakistan. The law existed in Bangladesh and gave specific provision of (13) marriage, divorce, inheritance, guardianship etc.
44. Ahmed, Neaz (2007), *Divorced Women in Bangladesh: Psycho-social and Economic Conditions,* A.H. Development Publishing House, Dhaka, pp. 125-126.
45. Dower or Mahr is a Sum of Money or other Property which the Wife is entitled to receive from the husband in consideration of the marriage.
46 It is the name of a silver coin 2.97 Grammes in weight. In India it is valued at 20 to 25 paisa. In India the value of 10 Dirhams may come Rs 3 to 40. see *Asma bibi Vs. Abdul Samad,* (1909) 32. All 167
47. *Zaker Begum vs Sakina Begum,* 19. 1A. 157., 1862.
48. The amount of dower is usually divided into to parts, one called prompt which is payable on demand and the other called deferred which is payable on dissolution of marriage by death or divorce.
49. *Komar-un nissa- vs Husaini Bibi*: 3 All 266. FB, (1926) I luck 83; 92 IC 265 (26) AO 186. (19 29) 4 Luck 343; 114 IC S04: (24) Ao 520.
50. *Jahuran Bibi vs Soleman Khan* (1933) 58 (al L3 251, 149 IC 1150; (34)
51. *Jyani Begum vs Umra Begum* (1908) 32 Bom, 612. (1877) All 483; (48) Al 135.
52. *Nurannessa vs. Mahomed* (1920) 47. Cal 537. 59. IC. 8; (1942) 44 Bombay. L,R 126; (42).
53. *Muhammad Taqi Khan vs Farmoodi Begum* (1941) All 326; (1941) AL
54. S. Ameer Ali, *Mohammedan Law,* Vol. 1, p. 432.
55. *Hefzur Rahman vs Shamsun Nahar Begum,* 47 DLR, (1995) 54
56. Ali Abdullah Yusuf (1979), The Holy Quran, Delhi.
57. An act to protect the rights of Muslim women who have been divorced by or have obtained divorce from their husbands and to provide for matters connected therewith or incidental thereto.
58. Tahir Mahmood, *Family Laws Reform in the Muslim World,* N.M. Tripathi, Bombay, 1972, Also see T.N.D. Anderson, Islamic Laws in the Modern World, Stevens, 1959, Cantwell Smith, Islam in Modern History.
59. Prof. Cantwell Smith in his book, *Islam in Modern History,* says regarding Turkey, "Turkey took the necessary salutary, reforming step of making religion what should be, an individual personal matter, a thing of conscience, a matter of private faith." pp. 162-166, 177. 193, 208 and 209.

VIOLENCE AGAINST WOMEN WITH SPECIAL REFERENCE TO SEXUAL HARASSMENT AT THE WORK PLACE IN INDIA

D. PULLA RAO*

INTRODUCTION

Discrimination and exploitation on the basis of gender constitutes a serious issue which effectively means that half the human race is unable to realize its potential and condemned to sub-optional standards of existence. This problem has received worldwide attention and several efforts have been made to bridge the seemingly ever-widening gap. Yet, even after years of efforts to integrate women into the mainstream development process, the effectivity of the same remains to be questioned owing to a multitude of factors which aid the continued marginalization of women. Women's equal access to education, health, employment and political space still remain distant goals in almost all the countries of the world. One of the most serious impediments to women's development is the phenomenon of continuing and increasing violence against them. Needless to say, this constitutes a serious violation of woman's human rights. Gender violence manifests itself in various forms – female foeticide and infanticide, sexual abuse, incest, molestation, sexual harassment at work and on the streets, marital rape, domestic violence in the form of wife assault and women battering. Of all the forms of violence that women face, domestic violence remains the least reported and largely suppressed.

Violence against women is socially a very sensitive issue and more so in our country where we have a special place for 'Family Honour'. Any act which affects the family honour is not tolerated and very strongly put down. Therefore the acts of violence are seldom talked-out of the family and its close confines.

Violence against women is widespread and viewed as one of the cruelest social mechanisms to suppress women. Unequal power relations have led to discrimination against women. Violence on women manifests even before birth and early life, married life as domestic violence, rape, murder, dowry death etc.

* Professor, Department of Economics, Andhra University, Visakhapatnam, A.P.

The basic reason for violence against women is their inferior status educationally, economically, politically, and socially-in a male dominated society. Other factors responsible for increasing criminalization of society, media images inadequate means to address the cause and consequences of violence's; poor enforcement of legal provisions, unabashed consumerism and erosion of family values have all added to it. Over the past decade, there has been growing awareness of this phenomenon and its long-term impact on women empowerment. The media reports extensively on dowry deaths, rape, molestation, incest, assault etc. and give out information that was virtually unavailable till a few years ago.

CATEGORIES OF VIOLENCE AGAINST WOMAN IN INDIA

Though woman's movement has had a long history of raising various concerns, violence was not the central issue till late seventies. Around late seventies the issues like dowry, wife beating were in the forefront and through them women's concerns were expressed. Initially the measure like legal aid centers and counseling services were taken by the Government and Non-Governmental Organisations. That was the starting point. The issue of violence against woman started coming in to the forefront from early eighties onwards. The issue was widely discussed and advocated due to continuous efforts of woman's organizations and activists. Very broadly, if we want to assess the situation of today, we can categorize violence against women in the following manner:

Violence within Family

- Wife beating and battering
- Dowry deaths
- Sexual abuse of female children
- Incest at all stages of a woman's life
- Unwanted pregnancy
- Female foeticide and infanticide
- Alcoholism
- Impact of patriarchal values
- Domination and control within family
- Cultural reasons

Violence within Community or Society at Large

- Sexual Harassment , molestation and intimidation at work
- Rape
- Kidnapping and abduction
- Sexual abuse
- Stripping and shaming of women
- Trafficking
- Forced prostitution
- Caste and communal violence
- Women's rights over their bodies denied
- Feminization of poverty
- commercial Interests of Sex work industry

Violence in Difficult Circumstances Like Wars and Riots

- Rape
- Sexual harassment and abuse
- Occupation by opponent's military
- War crimes

INCIDENCE OF OFFENCES AGAINST WOMEN BY CATEGORY

The data in Table 1 represents incidence of crimes committed against women during 1996-2004. Torture (by husband and relatives) occupies the first place and accounts for 37.66 per cent of crimes followed by molestation (22.40%). Both these crimes account for 55 to 60 per cent during 1996 to 2004. Rape, kidnapping and abduction cases account for 22 to 26 per cent while sexual harassment, dowry death and others account for the rest.

Of the nine categories of violence, crimes such as torture, rape, kidnapping & abduction, dowry death and others have increased in 2004 over 2003. Sexual harassment has decreased from 8.77 per cent in 2003 to 6.48 per cent in 2004 due to the intervention of government and follow up action taken to fulfill the directions of Hon'ble Supreme Court.

Andhra Pradesh (with 7.3% of population) has accounted for 12.3 per cent of total incidents of crime (18921 cases) in 2004. Uttar Pradesh (with 16.4 % population), has accounted for 10.0 per cent of crime against women (115485 cases) in 2004. Six states viz., Andhra Pradesh (12.3%) Uttar Pradesh (9.9%), Rajasthan (8.5%), Maharashtra (7.9%), and West Bengal (7.2%) contribute 56 per cent of total crimes in 2004.

SEXUAL HARASSMENT AT WORK PLACE

Even working women are not free from sexual harassment. The non-working are harassed at home while the workings are harassed at the work place. Sex discrimination and sexual harassment in employment are serious and pervasive problems for women throughout the world. Woman suffers from discrimination in every phase of the employment process—at the time of recruitment and hiring process; in the terms and conditions of women's employment, and harassment at work-place. Women's fundamental rights to employment opportunities as well as to just and favorable working conditions are not protected by any phase of legal process every where in the World.

Sexual harassment is not an expression of sexuality; it is an assertion of power in a situation of unequal power relations. Whether it takes the form of physical molestation, verbal comments or jokes of sexual nature, the result is the same; it undermines women professionally and their right to a respectful working environment.

Sexual exploitation of women by employers, contractors, middle-men and others is another serious issue related to working women. Such instances are more in the informal sector. Women workers in domestic service, fish processing and drying units, forest produce collection etc. are more vulnerable to sexual harassment. Those working under the control of contractors and middle-men, especially those working far away from home are sometimes, tortured, threatened, trapped or forced to submit to the lust of the contractor or his men. Instances of sexual harassment, though not that rampant are found

Table 1
Category-wise Incidence of Crime in India: 1996-2004

Types of crimes	*1996*	*1997*	*1998*	*1999*	*2000*	*2001*	*2002*	*2003*	*2004*	*Growth Rate (1996-2004) %*
Torture	35246	36592	41376	43823	45778	49170	49237	50703	58121	64.9
	(30.46)	(30.18)	(31.47)	(32.28)	(32.38)	(34.19)	(34.42)	(36.06)	(37.66)	
Molestation	28939	30764	30959	32311	32940	34124	33943	32939	34567	19.4
	(25.01)	(25..37)	(23.55)	(23.80)	(23.30)	(23.73)	(23.73)	(23.43)	(22.40)	
Rape	14846	15330	15151	15468	16496	16075	16373	15847	18233	22.8
	(12.83)	(12.64)	(11.52)	(11.39)	(11.67)	(11.18)	(11.45)	(11.27)	(11.81)	
Kidnapping & Abduction	14877	15617	16351	15962	15023	14645	14506	13296	15578	4.7
	(12.85)	(12.88)	(12.44)	(11.76)	(10.63)	(10.19)	(10.14)	(9.46)	(10.09)	
Sexual Harassment	5671	5796	8054	8858	11024	9746	10.55	12325	10001	76.3
	(4.90)	(4.78)	(6.13)	(6.52)	(7.80)	(6.78)	(7.10)	(8.77)	(6.48)	
Dowry Death	5513	6006	6975	6699	6995	6851	6822	6208	7026	27.4
	(4.76)	(4.95)	(5.31)	(4.93)	(4.95)	(4.76)	(4.77)	(4.41)	(4.55)	
ImmoralTraffic Act	7706	8323	8695	9363	9515	8796	6598	5510	5748	-25.4
	(6.66)	(6..86)	(6.61)	(6.90)	(6073)	(6.12)	(4.61)	(3.92)	(3.72)	
Dowry Prohibition Act	2647	2685	3578	3064	2876	3222	2816	2684	3592	35.7
	(2.29)	(2.22)	(2.72)	(2.26)	(2.03)	(2.24)	(1.97)	(1.91)	(2.33)	
Other Acts	278	151	336	223	726	1166	2584	1089	1467	427.7
	(0.24)	(0.12)	(0.25)	(0.16)	(0.51)	(0.81)	(1.86)	(0.77)	(0.95)	
Total	115723	121264	131475	135771	141373	143795	143034	140601	154333	33.4
	(100)	(100)	(100)	(100)	(100)	(100)	(100)	(100)	(100)	

Source: GOI, Crime in India, 2001, National Crime Records Bureau, 2003 and 2005.

in the organized sector also. Ill-treatment, threat of transfer to distant places etc. are the other forms of harassment in the organized sector.

For years, sexual harassment at the work place has been a grey area and due to workplace hierarchy, sexually harassed women are unlikely to complain. Often, she is economically and emotionally dependent on her aggressor. Most of the cases of sexual harassment go unreported for various reasons, for example, due to social stigma, fear of retaliation, and so on. Apart from fear of losing the job and economic security, a woman also faces psychological trauma and social stigma. Fear of re-victimization, by the legal system also compels her against reporting to higher authorities.

The brave women who come forward to report sexual harassment at the workplace are only the tip of the iceberg. Studies show that most of the women do not report harassment and that usually only the most outrageous behavior lead to lawsuits. Plaintiffs are more likely to lose their jobs than to win monetary compensations and settlements.

WHAT IS SEXUAL HARASSMENT?

According to the Supreme Court definition, sexual harassment in any unwelcome sexually determined behavior, such as:

- Physical contact
- A demand or request for sexual favours
- Sexually coloured remarks
- Showing pornography
- Any other physical, verbal or non-verbal conduct of a sexual nature.

SEXUAL HARASSMENT TAKES PLACE IF A PERSON:

- Subjects another person to an unwelcome act of physical intimacy, like grabbing, brushing, touching, pinching etc.
- Makes an unwelcome demand or request (whether directly or by implication) for sexual favours from another person, and further makes it a condition for employment/payment of wages/increment/promotion etc.
- Makes an unwelcome remark with sexual connections, like sexually explicit compliments/cracking loud jokes with sexual connections/making sexist remarks etc.
- Shows a person any sexually explicit visual material, in the form of pictures/cartoons/pin-ups/calendars/screen savers on computers/any offensive written materials/pornographic e-mails etc.
- Engages in any other unwelcome conduct of a sexual nature, which could be verbal, or even non-verbal, like staring to make the other person uncomfortable, making offensive gestures, kissing sounds, etc.

It is sexual harassment if a supervisor requests sexual favours from a junior in return for promotion or other benefits or threatens to sack for non-cooperation. It is also sexual harassment for a boss to make intrusive inquiries into the private lives of employees, or persistently ask them out. It is a sexual harassment for a group of workers to joke and snigger amongst themselves about sexual conduct in an attempt to humiliate or embarrass another person.

TYPES OF SEXUAL HARASSMENT

Sexual harassment at workplace is generally classified into two distinct types:

Quid Pro Quo

"Quid pro quo" means seeking sexual favour or advances in exchange for work benefits and it occurs when consent to sexually explicit behavior or speech is made a condition for employment or refusal to comply with a 'request' is met with retaliatory action such as dismissal, demotion, difficult work conditions.

Hostile Working Environment

"Hostile working environment" is more pervasive form of sexual harassment involving work conditions or behavior that make the work of environment "hostile" for the woman to be in certain sexist remarks, display of pornography or sexist/obscene graffiti, physical contact/brushing against female employees are some examples of hostile work environment, which are not made conditions for employment.

REASONS FOR SEXUAL HARASSMENT OF WOMEN AT WORK-PLACE

Through legal and constitutional supports are available, yet women are deprived of their rights, which is responsible for their suffering/harassment at work place. Some factors which make them stagnant are as follows.

(i) As the bureaucratic set-up is too complex, too slow, too distant even expensive, despite exploitation women do not want to enter in the troubled water. If bureaucrats were honest and serious, then situation would have been different. A few years back Kiran Vedi stood up against such powerful male bureaucrat and won the case. However, every woman is not a powerful woman like Mrs.Vedi.

(ii) As the judicial process is very time taking and expensive, a suffered woman does not want to enter in those jeopardized situation. Moreover, she chooses to keep silence as expression of her degenerated story would harm her reputation. A raped victim is more highlighted than the rapist.

(iii) When one exploited woman makes a report, it becomes an issue and attracts media. Till the case is not solved, the matter supplies spices to information world, which the already humiliated dislikes.

(iv) Today's modernization, mechanization, industrialization, urbanization have caused grater influence in the commission of sexual offence, like sexual harassment. Modern cinema also bears the major part of the responsibility for senseless violence. Hardly there is a movie in which the villain does not either modest the heroines or make attempt to seduce her.

CONSTITUTIONAL AND LEGAL RIGHTS FOR WOMEN IN INDIA

Constitutional

The Constitution of India guarantees both rights and privileges to women through Fundamental Rights and Directive Principles of State Policies.

- Article-14 confers on men and women equal rights and opportunities in political, economic and social spheres.
- Article-15 prohibits discrimination against any citizen on grounds of religion, race, caste, sex etc.
- Article-15(3) special provision enabling the state to make affirmative discrimination in favour of women.
- Article-16 provides for equality of opportunities.
- Article-39(a) Mentions policy security of state equality for both men and women, the right to a means of livelihood
- Article-39(c) Ensures equal pay for equal work.
- Article-42 Direct the state to make provision for ensuring just and humane conditions of work and maternity relief.

Above all, the Constitution imposes a fundamental duty on every citizen through Article-51(A/C) to renounce policies derogatory to the dignity of human.

Legal Provisions

In order to safeguard the various constitutional rights and provide free and fair justice, the state has enacted many women specific and woman related legislations.

- *Factories Act 1948 (Amended up to 1976):* Under this Act, a woman cannot be forced to work beyond 8 hours and prohibits employment of women except between 6 A.M and 7 P.M.
- *The Equal Remuneration Act of 1976:* This Act provides equal wage for equal work.
- *The Child Marriage Restrain Act of 1976:* This Act raises the age for marriage of a girl to 18 years from 15 years and that of a boy to 21 years.
- Maternity Benefits Act 1961: A woman is entitled 12 weeks maternity leave.

- Indian Penal Code-Sections 354 and 509 safeguard the interests of women.
- *The Dowry Prohibition Act 1961:* The amendment brought in 1948 made the husband or in-laws punishable, if a woman commits suicide within 7 years of her marriage.
- *The Medical Termination of Pregnancy Act of 1971:* The Act legalizes abortion by qualified professional on humanitarian grounds.
- Amendments to criminal law 1983: Provides for a punishment of 7 years in ordinary cases of rape and 10 years for custodial rape cases.
- *73rd/74th Amendment (Constitutional) Act, 1992:* It provides for reservation of 1/3 of seats in panchayat and urban local bodies for women.
- *The National Commission for Women Act, 1990:* It provides for set-up of a statutory body of National Commission for Women, to review the constitutional and legal safeguards for women. The commission was set-up in January, 1992.
- *The Protection of Human Rights Act, 1993:* This Act provides for the Constitution of National Human Rights Commission and state Human Rights Commission and Human Rights Court for better protection of Human Rights.

CONCLUSIONS

Women constitute almost about half of the nation's human resources. Their participation in the national building as equal partners is of vital importance. Discrimination and exploitation on the basis of gender constitutes a serious issue which effectively means that half the human race is unable to realize its potential and condemned to sub-optional standards of existence. This problem has received worldwide attention and several efforts have been made to bridge the seemingly ever-widening gap. All our efforts to integrate women into the mainstream development process could not solve the main problem. A number of factors are responsible for the continued marginalization of women. Women's access to education, health, employment, and political power still remain distant goals in many countries of the world. One of the most serious impediments to women's development is the phenomenon of continuing and increasing sexual violence particularly sexual abuse, incest, molestation, sexual harassment at work and marital rape.

The problem of sexual harassment can be treated as a form of sex discrimination and violation of human right to equality. It is not a problem between the two individuals, the harassment and harassed, but also an organizational problems since it occurs within the groups, such as academic institutions, commercial organizations and government agencies etc.

Sexual harassment at the workplace is pervasive and predominantly endured by females. Yet, despite the publicity given against sexual harassment, it remains hidden by most of its victims. Sexual harassment of women is not only a legal issue; it is also a psychological and social issue. The perpetration of sexual harassment at the workplace is a problem without any perceivable dimensions and the society needs to answer these legitimate questions through their corrective actions, so as to arrest the future degeneration in the society. While analyzing the ratio of sex crimes, the crime rate is phenomenally high, as the conviction percentage is very low. This displays the hedonistic attitude of this generation. Therefore, there is an urgent need to protect the basic human rights of working women against sexual harassment at the workplace and also it is essential that multi-dimensional intervention programme both individual and organizational level needs to be emphasized. It is essential for the government and the society at large to address this issue not only for safeguarding the dignity and person of women but also to realize the Constitutional goal of gender equality. There is a need for action plan to create awareness amongst women regarding their rights for better living along with full protection to the victims.

REFERENCES

Agnes, Flavia (1992), "Protecting Women against Violence? Review of a Decade of Legislation on Violence against Women: 1980-1989", *Economic and Political Weekly*, 27 (17): WS 21-34.

Baxi, Mamta (2001), Violence for Equality: A Report on Nari Adalat, Gujarat, Tata Institute of Social Sciences, Mumbai.

Chappell, D. and Martinon, V. D. (1998), Violence at work, *International Labour Gender Studies*, Vol. 5, No. 1, pp. 115-125.

Ellisberg, M., Heise, L. and Shrader, E. (1999), Researching Violence against Women: A Practical Guide for Research and Advocates, Centre for Health and Gender Equity, Washington D.C.

Jai Singh, I. (1995), "Violence against Women: The Indian Perspective" in J. Peters and A. Walpes (ed.) Women's Rights, Human Rights, Sage Publications, New Delhi.

Kelkar, Govind (1991), Violence against Women in India: Perspective and Strategies, Asian Institute of Technology, Bangkok.

Kishore, R. and Jain, S. (1993), Combating Sexual Harassment at work, Paper Presented at ILO Seminar, Manila, November, 22-26.

Mira Seta (2001), "Women and Development: The Indian Experience, Crime against Women", Sage Publications, New Delhi.

National Crime Record Bureau (2005), National Crime Record Bureau Report, New Delhi.

Pairvi (2001), A Study of Sexual Harassment of Women in the Work-place of NGO's of Rajasthan, Jaipur.

Prasad, Shally (1999), Medico-Legal Response to Violence against Women in India, Violence against Women, 5 (5) 478-506.

Sanhita (2000), Sexual Harassment at Workplace: The Campaign Report, April-September, Bhubaneswar.

VIOLENCE AGAINST WOMEN

P. SUNDARA PANDIAN* & R. SHOBANADEVI**

INTRODUCTION

For centuries past, women all over the world have not only, been denied full justice, social, economic and political but as "weaker section" they have been used, abused, exploited and, then discarded to lead immoral, street vagrant and destitute life till their death. Although they constitute about half the total population and have contributed and sacrificed not less than men in the national freedom struggles at any point of time, they have been deprived of their due shares in various areas of activities and have been subjected to inhuman and humiliating wrongs from birth to death for no sin.

KINDS OF VIOLENCE AGAINST WOMEN

Domestic Violence

The phenomenon of domestic violence remains one of the most prevalent yet largely invisibles forms of violence in the public domain. It is a manifestation of inequality within the home. Contrary to the general belief, violence faced by women in intimate relationships is neither restricted to certain social sections nor is it manifested only in its physical form. Domestic violence occurs in many forms -physical, emotional, sexual, economic, verbal and others, and a woman may face violence in any one, two or in combination of all of them. A woman may face this cycle of violence as a daughter, a sister, a wife, a mother, a partner or a single woman in her lifetime.

Traditional Practices

In many countries, women fall victim to traditional practices that violate their human rights. The persistence of the problem has much to do with the fact that most of these physically and psychologically harmful customs are deeply rooted in the tradition and culture of society.

* *Reader, Department of Commerce, VHNSN College, Virudhunagar.*

** *Research Scholar, Department of Commerce, VHNSN College, Virudhunagar.*

Female Genital Mutilation

According to the World Health Organization, 85 million to 115 million girls and women in the population have undergone some form of female genital mutilation and suffer from its adverse health effects.

There is a growing consensus that the best way to eliminate these practices is through educational campaigns that emphasize their dangerous health consequences. Several Governments have been actively promoting such campaigns in their countries.

Preference of Male Child

Giving priority to male child affects women in many countries, particularly in Asia. Its consequences can be anything from foetal or female infanticide to neglect of the girl child over her brother in terms of such essential needs as nutrition, basic health care and education.

Dowry-related Violence and Early Marriage

In some countries, weddings are preceded by the payment of an agreed-upon dowry by the bride's family. Failure to pay the dowry can lead to violence.

Early marriage, especially without the consent of the girl, is another form of human rights violation. Early marriage followed by multiple pregnancies can affect the health of women for life. The destructive effects of marriage of female children under 18 and has urged Governments to adopt relevant legislation.

Violence in the Community

Rape

Rape can occur anywhere, even in the family, where it can take the form of marital rape or incest. It occurs in the community, where a woman can fall prey to any abuser. It also occurs in situations of armed conflict and in refugee camps. It is the importance of education to sensitize the public about the special horrors of rape, and of sensitivity training for the police and hospital staff who work with victims.

Sexual Assault within Marriage

In many countries sexual assault by a husband on his wife is not considered to be a crime: a wife is expected to submit. It is thus very difficult in practice for a woman to prove that sexual assault has occurred unless she can demonstrate serious injury. It is noted that light sentences in sexual assault cases send the wrong message to perpetrators and to the public at large: that female sexual victimization is unimportant.

Sexual Harassment

Sexual harassment in the workplace is a growing concern for women. Employers abuse their authority to seek sexual favours from their female co-workers or subordinates, sometimes promising promotions or other forms of career advancement or simply creating an untenable and hostile work environment. Women who refuse to give in to such unwanted sexual advances often run the risk of anything from demotion to dismissal.

Prostitution and Trafficking

Many women are forced into prostitution either by their parents, husbands or boyfriends—or as a result of the difficult economic and social conditions in which they find themselves. They are also lured into prostitution, sometimes by "mail-order bride" agencies that promise to find them a husband or a job in a foreign country. As a result, they very often find themselves illegally confined in brothels in slavery-like conditions where they are physically abused and their passports withheld.

Violence Against Women Migrant Workers

Female migrant workers typically leave their countries for better living conditions and better pay—but the real benefits accrue to both the host countries and the countries of origin. For home countries, money sent home by migrant workers is an important source of hard currency, while receiving countries are able to find workers for low-paying jobs that might otherwise go unfilled. But migrant workers themselves fare badly, and sometimes tragically. Many become virtual slaves, subject to abuse and rape by their employers.

Pornography

Another concern highlighted is pornography, which represents a form of violence against women that "glamorizes the degradation and maltreatment of women and asserts their subordinate function as mere receptacles for male lust".

Violence Perpetrated Or condoned by States

Custodial Violence Against Women

Violence against women by the very people who are supposed to protect them—members of the law enforcement and criminal justice systems—is widespread. Women are physically or verbally abused; they also suffer sexual and physical torture. According to Amnesty International, thousands of women held in custody are routinely raped in police detention centres worldwide.

Violence Against Women in Situations of Armed Conflict

Rape has been widely used as a weapon of war whenever armed conflicts arise between different parties. It has been used all over the world: in Chiapas,

Mexico, in Rwanda, in Kuwait, in Haiti, in Colombia. Women and girl children are frequently victims of gang rape committed by soldiers from all sides of a conflict. Such acts are done mainly to trample the dignity of the victims. Rape has been used to reinforce the policy of ethnic cleansing in the war that has been tearing apart the former Yugoslavia.

Such rape is the symbolic rape of the community, the destruction of the fundamental elements of a society and culture—the ultimate humiliation of the male enemy. So, they need to hold the perpetrators of such crimes fully accountable.

Violence Against Refugee and Displaced Women

Women and children form the great majority of refugee populations all over the world and are especially vulnerable to violence and exploitation. In refugee camps, they are raped and abused by military and immigration personnel, bandit groups, male refugees and rival ethnic groups. They are also forced into prostitution.

CONCLUSION

The meaning of gender and sexuality and the balance of power between women and men at all levels of society must be reviewed. Combating violence against women requires challenging the way that gender roles and power relations are articulated in society. In many countries women have a low status. They are considered as inferior and there is a strong belief that men are superior to them and even own them.

Raising awareness of the issue of violence against women, and educating boys and men to view women as valuable partners in life, in the development of a society and in the attainment of peace are just as important as taking legal steps to protect women's human rights. Breaking the cycle of abuse will require concerted collaboration and action between governmental and non-governmental actors, including educators, health-care authorities, legislators, the judiciary and the mass media.

REFERENCE

www.womenaid.org

M. S. Gill, Human Rights Human Wrongs.

Praveen Yogi, Social Justice and Empowerment.

Na, Human Rights and Equal Opportunities.

WOMEN AND LAW

Himani* & Rajneesh**

Since the days of yore, the Hindu women are deprived of the fundamental rights. If we browse through the pages of history, we come through several aspects of their socio-economic life which was greatly confined to the cramped domestic environments. Thus their contribution in the developmental schemes of society was fairly limited. But there were a few exceptions with the active role of social reformers, particularly in the last two centuries, the scenario was changed and we find a great change for the benefit of the women folk.

The greatest tragedy has been the grave injustice done to half of the humanity, i.e. women. Woman is regarded as sub-species which she is not. Women and men are created by the same Creator. Their rights and duties are equally divided by him. Gradually, man started taking advantages of his strong physical power. As a result of this, the position of women was reduced to the mercy of men by imposing unreasonable customs upon women. There is still a need for improvement. At present, men are still under the impression that their position is very strong in the society. Women struggle for equality in the society is backed by the law and to some extent by the right thinking people in the society. Women have always played a specific and crucial role whether visible or not in society and history. Traditionally the Indian women has been the foundation stone of family and society in general. She is the transmitter of tradition, and instrument by which culture is preserved.

The position which women occupied in Hindu society at the dawn of civilization during the Vedic age is much better than what are ordinarily expect it to have been.

WOMEN IN VEDIC PERIOD

Undoubtly, the position of women during the Vedic period was glorious on account of freedom and equality. During this period the women participated in every walk of life. Women studied in Gurukuls and enjoyed liberty in every sphere. The was absence of *pardah* system, right to select life partners.

---

* *Academic Consellor, Public Administration (IGNOU) Centre, Govt. Post Graduate College Chamba, H.P.*

** *Lecturer in Sociology, P.U. Regional Centre, Ludiana.*

POST VEDIC PERIOD

During the post Vedic period the women has suffered drastic hardship and restriction as propounded by Manu. He attempted to set up male dominated society by increasing the authority of man. The birth of a child was treated as a disaster for the family. Girls were denied access to education.

In post Vedic period the women's *right to property* was recognized and the concept of *"stridhan"* (gifts and property etc. received by a women at the time of marriage) prevailed. As Manu defined- "stridhan" means- " that which was given to her before the nuptial fire, in bridal procession, in token of love and which she has received from father, mother, brother and husband."

MEDIEVAL PERIOD

The Medieval period proved to be highly disappointing for the Indian women, for their status further deteriorating during this period with invasion of India by Alexander and the Huns. Women could not inherit property. Girls were treated more as burdens or liabilities than as assets. The social evils/problems like *practice of child marriage, practice of sati, prohibition of widow remarriage, pardah system, devadasi system, female infanticide* was there in the society. Thus, during the medieval period the women were oppressed in every sphere.

WOMEN POSITION DURING THE BRITISH PERIOD

In the British period the position of women had undergone drastic changes mainly due to western impact on the Indian socio-cultural patterns. The father of nation *M. K. Gandhi* strongly criticized the system of *child marriage, sati, prohibition of widow remarriage and Devadasi system.* A number of reformers led the way in launching social movements like *Raja Ram Mohan Roy, Ishwar Chandra Vidyasagar, Maharshi Karve, Maharshi Dayananda Saraswathi, Maharaja Sayyaji Rao Gaekwar, Swami Vivekananda* to improve the position of women. These reformers and their social movements succeeded in arousing the social consciousness for the liberation and equal rights to women.

Consequently, a number of legislation were enacted like *The Prevention of Sati Act 1829, The Widow Remarriage Act1856, The Special Marriage Act 1872, The Child Marriage Restraint Act 1929, The Married Women's Property Act 1874 and The Hindu Women's Right to Property Act 1939,* which intended to eradicate certain social evils.

WOMEN IN INDEPENDENT INDIA

The status of Indian women has radically changed since independence. Both the structural and cultural changes provided equality of opportunities to women in education, employment and political participation.

WOMEN UNDER THE CONSTITUTION OF INDIA

The Constitution of India has certain provision relating to women. Parts III of the Constitution of India deals with the fundamental rights. The provision regarding fundamental rights have been enshrined in Articles 12 to 35, which are applicable to all the citizens irrespective of sex. Constitution of India guarantees all the rights to women which are given to men.

Right to Equality (Articles 14 and 15 of Constitution). It means the equality of opportunity, equality before law, equal protection in the laws, not discriminating against any person on grounds of sex, religion, caste and place of birth and no discrimination in the matters of public employment on the grounds of sex only as provided under *Article 16* of the Constitution.

Article 19 to 22 of the Constitution deals with the *Right to Freedom.* It includes right to freedom of speech, protection in respect of conviction for offences, protection of life and personal liberty and protection against arrest and detention etc.

Right against Exploitation. According to *Article 23* of the Constitution traffic in human beings and forced labour is prohibited. Employment of children is prohibited under *Article 24* of the Constitution.

Right to Freedom of Religion. Article 25 to 28 of the Constitution deal with the right to freedom of religion. It means professing, practicing and propagating religion freely.

Cultural and Educational Rights. The interest of minorities is protected under *Article 29* of the Constitution. Further *Article 30* of the constitution provides the right to minorities to establish and administer educational institutions.

Right to Constitutional Remedies. Every citizen has been provided the right to Constitutional remedies. *Articles 32 to 35* deal with the right to Constitutional remedies. Every citizen of India has the right to constitutional remedies, that is approaching courts for enforcing fundamental rights.

SOCIAL LEGISLATIONS SAFEGUARDING WOMEN'S INTERESTS

The Government of Independent India undertook a number of legislative measures to safeguard the interests of women. Some of them are:

(i) *The Hindu Marriage Act, 1955* the chief aim of this Hindu Marriage Act, 1955 was prohibiting polygamy. In the next amendment the age was raised to 18 years for girls and 21 years for boys and concedes equal rights to women to divorce and to remarry.

(ii) *The Hindu Succession Act, 1956* which provides for women the right to parental property. The women have the right to sue, sale, mortgage or dispose of the inherited property.

(iii) *The Hindu Adoption and Maintenance Act,1956* which gives a childless women the right to adopt a child and to claim maintenance from the husband if she is divorced by him.

(iv) *The Hindu Minority and Guardianship Act, 1956* this act has sanctioned women to guard her daughter throughout her life and in the case of a son for first five years.

(v) *The Dowry Prohibition Act, 1961* which declares the taking of dowry an unlawful activity and thereby prevents the exploitation of women. The act provides for punishment with an imprisonment of six months, or fine of Rs. 500 or both. Under this act, if a girl commits suicide within seven years of her marriage and it is proved that she was subject to cruelty, the husband-in-laws are liable to be punished.

(vi) *The Immoral Traffic (Prevention) Act, 1956* which gives protection to women from being kidnapped and or compelled to become prostitutes.

(vii) *The Medical Termination of Pregnancy Act, 1971* this act legalises abortion on health grounds.

(viii) *The Child Marriage Restraint Act, 1976* this act has raised the age of marriage of a girl to 18 years and that of a boy to 21 years.

(ix) *The Family Court Act, 1984* which seeks to provide justice to women who get involved in family disputes.

(x) *The Criminal Law Amendment Act, 1983* which seeks to stop various types of crimes against women.

(xi) *The Equal Remuneration Act, 1976* this act provides equal pay to men and women for equal work.

(xii) *The Indecent Representation of Women (Prohibition) Act, 1986* this act is made to prohibit indecent representation of women through advertisements or in publications, writings, paintings, figures, or in any other matter.

(xiii) *The Maternity Benefit Act, 1961* the act is made to regulate the employment of women in certain establishments for certain period before and after child birth and to provide for maternity benefit and certain other benefits to the working women.

(xiv) *The Pre-natal Diagnostic Techniques (Regulation and Prevention of Misuse) Act,1984* this Act is made to prohibit the misuse of pre-natal Diagnostic Techniques for determination of sex of foetus, leading to female foeticide and punish for violation of the provisions of the legislation.

(xv) *Protection of Women from Domestic Violence Act, 2005* the recently introduced the protection of women from *Domestic Violence Act, 2005* protects women from domestic violence.

CONCLUSION

Despite so many laws for the protection and betterment of women framed by Government of India, the plight of women has not improved. In the society which is still dominated by men, no one is serious to bring about any real change in the status of women. Even, the bill which was introduced in the parliament for bringing 33% reservation to women in parliament and state assemblies is still hanging-fire.

There are number of protective provisions in the Criminal Procedure Code, Indian Penal Code and Evidence Act for the offences against women. But still in most of the homes male-children are being preferred to female children. It appears that the societal approach towards women, their role and status has not radically changed. Hence, bringing about more and more legislations to ensure better opportunities to grant more rights and concessions, is of no benefit unless there is a basic change in the people's attitude towards women and women's role in society.

REFERENCES

Agnes, Flavia (2006), *Law and Gender Inequality: The Politics of Women's Rights in India,* New Delhi, Oxford Univ. Press.

Chandra, Sudhir, Monmayee Basu and Flavia Agnes (2004), *Women and Law in India.* New Delhi, Oxford Univ. Press.

Misra, Preeti (2006), *Domestic Violence Against Women: Legal Control and Judicial Response.* New Delhi, Deep and Deep Publications.

Ram, S. (2005), *Hindu Women and their Rights,* New Delhi, Commonwealth Publishers.

Rao, C. N. Shankar (2004), *Sociology of Indian Society,* New Delhi, S. Chand.

Rao, Mamta (2005), *Law Relating to Women and Children,* Lucknow, Eastern Book Company.

Seth, Mira (2001), *Women and Development: The Indian Experience,* New Delhi, Sage.

Singh, Devinder (2005), *Human Rights Women and Law,* Faridabad, Allahabad Law Agency.

Srivastva, A. B. and H. P. Gupta (2004), *Law of Dowry Prohibition,* Modern Law House.

Tripathi, S. C. and Vibha Arora (2006), *Law Relating to Women and Children,* Allahabad, Central Law Publications.

Universal Women Laws (2007), Delhi, Universal Law Publishing Company.

INDEX

J

K

N

S

Y & Z